CHANGING FACE AND CHALLENGES OF URBANIZATION

About the Author

Shahnaz Parveen *(b.1955)* is a senior faculty in Geography at Jamia Millia Islamia, New Delhi, with over twenty-two years of post-graduate teaching and research experience. Her field of specialization is urban geography, especially urban environmental studies. She has designed a course on '*Geography of Urban Environment*' for postgraduate classes at Jamia Millia Islamia. Her other fields of interest include cartography, inferential statistics, remote sensing and Geographic Information System. She owes to her credit a number of research papers. She has extended a cartographic consultancy to Oxford University Press for an Atlas. Besides attending several national and international conferences, she has been a UGC Visiting Fellow to the Centre for Urban Economic Studies, Kolkata University.

CHANGING FACE AND CHALLENGES OF URBANIZATION

A Case Study of Uttar Pradesh

SHAHNAZ PARVEEN

CONCEPT PUBLISHING COMPANY, NEW DELHI-110059

Cataloging in Publication Data—DK
Courtesy: D.K. Agencies (P) Ltd. <docinfo@dkagencies.com>

Parveen, Shahnaz, 1955-
Changing face and challenges of urbanization :a case study of Uttar Pradesh / Shahnaz Parveen.
p. cm.
Includes bibliographical references (p.)
Includes index.
ISBN 818069237X

1. Urbanization—India—Uttar Pradesh. 2. Urbanization —India—Uttaranchal. I. Title.

DDC 307.141 609 542 21

ISBN 81-8069-237-X

First Published 2005

Published and Printed by
Ashok Kumar Mittal
Concept Publishing Company
A/15-16, Commercial Block, Mohan Garden,
New Delhi-110 059

Phones : 25351460, 25351794
Fax : 091-11-25357103
E-mail : publishing@conceptpub.com

Dedicated

To

My (late) Parents, whose blessings and confidence in me has always kindled a ray of hope even in the darkest hour of my life

Prof. Mohammad Shafi
Professor Emeritus—Ex. Pro-Chancellor
President of India conferred 'PADMA SHREE', UGC-Award of SARASWATI SAMMAN—BHOOGOL RATNA—Highest Award of the Russian Academy of Sciences, ACADEMICIAN, POORVANCHAL RATNA, Laureat d'Honneur by IGU in Glasgow (U.K.).

DEPARTMENT OF GEOGRAPHY
ALIGARH MUSLIM UNIVERSITY
ALIGARH-202 002, INDIA

FOREWORD

It is a matter of great pleasure to write a foreword on a book that deals with urbanization in the biggest state of India from the viewpoint of population.

To day the world is facing an urban challenge. Almost half the world population to day is living in urban areas. In the developing countries the situation is more grim. The urban population jumped from 287 million in 1950 to 1904 million in 2000; nearly seven fold in a span of 50 years. The cities in the developing world do not possess the power resources and trained staff to provide their rapidly growing population with the lead services and facilities needed for an adequate human life: clean water, sanitation, schools and transport. Squatter settlements with primitive facilities, increased overcrowding related to unhealthy environment are the order of the day. Uttar Pradesh is no exception to the above-mentioned state of affairs.

The writer has done a commendable job by writing this book *Changing Face an Challenges of Urbanization.* After discussing the environmental setting of Uttar Pradesh, she has discussed the demographic aspect of Urbanization with specific reference to migration. The economic aspects of urbanization are interesting particularly active female workers: agricultural and non-agricultural. The discussion on women empowerment with reference to education is enlightening. The discussion on dynamics of applications throws new light on problems of urbanization.

All in all, the book provides a mine of information and the suggestions towards the end of the book are highly pragmatic. One can hardly resist the temptation of keeping this book on one's shelf.

(Dr. Mohammad Shafi)
Professor Emeritus

PREFACE

Urbanization is going to be one of the most significant demographic trends of the twenty-first century all over the globe. In fact, nearly all the population growth expected during 2000-2030 will be concentrated in the urban areas of the world in which the position of the less developed countries will be particularly vulnerable. The United Nations estimates that India's urban population will reach 600 million or 45 per cent of the total population by the year 2025. In India, though the urban economy accounts for about 60 per cent of GDP, the benefits of urbanization are not equally distributed both across different sections of population and over geographical space. Thus, core cities and core region of urbanization are developing with haphazard urban growth and resultant urban decay and decline. The specter of urban poverty haunts India's crowded cities.

In a low urbanized State of Uttar Pradesh the regional disparities in the economy along with the urban sphere of influence of National Capital Region of Delhi has given a significant direction to the course of urbanization in this State. The role of urbanization as a contributor of economic development has become questionable. The dynamics of urbanization in India in their spatial perspective, though extensively explored, for Uttar Pradesh researches in this direction have been fragmentary.

The present work is, therefore, a modest attempt to fill in the gap in developing the correct specification of local and regional urban systems using concepts and criteria that capture the ways in which patterns of urbanization are currently evolving in a low urbanized State of Uttar Pradesh. The study adopts a spatial analysis approach, focusing both on the patterns as well as processes that has generated them. The book is organized into six chapters. The first chapter relates to the environmental setting to trace the history of urbanization of Uttar Pradesh in twentieth century. From chapter second to chapter fifth, indicators pertaining to demographic, economic, social and living environmental aspects of urbanization, over 63 districts of the study area are analyzed. The sixth chapter attempts a synthesis of the results through Principal component Analysis to bring about underlying dimension of the problem.

The book would not have been completed without the all time guiding source of inspiration of my mentor—my late parents, my supervisor (late) Professor Abdul Aziz Tonki and (late) Professor Qazi Mohd. Ahmed. It is an honor for me to acknowledge Prof. Mohammad Shafi (Professor Emeritus) Department of Geography, A.M.U. for his keen interest and valuable suggestions during the completion of this book. I am also highly thankful to all my teachers, particularly Professor Mehdi Raza, Professor Azimuddin Qureshi, Professor Mohd. Farooq Siddiqui, Professor Abha Laxmi Singh. Sincere thanks are also due to all of my seniors and colleagues in the Department of Geography, Jamia Millia Islamia specially Professor Prof. Majid Hussain, Prof. Md. Feroz Khan, Prof. Md. Ishtiaq and Prof. Hasina Hashia for their moral support and active cooperation. Thanks are also due to the members of the administrative staff of the Department of Geography, AMU Aligarh and Jamia Millia Islamia particularly Miss Farzana, a research scholar in the Department of Geography, Jamia Millia Islamia for her generous help in cartographic work.

I also express gratitude to organizations like National Council of Applied Economic Research, School of Planning and Architecture, Centre for Environmental Studies, Housing and Urban Development Corporation that extended all possible support.

I am also highly thankful to my husband, Professor Mohd. Mazhar Ali Khan for his moral support and sustained interest in bringing about the book to its final shape and to my in-laws for their affection and blessings.

Dr. Shahnaz Parveen

Reader, Department of Geography
Jamia Millia Islamia,
New Delhi-110025
e-mail: sparveen_geog@yahoo.co.in

INTRODUCTION

The present study explores the levels of urbanization as is observed in Uttar Pradesh. It is basically a study of spatial analysis of emerging patterns of the distribution behaviour of selected indicators that are supposed to be a representative of urbanization in Uttar Pradesh. The unit of analysis is the district, which has been accepted as an administrative entity in the context of decentralized planning in India. The author, thus, attempts to explore the dynamics of urbanization in Uttar Pradesh through a set of indicators concerning with demographic, economic, social and environmental aspects of urbanization, over 63 districts of the study area. Multivariate statistical techniques are applied to explore the ongoing process of urbanization in a regional frame work. The area of study covers unbifurcated Uttar Pradesh which includes present Uttranchal as well.

The dynamics of urbanization in India though extensively researched upon, need a reappraisal in the present context of regional economic set up. The researches in this direction have been fragmentary for the state of Uttar Pradesh. The present work is, therefore, a modest attempt to fill in the gap in developing the correct specification of local and regional urban systems using concepts and criteria that capture the ways in which patterns of urbanization are currently evolving within a low urbanized but highly variegated state of Uttar Pradesh.

The overall aim of the study is to find out the degree of urbanization in Uttar Pradesh taking account of the major changes, which are currently taking place in the nature and magnitude of human settlement systems. Hence, ultimate aim of the study is to develop a comprehensive approach to study the spatial patterns of urbanization on one hand and to explore the dynamics of urban growth that is taking place on account of the changes currently occurring in the nature and magnitude of urban-economic systems at regional and national levels in a developing country like India on the other.

Contrary to the belief that urbanization promotes economic development and social upliftment of the society, the role of urbanization in Uttar Pradesh raises queries. With the second highest urban population of 27.61 millions and a percentage of 19.84 per cent, a trend towards metropolitan growth is noticed whereby 52.03 per cent of the total urban population is residing in class I cities (Census of India : 1991). Therefore, a duality in the spatial concentration of urbanization is noticed where a metropolitan growth seems to have thwarted the balanced development of the state's urban system. It seems rather a contradictory situation. On one hand, percentage share of the population of class I cities is increasing, on the other, the total urban population of Uttar Pradesh has recorded a sharp decline in terms of decadal growth rate. Thus Uttar Pradesh has been selected to study the dynamics as well as variations in the present levels of urbani-zation.

It is customary to define the degree of urbanization in terms of the percentage of urban population to total population for all practical purposes. The level of urbanization is related to the levels of economic development of productive forces, the level of industrialization and the rate at which urbanization is taking place. Consequently, it becomes an indicator of overall socio-economic development of an area At any given point of time recording all pull and push factors operative in urban and rural areas respectively. If the level of urbanization is not at par with the economic potentialities of the region, under-urbanization results and vice-versa. Each of these two conditions results in regional imbalances and affect the future course of urban-economic development of any area. In an under-urbanized region, economic resources are not properly harnessed, urban centers providing urban facilities are relatively few, quality of life comparatively inferior, population remains less mobile and consequently more tradition bound and less dynamic. As against this, over-urbanization implies a situation in which, though the urban infrastructure is sufficient enough to sustain the increasing urban population, there is great strain on existing urban amenities. As a result, larger proportion a country's population lives in urban areas than their degree of economic development justifies. Under economic pressure from countryside fresh flow of migrants move towards the cities. This leads to a marked deficiency in urban facilities and services creating great peripheral slums, congestion, gross inadequacy for employment for larger masses of migrants, and shortage of fund for urban re-development plans. It follows that there should be a balanced and integrated development of a region so that urbanization could proceed in accord with the economic and social potentialities of a region.

The impact of the policies of the government during the colonial era in this context has a significant role in shaping the economy of Uttar Pradesh. Consequently, even after the Independence, the polarized regions of urban economic development are still flourishing. Furthermore, the scene of urbanization in Uttar Pradesh is instigating since the obvious low levels of urbanization is curtailing the problem of urban growth, which is a distinctive feature of urbanization process in the third world countries. The regional disparities in the form of its rate and spatial patterns of urbanization apprehend an analysis for which the present study promises an implication for the urban planning of Uttar Pradesh.

The present study assumes a greater significance in view of the fact that the process of urbanization is going to be one of the most alarming demographic trends of the twenty-first century all over the globe. In fact, nearly all the population growth expected during 2000-2030 will be concentrated in the urban areas of the world in which the position of the less developed countries will be particularly vulnerable, with an average growth rate of 2.3 per cent per annum during 2000-2030 and consistent with a doubling time of 30 years (United Nations: 2000). In India, the process of urbanization though a recent phenomena, is posing serious threats to the sustainability of urban environment in general. India had a population of 218 million, about 26 percent of the total population in 1991 residing in urban areas, and it It is projected that the number will reach 45 percent of the total population by the year 2025.

In the developing world in particular, new forms and dimensions of urbanization are emerging up. In response to the emerging dynamics of urban growth, the Bellagio meeting at its initial planning meeting held at Newcastle upon Tyne, England, in April 2000, has decided that top priority should be given to the better measurement and understanding of urban population dynamics. The overall aim of the meeting was to work towards a new approach to study urbanization trends occurring on account of the major changes in the nature and architecture of human settlement systems around the world.

Though during 1990s, the world's urban population increased by 36%, in the future, such growth rates are likely to continue. It is basically an outcome of the lopsided economic development programs of the past three decades. A multitude of economic policies like trade liberalization and massive subsidies in agriculture by the world's affluent nations have confounded rural incomes in many parts of the world, pushing people towards the cities. Neoliberal growth strategies have not produced decent and sufficient employment opportunities; instead, unregulated and uncertain informal employment opportunities have flourished adding up to urban decay and decline in many parts of the world including both poor and rich nations. For example, in high-income countries, about 54 million people in urban areas live in substandard conditions similar to those in developing countries. Poverty is expected to be progressively more urbanized across the globe. Within 30 years, if current trends continue, one out of every three people on the planet will live in urban areas characterized by poor public health, a lack of basic infrastructure (including water delivery), inadequate public services, substandard sanitation, and widespread violence and insecurity. Without new strategies for development, which take into account these fundamental shifts in the world's population, a human disaster of global proportions is inevitable.

The 1996 *UNDP Human Development Report* has called the present pattern of growth as 'jobless growth' where the economic growth does not necessarily result in opportunities of employment. In India, from 1975 to 1989, yearly GDP growth was about five percent, while yearly employment growth lagged behind at two percent. . The focus of the UN development programmes, *Common Country Assessment (CCA)-INDIA 1997* has been upon the identification of major issues of urbanization and its related problems. Identification of urban poverty in its various forms has been the prime objective of all the developmental programmes of the government. Lack of the basic amenities and infrastructure in urban areas has a telling effect on the morbidity and mortality rates among the slum population. The *1992 National Housing Policy* has also recognized " ...the rapid growth of urban population and its concentration in 300 cities with a population exceeding 100,000 has led to increasing congestion and overcrowding in small houses, steady growth of slum and informal settlements and severe pressure on civic services..."

Since the study is exploratory in nature, no initial hypothesis could be formulated for testing the results, however, few fundamental questions are addressed. Firstly, to find out the existing levels of urbanization in terms of emerging spatial patterns and to probe into the process of urbanization in Uttar Pradesh with the help of a given set of indicators which are mainly status variables instead of process variables. However, the resultant levels of urbanization at any point of time are an outcome of the process of urbanization itself. Secondly, to evaluate the regional variations in levels of urbanization in Uttar Pradesh and analyze the regional imbalances in terms of the degree of urbanization with special reference to its regional economic set up. Thirdly, to demarcate the areas suffering either from under urbanization or over urbanization with resultant levels of urban development and urban decay. Finally, to suggest, if any, plan or strategies to cope up with the distortions introduced in the patterns of urbanization of Uttar Pradesh.

Literature Review

Urbanization is a highly diverse phenomenon manifesting itself in a multi-functional space. This process encompasses the margins of various disciplines like economics, sociology, demography, political geography, environmental sciences and many other allied disciplines. The literature on urbanization as a process and its spatial manifestation in terms of levels of urbanization has been extremely varied and intensive.

The conditions, which exist in few large urban centers of the developing countries especially in connection with the on-going mechanism of urbanization in India have been widely criticized. The process of urbanization in India was labeled as 'pseudo' (Gee: 1967) as it was different from the urbanization process of the western world where industrialization and urbanization occurred sequentially and gradually. In India the process of population concentration in cities was not backed by corresponding economic progress. Mills (1983) has given the concept of 'over urbanization'. Considering the level of urbanization, India was identified as 'over urbanized' by Sovani (1966) in which larger proportions of a country's population lives in cities than their degree of economic development justifies.

In contrast to the western pattern of urbanization, Indian urbanization is more tilted towards primate city distribution where the colonial heritage of urbanization pattern continued even after the Independence. Therefore, polarization of urban economy and pockets of highly urbanized areas continued to dominate in face of under developed agricultural sector of economy. Several Indian geographers have analyzed this phenomenon from various points of view. Core periphery exploitative relationship was noticed by Raza, (1979). The process of primate city distribution and its resultant impact on the urban environment was analyzed by Berry (1973) in which Indian urbanization was considered as a case of dual and transitional pattern of economy with a highly polarized and spatially imbalanced urban system.

As noted by Bourne (1975) and Gohman (1976), urbanization in India is related to the national urban development. Raza and Habeeb (1980) have also identified the role of urban system in the national development in India from a regional policy perspective. Raza and Kundu (1978) have defined Indian urbanization through urban accretion in which disproportionate growth of large cities is a major cause for imbalanced urban regional hierarchy. The characteristics and correlates of Indian cities were critically summarized by Qazi (1965). Premi (1981) has studied the role of migration in urbanization process in India. Singh (1976) has focused upon a functional typology of the cities of Uttar Pradesh. The demographic profile of metro-hinterland in Delhi was critically analyzed by Nangia (1980). The urban system of cities of India was explored by Aziz (1981b). The spatio-temporal pattern of urbanization in India was attempted by Bose (1965). A critical evaluation of urban policies and growth trends of Indian urbanization was done by Mohan (1981). Goryacheva and Lipyets (1976) have identified the interrelation of factors for the system of evolution of Indian cities. Sinha and Phadke (1980) have noticed the declining towns of India. The urban poverty and its reduction were suggested by Sundaram and Tendulkar(1983). Mahmood and Raza

(1982) have explored the urban redistribution of population in regional space of India.

Various studies on trends and patterns of urbanization and consequences of urbanization at regional city level were conducted among which Jones (1975), Berry (1979), Preston (1984), Pathak (1975), and Alam, Rao and Gopi (1976) are significant. The growth and spatial structure of Indian cities was also identified by Buch (1977). The mechanism and dynamics of urbanization were observed by Munshi (1975) and dysfunctionalities of Indian urban system were identified. Bose (1978) traced the trends and patterns of Indian urbanization during twentieth century along with its dynamics of city growth and development. Environmental implications of contemporary urbanization were analyzed by Shafi (1994).

Studies on urbanization of Uttar Pradesh as a whole especially for analyzing the levels of urbanization are sectoral and fragmentory. A significant contribution is made by Aziz (1981a) for relating the dimensions of urbanization with quality of life in Uttar Pradesh. Another study by Aziz (1982) aims for evaluating the dynamics of urbanization in terms of city growth and development. Aziz (1983) has also researched on the man-land ratio in the towns of Uttar Pradesh. The phenomenon of urban sphere of influence was analyzed for Lucknow district by Ara (1980). The urban amenities provision was analyzed for Saharanpur city by Bansal (1974). Hussain and Siddiqi (1977) analysed the impact of encroachment of Ghaziabad city on its hinterland. Saxena (1970) has treated the history of urbanization of cities of Uttar Pradesh. Mukherjee (1976) has explored the small towns of Uttar Pradesh in terms of the dynamics of urban growth. Sinha (1980) has studied urban growth and urbanization in Uttar Pradesh on a 30% sample base to assess relation between urbanization and urban growth. Singh (1977) has tried to extrapolate the population of small towns of Uttar Pradesh. Parveen (1992) has studied the levels of urbanization of Uttar Pradesh.

Though a vast literature on various aspects of urbanization is available for district level studies, no comprehensive work is done to assess the levels of urbanization in Uttar Pradesh by taking into consideration all major aspects of demographic, economic, social and quality of living environment of Uttar Pradesh. Thus, the study under concern is a pioneer work in this direction.

Methodological Issues

Approach to the Study

The growing concern about handling the distribution of population in relation to geographical space has given rise to evolution of concepts for a whole philosophy of geography (Harvey: 1969). The earlier concept recognized this phenomenon through 'landscape studies', 'areal differentiations', 'spatial analysis' and so on. Regardless of the methodological issues, the focus has shifted from distances and space in absolute terms to a relative spatial context of economic and social space (Haggett: 1979).

Traditionally, spatial analysis approach explains the arrangement or locational patterns of objects in their physical configurations ignoring the process involved in the resulting patterns (Coffey: 1981). To understand the spatial arrangement of the objects including population, the role of external realm like movement or interaction has to be identified through space-time process. Berry (1968) argues that behaviour (interaction) creates and is created by the structure (attribute of the place). Hence, the true notion of space as an interaction field transcends the boundaries of various disciplines. The concept of relative space best represented by a map (Gould: 1975), considers both similarities (nearness) and dissimilarities (spatial segregations) which according to Gatrell (1981) is theorized as proximities. Any change in behaviour leads to alterations in urban structures through the interaction of urban processes best captured in the form of spatial patterns.

Thus, the study of urban spatial analysis aims at relation between the spatial structure of an urban unit and its basic character in terms of organization of people over the geographical space. The geographical space, thus, serves as both economic and social space in which the urban activities are being organized as a result of urbanization process.

The basic approach of the present study is therefore, firstly, analysis of the degree of areal segregation on the basis of locational pattern of population concentration, secondly to study the degree of concentration of population as a result of functional linkages. Both of these approaches are adopted for analyzing the levels of urbanization in Uttar Pradesh.

Choice of Indicators

The study is basically analytical in treatment of the data. The basic aim was to find out the underlying dynamics of urbanization for emerging levels in a developing state like Uttar Pradesh. The major aspects of urbanization relevant in Indian context were selected. The selection of indicators under each aspect of urbanization is made with a view that it is a reflective of the nature of urbanization process of Uttar Pradesh. Since the study area is poorly urbanized with high regional variations in the degree of urbanization, simple and direct measures of urbanization are attempted. The list of indicators is not given here separately since it is included in the text itself along with a brief justification about the broader aspect of urbanization from which the indicator is derived.

Data Base

The present study is empirical in its nature of treatment of the data. The basic design of the present study is aimed for areal segregation of the values in which the appropriateness of the scale of unit of analysis assumes a greater importance. The district as an administrative unit has been accepted in context of decentralized planning in India therefore, it is selected for the collection of relevant data. However, districts occupy considerable area on the geographical surface based upon administrative propinquity, it was not possible to collect primary data through field survey. The Census of India is the government agency, which reliably collect data on decadal basis on district level. Therefore, concerened series of Census reports on Uttar Pradesh were referred and data were collected related to major aspects of the present study. In addition, Housing and Urban Development Corporation (HUDCO), National Institute of Urban Affairs (NIUA), Town and Country Planning Organization (TCPO), National Council of Applied Economic Research (NCAER) and various other concerned offices provided ancillary information. The base map and physical map of Uttar Pradesh were procured from The Survey of India, which is the sole authorized mapping agency of the government of India.

Selection of the Statistical Techniques

The rationale behind the selection of indicators pertaining to any aspect necessitates either some theoretical constructs or some operationalization technique to discover the mechanism underlying the particular phenomena. This concern has given rise to a number of statistical techniques among which the earlier employed simple additive technique gave way to more sophisticated multivariate analysis like multivariate regionalization scheme by Ginsberg (1961). In recent years Principal Component Analysis is widely used in geographical studies dealing with the complex multidimensional realities of the modern life.

The choice of *Principal Component Analysis* to measure the complex concepts and process of urbanization and emerging spatial patterns arises from the fact that simple measures of urbanization are able only to identify spatial patterns in which all the variables were thought to be contributing equally in the process of urbanization. Many queries remain unanswered like the relative importance of a set of variables, or any group of variables, which can be weighted according to its degree of effectiveness in explaining the urbanization process.

Thus, Principal Component Analysis—a branch of Factor analysis was selected which is designated primarily to synthesize a large number of variables into a smaller number of general components, that retain maximum amount of descriptive ability (Soja: 1968). The major role of this technique lies in its ability to identify group of variables, which are correlated within themselves but orthogonal to each other. It also includes overlapping groups, which tend to occur when variables have high loadings on more than one component. Although as many components as number of variables are extracted, only a few dimensions particularly those with one or more eigen values are retained for analyses.

The method includes the derivation of the matrix of Spearman's Rank Correlation Coefficients from the original data set upon which the Principal Component Analysis operates. Each principal component is composed of a cluster of interrelated variables, which show the general pattern of co-variation within the data set. The extraction of the component includes locating the new set of variables in the vector space by its correlation with the original variable. Each principal component is a linear combination of the observed variables and the linear functions are chosen to be orthogonal due to the orthogonal nature of the vector space. Thus, the first principal component is defined as the linear combination of variables, which has the maximum variance of all linear functions derivable from the given variable. The second component, independent of the first one, absorbs maximum variance from the remaining variables. Therefore, each successive principal component accounts for lesser absorption and consequently lesser accountability in the interpretation of the data set. Factor loadings are the weights assigned to the set of new variables expressed as correlation between the original variables and the corresponding component. Each squared component loading indicates the degree to which the new variable, which is the average of all the original variables, subsumes or replaces the original variable. The sum of the squared loadings gives eigen value that explains the total variance in the data set accounted by the component.

The derived components explain the emerging dimensions of the process under study. It is also required to measure the spatial manifestation of the process onto the geographical surface at its respective unit of analysis. Component scores are values for the observation on the new variables, reflecting their values on the original variables and the contribution each component (new variable) makes to the variance of these. Thus, component scores provide spatially map able data of various components for the corresponding areal units. For the analytical purpose of data two, statistical techniques are used.

1. *Simple bi-variate correlation* based upon Spearman's Rank Correlation Coefficient, which helped in examining each individual variable that is most strongly correlated. It helps in finding out the dynamics of spatial process in terms of the variable under consideration.

2. *Principal component analysis*, which has economized the details of description and has helped to come out for analytical purpose, with most pertinent dimensions of the levels of urbanization in Uttar Pradesh. Considering the diversity in socio-economic and

demographic profile of the area, the techniques, thus, selected are supposed to fulfill the objectives of the study.

Selection of the Cartographic Techniques

The spatial data was generated from the base map and physical map of Uttar Pradesh through digitization. For final mapping, the GIS software—Arc View was used under which after linking the spatial data with the non-spatial data, different layers of thematic maps were generated. Depending on the nature of analysis of the data both diagrammatic and choropleth maps were drawn. To enhance the explanatory power of the indicator, choropleth maps and located diagrams are also superimposed on the same map in order to synthesize the information to be depicted for effective display of the data.

The data are in an abstract form that have to be analyzed in its spatial perspective. The configuration of any statistical surface thus depends on the nature of the distribution of data both in its series and over the geographical space. The amount and nature of information to be extracted depends on the expertise in data manipulation through value judgment of the generalization techniques. The desirable degree of generalization involves compression of data set in a few most easily readable number of classes which could also be areally be differentiated. Hence, for the purpose of this study the *Irregular Series of Class Intervals* is chosen which by default takes care of error aspect of calculating mean from the series. It also highlights the elements of the surface configuration that can be obscured by a regular class interval.

The *Natural Break Series* as developed by Jenks and Coulson (1963) uses the cumulative frequency curve to determine the number of classes on the basis of natural breaks that occur in a clinographic curve. The break points in the general gradient give information about the tendency of values to cluster together within a specific data range over geographical surface. Therefore, to highlight the dynamics of urbanization in terms of its selectivity over area this technique is preferred.

CONTENTS

LIST OF FIGURES

1

ENVIRONMENTAL SETTING OF UTTAR PRADESH

INTRODUCTION

Uttar Pradesh, the most populous state of India occupies a prominent place in Indian Territory. Viewed in the national context, it has a very important role in shaping the history of India. Formerly known as United Provinces of Agra and Oudh (now spelled as Avadh) in British Period, it was re-named as Uttar Pradesh in 1950 and further bifurcated into Uttranchal and Uttar Pradesh in 1996. In the historical past, Uttar Pradesh had a very well developed agricultural economy and was occupied by some of the finest and most industrious races, the imprints of which are still seen in the form of rich culture and heritage. However, after 50 years of independence and 46 years of planning, the state of Uttar Pradesh remains one of the backward states of India. It has also lost its glorifying past although it tops the population scenario of India with fourth largest state in terms of area.

Uttar Pradesh has a significant geo-political location. It shares its northern boundary along Himalaya with China and Nepal. The eastern, southern, western and north-western boundaries are shared by the states of Bihar, Madhya Pradesh, Rajasthan, Delhi, Haryana and Himachal Pradesh respectively. It extends between 23° 52' N to 31° 28' N and 77° 03' E to 84° 39' E and covers a total area of 294,4411 km^2 which is approximately 8.97 per cent of the total national territory. The state has a total population of 139.1 million persons contributing about 16.5 percent of the total population of India (Census of India, 1991). With 63 districts and 1,12,804 villages in 1991, Uttar Pradesh is divided into broad physiographic divisions of the Kumaon Himalayas, the Bhabhar and Tarai region, the Ganga-Yamuna Plain and the Southern Plateau Region (Fig. 1).

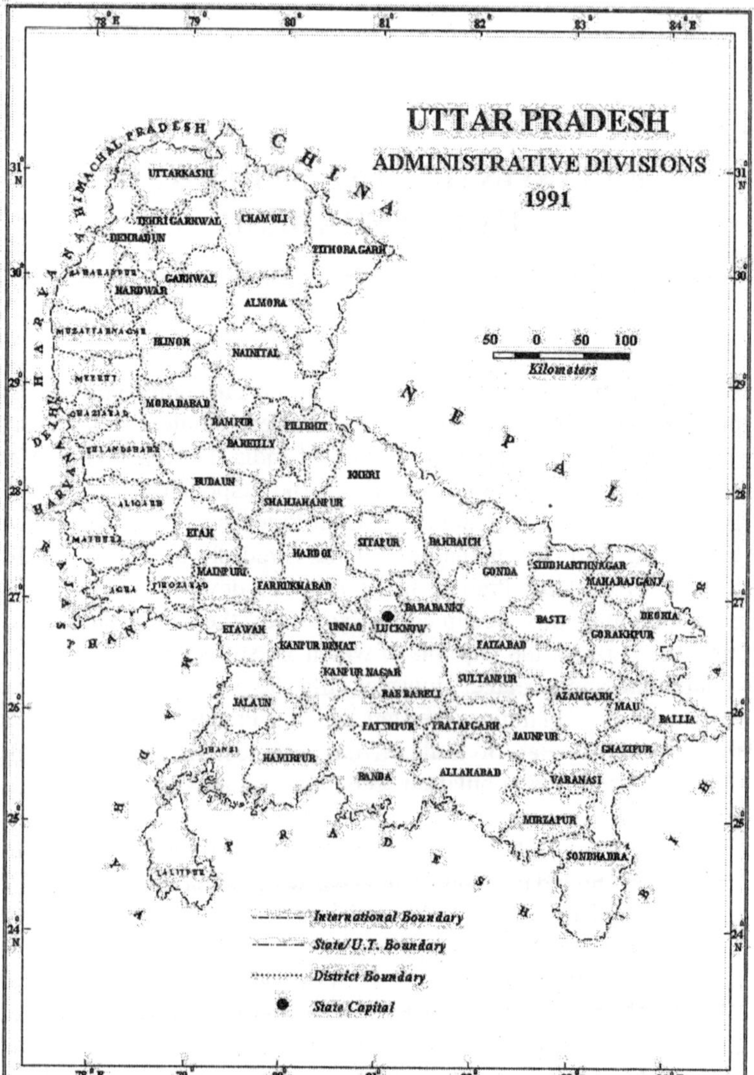
UTTAR PRADESH
ADMINISTRATIVE DIVISIONS
1991
CHINA
NEPAL
50 0 50 100
Kilometers
International Boundary
State/U.T. Boundary
District Boundary
State Capital
UTTARKASHI
CHAMOLI
DEHRADUN
PITHORAGARH
GARHWAL
HARDWAR
ALMORA
NAINITAL
MORADABAD
RAMPUR
PILIBHIT
BAREILLY
BUDAUN
KHERI
SHAHJAHANPUR
ETAH
SITAPUR
BAHRAICH
HARDOI
GONDA
MAINPURI
FARRUKHABAD
BARABANKI
BASTI
DEORIA
GORAKHPUR
LUCKNOW
ETAWAH
UNNAO
FAIZABAD
KANPUR NAGAR
SULTANPUR
RAE BARELI
JALAUN
AZAMGARH
MAU
BALLIA
JAUNPUR
GHAZIPUR
HAMIRPUR
BANDA
ALLAHABAD
VARANASI
MIRZAPUR
SONBHADRA

Fig. 1

Uttar Pradesh has a diverse religious and ethnic composition. Around 83 per cent of the population is represented by Hindus, 16 per cent by Muslims, and remaining 1 per cent consists of diverse small religious groups like Christians, Sikhs, Budhists and Jains etc. Scheduled castes are the traditionally backward and historically exploited section of the society; which constitute about 21 per cent while about 0.02 per cent are scheduled tribes. A sizeable section of the population is both educationally and economically backward. The per capita income of the state is about two-third of the national per capita income of Rs. 10,771. In 1993-94 as per the estimates of the expert group of the Planning Commission on Estimation of Proportion and Number of Poor, 42.3 per cent of the rural population and 35.4 per cent of the urban population were below the poverty line.

Geology

Uttar Pradesh forms a part of old Gondwana and traces its geological records in lower Palaeozoic, Archaean, Upper Peterozoic (Vindhyan), Mesozoic, Tertiary and Quaternary (Recent) periods. There is a close correspondence between the geological structure and resultant landscape. Therefore on spatial basis, broadly, Uttar Pradesh can be divided into three physiographic divisions: the Mountainous and Hilly tract in the north, the Plateau region in the south and the Ganga-Yamuna Plains lying in between.

The Mountainous and Hilly tract of Uttar Pradesh is known as Kumaon Himalayas. It exhibits rocks belonging to Lower Palaezoic period in the extreme north-western part of the state covering the upper part of Uttar Kashi district. The Archaean rocks extend in the form of narrow belt running in east-west direction immediately to the south of it consisting of rocks like gneisses, granites, schists, phyllites etc. It covers parts of Uttar Kashi, Rudra Prayag, Chamoli, Bagheshwar and Pithoragarh. To the south of the Archaean rocks are the rocks belonging to Upper Peterozoic mostly of Vindhyan age with significant concentrations of un-fossiliferous metamorphic rocks like slates with some limestone and mudstone. Vindhyan rocks extend over the lower parts of almost the whole of Tehri Garhwal, Almora and Champawat as well as the upper parts of the districts of Dehradun, Garhwal and Nainital. To the south lies a belt of Tertiary rocks like micaceous sandstone, greenish shale, impure limestone. It extends over the parts of Dehradun, Garhwal and Nainital as well as whole of Hardwar, Uddam Singh Nagar along with the upper parts of Saharanpur, Bijnor, Rampur and Pilibhit districts.

The Ganga-Yamuna Plain extends between Himalayas in the north and Peninsular India in the south and forms a part of the Indo-Ganga synclinorium. It is a plain of aggradations termed as *fore-deep* by the eminent geologist Edward Suess while Sydney Burrard considered it as a *rift valley*. The Ganga-Yamuna Plain stretches over a vast area of the state of Uttar Pradesh from west to east and is covered largely by Quaternary (Holocene) newer alluvium, the Khadar in the eastern part and the Pliestocene deposits of older alluvium, the Banger in the western part. The thickness of the alluvium is more in the north than in the south. The rocks are generally of fluvial and sub-aerial formation with beds of massive thickness of clay of either sandy or calcareous nature. Underlying the alluvium are the unconsolidated older formations belonging to Gondwana and the Cretaceous.

The southern part of Uttar Pradesh is an extension of the Indian Peninsula. The western part of it is designated as Bundelkhand. Bundelkhand gneisses dominates the landscape and is a coarse grained gneiss which looks like a granite. The Upper Vindhyan system consisting of Kaimur and Rewa series, extends over the south-eastern part of Uttar Pradesh comprising of Allahabad, Sonbhadra and Mirzapur districts.

Relief

The state of Uttar Pradesh is divided into four physical divisions consisting of Kumaon Himalayas, Bhabhar and Tarai Region, Ganga-Yamuna Plain and Southern Plateau Region (Fig. 2).

Kumaon Himalayas

This physical division extends between River Satluj and River Kali. It is about 320 kms. long with an area of 38,000 sq. kms. covering the districts of Uttar Kashi, Rudra Prayag, Chamoli, Dehradun, Tehri Garhwal, Garhwal, Bhageshwar, Almora, Nainital, Champawat, Udham Singh Nagar and Hardwar. Kumaon Himalyas is also known

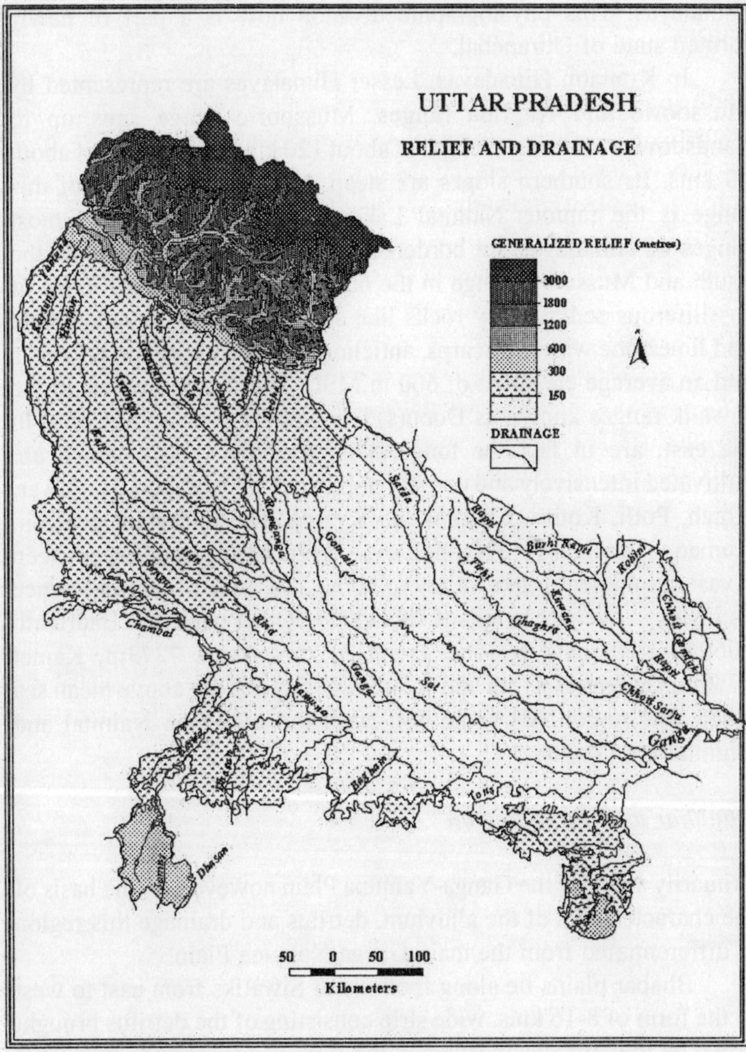
UTTAR PRADESH
RELIEF AND DRAINAGE
GENERALIZED RELIEF (metres)
3000
1800
1200
600
300
150
DRAINAGE
Yamuna
Hindon
Ganga
Kali
Ramganga
Gomati
Sarda
Rapti
Burhi Rapti
Kohini
Ghaghra
Chhoti Gandak
Rapti
Chhoti Sarju
Ganga
Sai
Yamuna
Ganga
Chambal
Sengar
Isan
Rind
Betwa
Tons
Belan
Dhasan
50 0 50 100
Kilometers

Fig. 2

as Uttar Pradesh Himalayas and include Lesser Himalayas as well as Sub-Himalayas, which are also known as Siwaliks or Outer Himalayas. This physiographic division now is a part of newly formed state of Uttranchal.

In Kumaon Himalayas, Lesser Himalayas are represented by Mussoorie and Nagtiba ranges. Mussoorie range runs up to Landsdowns covering a length of about 120 kms and a width of about 40 kms. Its southern slopes are steep. On the eastern side of this range is the famous Nainital Lake. Siwaliks, the southern most ranges of Himalayas are bordered by Ganga-Yamuna plain in the south and Mussoorie range in the north. These are largely made of fossiliferous sedimentary rocks like sandstone, clay, conglomerate and limestone with flat scarps, anticlinal crests and synclinal valleys and an average elevation of 600 m MSL. The discontinuities in the Siwalik ranges known as Doon(s)/Duns in the west and Duar(s) in the east, are in fact the longitudinal tectonic valleys which are cultivated intensively and densely populated in Dehradun, Haridwar, Kotah, Potli, Kothri, Chumbi and Kyarda. The important peaks in Kumaon Himalayas are Nanda Devi (7817m MSL) standing between a vast amphitheatre like valley of about 112 kms. of circumference and with an average height of 700m MSL. Other peaks are Badrinath 7069m, Kedernath 6940m, Trisul 7120m, Mana 7273m, Kamet 7756m, Gangotri 6615m and Jaonli/Shivling 6638m above mean sea level. The region has some 360 lakes out of which Nainital and Bhimtal are famous.

Bhabhar and Tarai Region

Primarily a part of the Ganga-Yamuna Plain however, on the basis of the characteristics of the alluvium, detritus and drainage this region is differentiated from the main Ganga-Yamuna Plain.

Bhabar plains lie along foothills of Siwaliks from east to west in the form of 8-16 kms. wide strip consisting of the detritus brought down by the Himalayan rivers in the form of gravel and unassorted sediments like kankar and boulders. The beds of these pebbles, cobbles and boulders are usually parallel to the slope of the riverbeds. Here the porosity is so high that all streams loose their identity and only big rivers are seen flowing over the surface within this belt.

Tarai Plain is in the form of a 15-30 kms. wide marshy tract lying south of Bhabar. Due to its gentle gradient and deranged drainage, water spreads over the surface giving an impression of a marshy land. The Tarai region extends from Saharanpur in the north-west to Deoria in the east and also the districts of Bijnor, Bareilly, Pilibhit, Lakhimpur, Bahraich, Gonda, Basti, and Gorakhpur. Excessive dampness, thick forest, rich wild life and insects like mosquitoes make this area difficult for human habitation and cultivation except sugarcane and paddy.

Ganga-Yamuna Plains

Being part of The Great Plains of the northern India, Ganga-Yamuna Plain owes its origin to alluviation of the Fore-deep or to the infilling of the *Rift Valley.* It is an aggradational plain of R.Ganga and its tributaries like Yamuna, Ram Ganga, Gomti, Ghaghra, Sharda, Rapti, Chambal and Son. It is composed of detritus and alluvium consisting of mud, clay and sand. The Ganga-Yamuna Plain extends between R.Yamuna in the west, Siwaliks, Bhabar and Tarai in the north, inter-state boundary of Bihar and West Bengal in the east, and Peninsular Uplands in the south. The average gradient of the plain is about 1 in 7000, with a maximum height of 276m MSL near Saharanpur. The height decreases towards the south and south-east. Roorkee is at 274m, Delhi 216m, Meerut 222m, Aligarh 111m, Allahabad 98m, and Varanasi is at 76m above mean sea level. The depth of alluvium according to Oldham, ranges between 4000m-6000m, while Sydney Burrard considered the existence of a fault with a down throw of 32000 meters gradually filled up by alluvium. However, recent studies show that thickness of the alluvium in Ganga-Yamuna Plain varies between 1300-1400 meters that decreases towards the south till the irregular edges of the Indian Peninsula. However, along the foothills of Siwaliks, the maximum depth of the alluvium is recorded more than 8000 meters.

The Plain is fertile from the viewpoint of agriculture. The general slope of the plain is from north-west to south-east. The monotony of the physical landscape is breached on a micro-level by the river bluffs/levees, dead arms of the channels, the ravines, and 'khols'. On the basis of relief, the Ganga-Yamuna Plain of Uttar Pradesh is divided into Upper Ganga Plain and Middle Ganga Plain.

Upper Ganga Plain

Upper Ganga Plain is bounded by river Yamuna in the west and south, Siwaliks in the north, 100 m. contour line (Allahabad-Faizabad Railway line) in the east and the northern edges of the Indian Peninsula in the south covering approximately 1,49,029 sq. kms. with an average elevation of 100-300 m. above mean sea level and an average gradient of 1 in 4000. The plain is drained by river Ganga and its tributaries like Yamuna, Ram Ganga, Sarda, Gomti and Ghaghra. The plain is 350 kms. long from east to west and 380kms. wide from north to south. The Upper Ganga Plain is sub-divided into three micro-regions of the Ganga-Yamuna Doab, the Rohilkhand Plain and the Avadh Plain.

Middle Ganga Plain

The portion of the Middle Ganga Plain falling within Uttar Pradesh, extends from Allahabad-Faizabad Railway line roughly along the 100 m. contour line, eastwards till the inter-state boundaries of Bihar and West Bengal. The northern boundary of the plain is shared by the Indo-Nepal international boundary. The contour line of 150 m. demarcates the southern boundary of the plain along with the Vindhyan-Rohtasgarh-Chotanagpur plateux. The plain is 600 kms. long in east-west direction and 330 kms. wide from north to south, covering an area of 1,44,409 sq. kms. The relief is between 100 m. in the north-west to 75 m. in the north-east and 30 m. in the south-east. To the north of R. Ganga the general slope is from north-west to south-east with a gradient of 1 in 5000, while to the south of R.Ganga the slope is from south-west to north-east with a gradient of about 1 in 11,000.

The Middle Ganga Plain is divided into two sub-regions of the Northern Ganga Plain and Southern Ganga Plain. The Northern Ganga Plain is further sub-divided into the Ganga-Ghaghra Doab, the Saryupar Plain, and the Kosi Plain. The Kosi Plain terminates in Bihar out side the boundary of Uttar Pradesh. The Southern Ganga Plain also has three micro-regions of the Ganga-Son Divide, the Magadh Plain, and the Anga Plain. Out of these three, only a part of Ganga-Son Divide lies within the boundaries of Uttar Pradesh.

Lithologically and structurally, the Ganga-Yamuna Plain is divided into *'Bangar'* and *'Khadar'*. *'Bangar'* spelled also as 'Bhangar,' is the part beyond the reach of flood waters and is composed of older alluvium of a dark colour of pale reddish brown. It is generally rich in the concentrations of nodules of impure calcium carbonates locally known as *'Kankar'*. At places it also exhibits the traces of sodacity and alkalinity that require different types of treatment for reclamation. Clay being the main constituent of Bhangar, gives way to loam and sandy loam (Shafi: 1968). All these deposits date back to Middle and Upper Pleistocene. *Khadar* is a low lying area within the reach of floodwaters which deposits a layer of fresh fertile soil every year. This younger alluvium of the flood plains of numerous rivers is light coloured, poor in calcareous matter and consist of deposits of sand, silt, mud and clay, which dates back from Upper Pleistocene to Recent.

Southern Plateau Region

The Southern Plateau of Uttar Pradesh stretches partially over three macro-regions of Indian Peninsula namely the North Central Highlands, the South Central Highlands and the Eastern Plateau. The plateau is dissected into narrow valleys of Chambal, Ken and Betwa rivers, which join river Yamuna, while Son and Ton merge with river Ganga. It is sub-divided into Bundelkhand Uplands and Vindyachal-Baghelkhand Plateau.

The Bundelkhand Upland form a part of the North-Central Highlands bounded by R.Yamuna in the north, Vindhyan Plateau in the south, R.Chambal in the north-west and Panna-Ajaigarh ranges in the south-east. These uplands cover the districts of Jalaun, Jhansi, Lalitpur, Hamirpur and Banda where crystalline igneous and coarse-grained metamorphic rocks like Bundelkhand gneisses are common. In the north-west and the north-east, the alluvial deposits of Ganga and Yamuna are dominant. The plateau occupies an area of 45,200 sq. kms. The general height is 300 m., however, the Sonpar and Kaimur ranges are more than 600 m. above mean sea level. The plateau has a gently undulating surface with occasional flat-topped hills and a general slope from south to north

The Vindhyachal-Baghelkhand Plateau forms a part of South

Central Highlands and the Eastern Plateau. The general elevation varies between 150m. to 1200m. with highly un-even relief. The scarps of Vindhyan sandstone are commonly found between Ganga Plain and Narmada-Son trough. Between the two scarps are the plateauex of Sonbhadra and Mirzapur.

Drainage

The Ganga system, which is a sub-system of Himalayan Drainage System, forms the main drainage of Uttar Pradesh. The origin of this system can be traced back to River Indobrahm (Pascoe: 1919) or River Siwalik (Pilgrim: 1919). The Ganga drainage system can be grouped into two main categories: the rivers emerging from Himalayas and Himalayan foot hills and the rivers emerging from Peninsular India (Fig.2).

The River Ganga arising from the Gangotri glacier near Gaumukh (3900m, MSL) in Uttar Kashi district, as River Bhagirathi, which cuts across the Central and Lesser Himalayas in deep and narrow gorges. At Deva Prayag, River Bhagirathi is joined by River Alaknanda, which originates from Satopanth glacier above Badrinath and Mana Pass. After the confluence of Bhagirathi and Alaknanda, the main channel of River Ganga is formed which leaves Himalayas at Rishikesh. Alaknanda is joined by the River Dhauli and Vishnu-Ganga at Joshimath, also called as Vishnu Prayag. The River Pindar rising from Nanda Devi and East Trisul joins Alaknanda at Karana Prayag while River Mandakini also called as River Kali Ganga joins it at Rudra Prayag.The River Ganga after reaching the Great Plains at Rishikesh, follows a course in south and south-east direction up to Allahabad beyond which it flows in easterly direction outside the boundary of Uttar Pradesh up to Farakka in West Bengal to finally join Bay of Bengal. Out of a total length of 2,525 kms. only 1,450 kms. falls in Uttar Pradesh.

River Yamuna, the most important tributary of River Ganga, is 1,384 kms. long from its source to its confluence with River Ganga at Prayag. It rises from the western slopes of Bandarpunch (6,316m, MSL) in Jamnotri glacier. In its upper course River Yamuna is joined by Tons, Giri and Asan. The important tributaries of River Yamuna on its right bank are Chambal, Betwa, Ken and Sind while Hindan,

Rind, Sengar, Non, Baruna, and Sasur Khaderi join River Yamuna on its left bank.

Ramganga is a small river having its source near Nainital in the southern part of Kumaon Himalayas in Garhwal district. It flows through the hilly country for 144 kms. and enters into the plains near Kalagarh Fort in the district of Bijnor. After traversing a distance of about 600 kms. in the plains, River Ramganga merges with River Ganga near Kannauj.

River Gomti after emerging from marshland in Pilibhit, passes through Shahjahanpur, Kheri, Sitapur, Lucknow, Sultanpur and Jaunpur before joining River Ganga near Ghazipur. Sai is its main tributary.

The River Ghaghara is also known as Karnali in hilly area, has a Trans-Himalayan origin with 1,080 kms. length. It rises in the glaciers of Mapchachung (Mandhata Peak, 7,720m, MSL), which is just 57 kms. north-west of Taklakot. It is joined by the waters of Tilla, Seti, and Beri. The Rapti and Chhoti Gandak rivers join it near Gorakhpur. It carves out a 600 m. deep gorge at Shishapani. In plains it is joined by Sharda and flows south-eastward to join River Ganga at Chapra, Bihar.

River Kali or Sharda rises in Milam glacier in Nepal Himalayas as Gori Ganga while in its initial course, it is called as Kali Ganga. In its upper reaches, Dharma and Lisar join it. After traversing a distance of 160 kms., River Saryu and Eastern Ram Ganga merge with it near Pancheshwar. From this place the river enters the plains near Brahmadev and is called as Saryu or Sharda. At Braham Ghat it joins River Ghaghra on its right bank.

The River Rapti rises from the southern part of Dhaulagiri of Middle Himalayas of Nepal. After flowing through Bahraich, Gonda, Basti and Gorakhpur, it joins Ghaghra near Barhag. The course of the river is 640 kms. long. The Rohini and Budhi Gandak are its main tributaries.

Chambal is an important tributary of River Yumuna, which rises from the Vindhyan range of Malwa plateau near Mhow and flows in northward direction through a gorge upto Kota. Below Kota it flows in north-east direction to join Yamuna about 40 kms. west of Etawah.

River Betwa emerges from the south-west of Bhopal in

Madhya Pradesh. In Uttar Pradesh it passes through Jhansi, Ourriya, Jalaun and merges with Yamuna in Hamirpur.

Ken is also called Karanwati. It arises from Kaimur Hills and after flowing through Bundelkhand, it joins Yamuna at Bhojah.

River Son rises near Shoshakund in Madhya Pradesh with Rhind and Kunhar as its main tributaries. It passes through the southern part of Mirzapur district to join River Ganga at Danapur, 16 kms. away from Patna.

River Tons also called as Tamsa, arises from Tamsakund dam located at Kaimur hills. It joins Ganga at Sirsa, which is about 32 kms. away from Allahabad.

Climate

Uttar Pradesh has a tropical monsoon type of climate characterized by significant seasonal and regional variations. Indian Meteorological Department has classified the climate of India into two broad seasons: the season of south-west monsoon and the season of north-east monsoon and four sub-seasons viz. the cold weather seasons, the hot dry weather season, the wet session and the season of retreating monsoon.

During *cold weather season* (October 15–March 15), the temperature falls and by December the whole of north India including Uttar Pradesh comes under the grip of severe cold. For the coldest month of January, the average temperature is 10° C in hilly parts of Uttar Pradesh, while it ranges between 10°–20°C in the rest of the state. In general the temperature declines southwards..In January an isobar of 1018 mbs. divides the study area into two longitudinal halves. To the north of isobar of 1018 mbs., the air pressure is further higher with variable rainfall. It is above 5.0 cms. in the month of January in hilly parts, and ranges between 2.5-5.0 cms. in the foot hills of Siwaliks and Tarai region while to the south, in rest of the state, the winter rains are below 2.5 cms.

In the *hot-dry weather season* (March 15–June 15), the thermal heating over the northwestern parts of the Indian sub-continent becomes intensified during the months of May and June when mercury soars upto 42°C . in plain areas with occasional recording of

46°C. In the Ganga Plains, places like Kanpur, Agra, Allahabd, Lunckow, Orai remain very hot. The whole of the northwestern part of the state including Bundelkhand, also record high temperatures with minimum temperatures varying between 21°C. and 23°C. Even the hilly tract of the state experiences temperature ranging between 20°C. and 30°C. However, the average temperature of the state remains between 36°C. and 39°C.

On account of high temperatures, a fairly strong low-pressure belt over the plains of Uttar Pradesh is established which is comparatively weaker than that of north-western part of the sub-continent. Hence, strong extremely hot, dry and dusty westerly winds called *'Loo'* blows unabated throughout the plains and plateau between 10 a.m. and 5.00 p.m. with a temperature of 42°–47°C.

During this season, the air remains extremely dry and the relative humidity is recorded as low as 5 percent with less than 5 cms. of rainfall accompanied by occasional thunderstorms.

During the *wet-weather season* (June 15–September 15), with the disappearance of Equatorial Lows and further intensification of pre-existing low pressure area over the north-western part of India, a steep pressure gradient is developed between Indian Ocean and the north-western part of India. An elongated zone of low pressure within 998 mbs. and 999mbs is formed over the Indo-Gangetic plains, the axis of which is approximately lying in a north-west to south-east direction. The Bay of Bengal Branch of south-west monsoon reaches eastern part of Uttar Pradesh around 15th of June and in the western part of Uttar Pradesh around 1st of July. With the onset of monsoon, the soaring temperatures fall by 1 to 7 degrees in July ranging between 32° to 36°C. In hilly region of the state, the temperature remains less than 30°C. The amount of rainfall received in Uttar Pradesh during this period decreases from east to west and north to south. The hilly area gets an average rainfall of 170 cms., while the eastern, central, western and southern parts of the state receive 112 cms., 94 cms., 84 cms. and 91 cms. rainfall respectively. Approximately 75 to 80 per cent of the rainfall in the state is received from the Bay of Bengal Branch out of which 60 per cent amount is received in the months of July and August. The humidity during this period remains almost 80 per cent.

During the *season of retreating monsoon* (September 15–December 15), the south-west monsoon begins to retreat by the middle of September with the apparent shifting of the sun to the south of equator. By the first week of October, the monsoon withdraws from Uttar Pradesh.The temperature during this season is uniformly high, about 26°C. in early October. The night temperatures are comparatively low and the diurnal range of temperature is high. In hilly parts, the temperatures are lower generally less than 25°C. The low-pressure area of the north-western part of India is dissipated and westerly winds prevail over the Ganga-Yamuna Plain of Uttar Pradesh. The relative humidity remains below 50 per cent in October.

Agriculture

Uttar Pradesh is predominantly an agricultural state and its economy is basically an agrarian economy. In 1991, agriculture accounted for 43.4 per cent of the state domestic product against the national figure of 32.9 per cent. The general land use figures reveal that out of 29.80 million hectares, total reporting area for land use, 58.39 per cent was the net area sown which was above the corresponding national figure to the tune of 11.75 per cent (Table 1.1).

Table 1.1 : General Land Use : 1995-96

Land Use Category	*India (%)*	*Uttar Pradesh (%)*
Forest	22.85	17.33
Area under Non agricultural (Barren and Uncultivable)	13.57	11.80
Permanent Pastures and Grazing Lands	03.63	01.01
Miscellaneous Tree Crops	01.14	01.77
Culturable Wasteland	04.63	03.22
Fallow Land	07.81	03.22
Net Sown Area	46.64	58.39
Total Reporting Area for Land use, (000,000 Hects.).	304.89	29.80

Source: Profiles of States, Centre for Monitoring Indian Economy, March 1997.

However, with regard to forest cover, the study area is below the national average by 5.52 per cent. In general, a good climate, wide spread fertile alluvial soils with perennial rivers and abundant ground water resources are ideally suited for agricultural operations. However, in Uttar Pradesh 67.1 per cent of the net-cropped area is irrigated. Out of the total irrigated area, 69.9 per cent is irrigated by wells and tube-wells, 26.3 per cent by canals and 3.8 per cent by other sources.

The state is the largest producer of food grains and oil seeds in the country besides sugarcane and potatoes. However, the average yield of food grains per hectare is not satisfactory as compared to Punjab and Haryana, the two pioneer states in green technology. A comparative statement of yield of selected crops in selected states is provided in Table 1.2.

Table 1.2 : Yield of Selected Crops in Selected States of India

(Quintals per Hectare: 1997-98)

Commodity	*India*	*Uttar Pradesh*	*Rank*	*Punjab*	*Haryana*	*T.Nadu*	*Karnataka*
Wheat	24.8	25.0	III	38.5	36.6	—	4.6
Paddy	19.0	21.5	VIII	34.7	28.0	29.9	24.2
Sugarcane	696.0	610.0	V	568.0	532.0	1108.0	914.0
Barley	19.5	21.6	III	30.0	28.0	—	—
Gram	08.1	08.3	V	08.5	08.7	—	03.3
Maize	17.2	15.4	X	21.0	19.2	16.2	29.9
Pulses	05.7	08.3	II	06.9	8.9	04.5	02.9
Oil Seeds	08.5	08.8	VI	11.3	07.1	14.3	05.8
Cotton	2.1	01.5	VII	02.2	03.0	02.8	03.2

Source: Profiles of States, Centre for Monitoring Indian Economy, March 1997.

A comparative assessment of the yield of major crops in relation to the national average reveals that Uttar Pradesh ranks second in case of pulses, third in case of wheat and barley, fifth in case of gram and sugarcane, sixth in case of oilseeds, seventh in case of cotton, eighth in case of paddy and tenth in case of maize. The explanation of lower yields partially lies in marginal land holdings (less than one hectare), which occupies about 74 per cent of the total area with all land holdings. However, a rise in the yield of major crops can be achieved through mechanization of agriculture and optimum use of HYVs, manures, fertilizers, pesticides, herbicides and irrigation facilities.

However, in terms of total production of wheat and sugarcane, Uttar Pradesh ranks first. Wheat is the staple crop of western Uttar Pradesh, which occupies 9.2 million hectares or about 34.45 per cent of the national acreage of wheat with a production figure of 23.03 million tonnes or about 34.95 per cent of the national production of wheat. Sugarcane, the most important cash crop of the study area, is grown over 2 million hectares of land or 49.48 per cent of the acreage of sugarcane at national scale. The production of sugarcane in Uttar Pradesh is about 120 million tonnes, which is about 43 per cent of the national production of sugarcane. This crop is produced almost everywhere except the southern plateau region and the hilly part of the state. Paddy occupies about 7.5 million hectares and its production accounts for about 12.2 million tonnes. Uttar Pradesh ranks second after West Bengal both in terms of acreage and production of paddy. Table 1.3 provides a comparative statement of the acreage and production of selected crops in Uttar Pradesh.

Table 1.3 : Area and Production of Selected Crops in Uttar Pradesh (1997-98)

Crop(s)	*Area (,000,000 Hects.)*	*Production 000,000 (tons)*	*Share at national Scale*		*Main producing Area(s)*
			Area(%)	*Prod.(%)*	
Wheat	09.22	23.04	34.45	34.95	Western Central parts
Sugarcane	02.00	120.00	49.48	43.43	Except hilly part every where
Corn	01.04	01.66	17.03	15.27	Southern and Eastern part
Paddy	05.66	12.17	13.04	14.78	Eastern part
Barley	00.34	00.74	40.16	44.34	Central, Southern and Eastern
Gram	00.90	00.73	11.54	11.85	Western Central and Eastern
Oil Seeds	01.70	01.00	06.63	04.57	Western Central Eastern and Southern

Source: Profiles of States, Centre for Monitoring Indian Economy, March 1997.

As far as the crop combination is concerned, R.L. Singh (2002) has divided Uttar Pradesh into several crop combination regions. The eastern part of Uttar Pradesh is mainly a wheat-rice-sugarcane producing region. The northern and hilly part of the state is designated as wheat-maize-rice region. The western part of Uttar Pradesh is basically a wheat-sugarcane-rice region. The Rohilkhand and central part of Uttar Pradesh is a wheat-rice-gram region. Between Rohilkhand and Bundelkhand and also in some parts of the southern Ganga Plain lies a wheat-maize-gram combination region. Along the southern border of Nepal, lies a wheat-maize-rice region. The Bundelkhand is gram-wheat-maize crop combination region.

Considering the above crop combination regions, it can be inferred that the state of Uttar Pradesh represents a medium type of cropping diversity.

Mineral Resources

The role of mineral wealth in the development of the economy of Uttar Pradesh is negligible. For the year 1990-91, the total mineral production was equivalent to only Rs. 3953 millions. Table 1.4 provides information about the total reserves and production of important mineral resources of Uttar Pradesh.

The minerals like diaspore, magnesite, pyrophallite, phosphorite, along with coal, are significant in Uttar Pradesh.The less important mineral resources are iron ore, mica, glass sand, lead, silver, graphite, copper and gypsum etc. Deposits of limestone are also found in Barabanki, Lucknow, Unnao, Rai Bareli, Sonbhadra, Nainital, Garhwal and Dehradun. Iron ore deposits are located in the districts of Sonbhadra, Dehradun, and Garhwal. Mica is found generally in Sonbhadra, glass sand in Jhansi, Allahabad and Chandauli. Lead, silver and graphite are found in Tehri Garhwal and Almora. Graphite and copper deposits are located in Garhwal and Almora. Coal is obtained from Chandauli.

Industry

Although industrial/manufacturing sector enjoys highest place after agriculture in the economy of Uttar Pradesh, yet it is still backward compared to many states of India. Until recently, the organized industrial sector of the state was composed of agro-based industries such as sugar, cotton textile, edible oil, paper etc. However, the electricity generation, railroad equipment, electrical machinery and basic industrial chemicals are coming up. The traditional industries for which India is known, Uttar Pradesh is still a home for many of them. Varanasi, Mirzapur, and Azamgarh are known for hand-woven carpets and silk cloths, brass works of Moradabad, terracotta of Gorakhpur, woodcarving for Saharanpur, *'chikan'* (hand embroidery) of Lucknow and handicraft of Farrukhabad, Aligarh has excellence in craftsmanship.

Table 1.4 : Reserves and Production of Minerals in Uttar Pradesh (1990-91)

Minerals	*Reserves*		*Production*		
	(,000m, Tonnes)	*(National Percentage*	*(,000,m, Tonnes)*	*(Rs. 000,000)*	*(National Percentage)*
Barytes	20.0	0.0	—	—	—
Bauxite	9,400.0	0.4	—	—	—
Calcite	07.0	0.1	—	—	—
China Clay	12,000,00	—	—	—	—
Coal	—	—	10,460,00	2,123.0	5.2
Copper Ore	01.0	0.3	—	—	—
Diaspora	52.0	4.3	2.0	0.9	68.4
Dolomite	2,44,000.0	4.50	52.0	2.4	1.3
Feldspar	100.0	0.6	—	—	—
Phosphorite	32.0	—	154.0	46.0	7.8
Gypsum	1,200.0	0.5	7.0	0.6	0.2
Lead-Zinc ore	1,000.0	0.1	—	—	—
Lime stone	13,37,400.0	1.7	10,72.2	122.0	2.6
Magnesite	1,80,600.0	77.4	80.0	48.0	9.0
Pyrophallite	1,200.0	36.5	15.0	2.2	8.8
Quartz and Silica Sand	73,000.0	7.5	104.0	5.3	4.7
Talk and Soap Stone	16,100.0	19.2	—	—	—

Source: Profiles of States, Centre for Monitoring Indian Economy, March 1997.

A large scale, rapid industrial growth of the state was not possible on account of deficiency of mineral resources. Another major factor impeding the industrial development of Uttar Pradesh is the lack of other industrial raw materials, shortage of power supply, inadequacy of transport and communication facilities in face of rapidity of population growth, paucity of capital and lack of local entrepreneurs.

The sectoral share of income shows that, the share of agriculture in state's income was 52 per cent in 1980–81, which declined to 43 per cent in 1990–91. The industrial sector during the corresponding period changed from 16 per cent to 20 per cent. In service sector, the figures recorded an increase from 32 per cent and 37 per cent within a span of ten years. Thus, a sectoral shift in the economy is noticed whereby agricultural sector has declined by 9 per cent, industry has registered an increase of 4 per cent, however, the major rise by 5 per cent was recorded in service sector. Hence, service based activities followed by industrialization characterizes the changing economic scenario of Uttar Pradesh.

The credit by sector reveals that out of the total, 116270 million rupees in 1992-93 agriculture accounted for 21.2 per cent, industry for 40.1 per cent, transport operators 11.8 per cent, personal loans and professional services 11.8 per cent, wholesale trade 4.9 per cent, retail trade 9.2 per cent and others 9.58 per cent (CMIE: 1997).

The indices of net state domestic product at factor cost by major sectors recorded in Uttar Pradesh are given below in Table 1.5.

Table 1.5 : Indices of Net State Domestic Product at Factory Cost by Major Sectors (at Constant 1980– 81)

Sectors	*1980-81*	*1990-91*	*1991-92*	*1992-93*	*1993-94*
Primary Sector	2.5	7.6	3.1	–2.2	3.7
Secondary Sector	–0.3	6.4	–3.8	1.9	2.8
Tertiary Sector	3.4	3.2	–0.5	6.3	2.1
Total Net Product	2.4	5.7	0.5	1.7	3.0

Source: Profiles of States, Centre for Monitoring Indian Economy, March 1997.

The state income is recording a decline in primary sector from 2.5 index value in 1980-81 to 1.2 in 1995-96. The changes in secondary sector are more intriguing as in 1980-81, the index value was –0.3, which rose to + 4.6 in 1995-96. Tertiary sector also increased from 3.4 in 1980-81 to 4.5 in 1995-96. Therefore, state income index is showing a considerable rise in secondary sector as for the corresponding period in India the index for secondary sector income was only doubled (CMIE: 1997).

The key indicators on factory sectors reveal that out of 7,87,961 factory workers, the dominant industry is food product, providing employment to 26.14 per cent, machinery and equipment to 11.2 per cent, electricity to 10.3 per cent, cotton textiles to 6.5 per cent, transport equipments to 5.7 per cent, basic chemicals to 6.2 per cent and non-metallic mineral products to 5.46 per cent of the total factory workers (CMIE: 1997).

On profitability scale, it is the basic chemical industry which contributes 43.62 per cent out of the total of 11,877.4 million rupees, food products contribute about 30.50 per cent, machinery and equipment 24.47 per cent, gas and steam 36.28 per cent beverages and tobacco 21.18 per cent (CMIE: 1997).

The industrial companies are located in both private and public sectors. The major industrial group of companies include Indian Oil Corporation at Mathura, which is known for producing petroleum products. Lucknow has Hindustan Aeronautics and commercial vehicle company. Ghaziabad is the major producer of electronics, tyres and tubes, motorcycles, computers, plastic films and food processing industries. Kanpur Nagar has aircraft, two wheelers and urea manufacturing plants and leather industry. Meerut produces tyres, tubes, and various synthetic products besides textiles. Saharanpur has important sugar mills, cigarettes, ammonia and urea. Allahabad, Nainital, Haridwar and Jhansi have a number of electrical machinery plants including computers and telephones. Sultanpur has important weaving plants of rugs and carpets.

The industrial development is generally assessed in terms of the ratio of manufacturing workers to total population. The manufacturing industry in Uttar Pradesh is employing 7,88,000 persons, which accounts for about 8.92 per cent of the total workers in this sector on the basis of which Uttar Pradesh ranks eighth on value addition in manufacturing sector in 1993-94. The total investment in manufacturing industry in Uttar Pradesh shows that it is 7.92 per cent of India's total investment in this sector. The state average comes to 23.04 workers per thousand persons (1991). However, the regional variations highlight the nature of uneven development of industrial economy. The western region records highest of 28.38 per thousand followed by eastern region, which is about 21.24 per thousand. The central region has 19.39, hill region 18.43 and Bundelkhand has only 14.97 per thousand.

The total value added by all manufacturing units in millions of rupees shows that during 1980-81 and 1990-91, the value added has increased by 2.7 times from 7032.2 to 34235.9, however, the per capita gross value output of manufacturing in million rupees is recorded 0.327 for Uttar Pradesh as a whole which in case of western region is 0.337, followed by central region with 0.208. Mathura records the highest per capita gross value output of manufacturing with 3.689 million rupees.

As per National Commission of Urbanization criteria of Generator of Economic Momemtum (GEM), the districts with 30 per cent urban population have been considered for the value added per worker in registered factories in thousands of rupees. Kanpur Nagar records a value of 50.45 per cent, Lucknow 40.82 per cent, Dehradun 55.41 per cent, Ghaziabad 86.95 per cent, Agra 31.66 per cent, Jhansi 1.45 per cent, Meerut 81.51 per cent, Bareilly 91.05 per cent, Nainital 46.66 per cent, and Hardwar 0.0 per cent.

The contribution of percent share of registered factories in the net value added by industries shows an index of 50.44 per cent for Uttar Pradesh as a whole. On the regional scale, hill region shows 72.63 per cent, western region 58.97 per cent, central region 53.36 per cent, eastern region 38.83 per cent, and Bundelkhand 37.14 per cent. On district level the highest value is recorded by Ghaziabad with 90.71 per cent and the lowest by Hamirpur with 1.36 per cent. Amongst the districts with above 30 per cent of urban population, identified as GEM as per NCU criteria, Kanpur Nagar with 72.76 per cent, Lucknow with 57.91 per cent, Dehradun with 74.11 per cent, Ghaziabad with 90.71 per cent, Agra with 37.99 per cent, Jhansi with 52.66 per cent, Meerut with 48.17 per cent, Bareilly with 49.88 per cent, Nainital with 89.43 per cent, and Hardwar with 65.59 per cent record share of registered factories in net value added by industries.

The number of large and medium industries per lakh of population records a figure of 5.4 for Uttar Pradesh. On regional scale, the western region has a value of 9.3, central region 5.8, eastern region 1.8, hill region 7.8 and Bundelkhand 1.5 only. Among the group of GEM districts, lie Kanpur Nagar with 15.2, Lucknow with 11.60, Dehradun with 11.70, Ghaziabad with 42.80, Agra with 19.20, Jhansi with 4.60, Meerut with 13.70, Bareilly with 5.40, Nainital with 20.50, and Hardwar with zero index value.

Another important indicator for industrial development is the per capita net value added to industrial production. It was only Rs.60 in 1980-81 as against the national average Rs.175 that subsequently increased to Rs.335 during 1990-91 against the national average of Rs. 614. Thus, employment and per capita net value added in manufacturing sector is definitely one of the lowest, making Uttar Pradesh one of the industrially backward states of the country.

Thus, industrial sector in general is dominated by low value added industries mainly cottage and handloom that dominate the economic scenario of Uttar Pradesh causing its present level of economic backwardness.

History of Urbanization

Uttar Pradesh has a history rich in culture and heritage. During the phases of historical growth, urban centres evolved in response to changing socio-economic and political scenario. In this context, four phases of the origin and evolution of cities can be traced in the urbanization history of Uttar Pradesh.

First Phase: Pre-Buddhist and Buddhist Period

This period roughly coincides with 700 A.D., in which the origin and evolution of cities in the Ganga Valley can be traced back to the Aryan period. Since pre-historic times mention of the aboriginal groups like Cherus and Bhars in the northern plains of India are made. During the 6th century B.C., Buddhism and Jainism evolved gradually as republican groups (500-700 B.C.) were powerful tribes occupying specially most of Oudh (Awadh), Benaras (Varanasi) and Gorakhpur divisions.

The initiatives for early urbanization were provided by Prayag, Vindhyachal, Hastinapur, Kaushambi etc., around which at present are located Faizabad (Ayodhya), Meerut (Hastinapur) and Parikshitgarh. Mathura is described as a prominent trading centre. Prayag situated at the confluence of Ganga-Yamuna and the legendary Saraswati, was a capital town. Eight of the sixteen Mahajanpadas of the Grand Mahajanpada Agra fell within the present frontiers of Uttar Pradesh. The whole territory of Uttar Pradesh was contained within the empires of The Great Mauryan Monarchs—Chandragupta Maurya, Bindusara, .and Ashoka The Great in 3rd Century B.C. The Lion Capital of Sarnath erected by Ashoka near Varanasi, is the national emblem of India. During the reign of Gupta Dynasty, the Golden Age of Indian history, this region experienced phases of peace and prosperity. When Harsha Vardhana ascended the throne in the 7th A.D., Kannauj became the hub of then political activities. The downfall of Harsha Vardhana culminated into the resurgence of the Hindus, more specifically of Rajputs, during 7th-12th A.D. Rajputs had already established their feudal state in the western part of the country. This was a period of insecurity as invaders were arriving from the west.

Second Phase: Mughal Period

Mohammed Ghori captured Delhi and Kannauj. However, the cultural grandeur of the state touched new heights during the Mughal period in the Middle Ages of Indian history. Muslim architects added new dimensions to the built environment of urbanization scenario in India. Agra became the capital of Mughal Empire and Shahjahan fulfilled the dream of fascinating monument, The Taj Mahal. Agra also emerged as one of the new centres of fortification like Allahabad. Allahabad was the capital of the united province of Agra and Oudh. Ayodhya, became the capital of the state of Oudh which later on was shifted to Faizabad and finally to Luncknow. Muzaffarnagar, Moradabad, Shahjahanpur, Firozabad, Farrukhabad, Azamgarh, Jhansi, Rampur, Meerut and Bareilly and other towns subsequently also became important on the scene of urbanization of Uttar Pradesh.

Third Phase: British Period

After the death of Aurangzeb, the glory of Mughal Empire started fading. The British power, under the name of East India Company came into contact with the Awadh ruler during the reign of 3rd Nawab of Awadh. By 1856, India was under British rule under which important institutional reforms like police, health and hygiene were introduced. The infrastructure was considerably improved through the development of transport and communication, and important centres of production werc connected to the market centres as well as port cities. Inland water transport was replaced by speedy and efficient railroad network. It boosted the economic growth of important trade and transport centre like Jhansi, Moradabad, and Tundla on one hand while induced decay of some off the route centres like Ghazipur and Mirzapur on the other. The traditional artisans based cities like Prayag, Ayodhya, Zafrabad, Kannauj and Mathura were facing a threat for their survival from newly established mechanized large and small scale centres. Kanpur, Lucknow, Varanasi, Meerut, Dehradun and Jhansi were established for cantonment, military centre and base camps. The trade, transport and communication related railway yards of Jhansi, Gorakhpur, Bareilly, Saharanpur, Shahjahanpur, Moradabad, the industrial base of Kanpur and the hill resort of Dehradun, Nainital were all acting as pull centres for increase in urbanization through in-migration in Uttar Pradesh as a whole.

Fourth Phase: Post-Independence Period

The British period culminated into India's struggle for freedom as a result of the National Freedom Movement in which the contribution of Uttar Pradesh was highly significant. In 1947, after the partition of the sub-continent, the influx of refugees from Pakistan as well as exodus of population from India had a very destabilising effect on every sphere of economy and society all over India but more specifically for Uttar Pradesh. After the phased partition and migration was over, the National Government took initiatives for the phenomenal industrial development of then industrialised cities like Kanpur and reclamation of the Tarai region causing heavy migration towards selected cities. The uneven development of agricultural sector in the following decades along with a failure in decentralising industrial centres had a localizing impact on urban scenario in this part of the region. Few selected sites like already crowded large cities of Kanpur, Lucknow, Allahabad and Rampur were preferred by in-migrants due to the comparatively better job opportunities and obvious galore of the city life.

Trends of Urbanization in Twentieth Century

The level of urbanization as measured in terms of percentage of urban to total population in Uttar Pradesh at the start of 20th century had made a niche on Indian urbanization scenario with slightly higher percentage of urban population against the national average. In 1901, Uttar Pradesh had 21 per cent of India's total urban population share, which declined to 12.97 per cent in 1991. From 1901-1991, India's total urban population increased more than 8 times, in the corresponding period Uttar Pradesh recorded an increase only by 5 times. In India, the total number of cities recorded an increase by 2 times from 1811 in 1901 to 3609 in 1991 while in Uttar Pradesh the increase was only by 1.64 times from 458 to 753 during 1901-1991. Thus, the tempo of urbanization during the last decade has shown both slowing down the intensity of urbanization as well as its increase in selectively in space.

The evolution of urban system in Uttar Pradesh, as revealed by the changing number of towns over the last decade, clearly reflects the lopsided development of urban hierarchy both in terms of population and space. This further implies that in Uttar Pradesh, the percentage urban population increase was not just a result of the emergence of new towns rather the promotion of already existing towns in the ladder of urban hierarchy. Uttar Pradesh has a rich history of urbanization as the foregoing discussion reveals. However, continuance of the already existing towns is both an indicative their ability to serve the hinterland as well a lack of other competitive urban centres to weaken their powers. The colonial history of the region in face of its traditional agricultural economy has had an important role to play. Thus, urbanization in Uttar Pradesh reflects distortions inherited from its colonial past.

During the pre-independence period, Uttar Pradesh had a purely subsistence agro-based economy. However, during 1901-11, Uttar Pradesh had an initial lead with 11.1 per cent of urban population compared to the national average of 10.8 per cent with 7 class I cities out of a total of 24 for whole of India. The point of consideration is that these cities like Kanpur, Lucknow, Agra, Varanasi, Allahabad and Bareilly enjoyed the status of Class I cities even during 1891 census enumeration. During this period, the outbreak of epidemics and famines resulted in heavy loss of life and large-scale exodus of population from urban to rural areas. However, there was also a back migration from rural to urban areas, as per the records of census 1911 which presented a marginal increase in the percentage of urban population.

During 1911-1921, the level of urbanization of Uttar Pradesh increased marginally from 10.2 to 10.6 per cent which was slightly less than India's average of 10.3 per cent and 11.2 per cent for the corresponding period. Influenza broke out in the form of an epidemic between 1918 and 1920, hence, for reasons of availability of better medical facilities, rural to urban migration was initiated especially towards the cities of larger population size. Thus, class I and Class II cities in Ganga Plain recorded a marginal percentage increase in population concentration. However, the cities and towns in hilly areas recorded a decline in the concentration of population during this period.

From 1921 onwards, the urbanization process was accelerated. The impact of the British policy of sectoral economic development became conspicuous. The foundation of modern industrialisation in India though laid down during colonial rule, the process of industrialization was structurally weak and regionally un-integrated. Uttar Pradesh being a land locked state was not a direct recipient of industrialization impacts of colonial era. In fact the traditional industries of Uttar Pradesh recorded a set back. Only large ancient and medieval towns were selected for either administrative or allied purposes. The basic aim was to regulate the Mughal administrative power with the minimum of technical supplement except in the field of transport. Thus, during British period, Allahabad because of its good connectively as a transport node was selected as the capital of United Provinces of Agra and Oudh till in 1935 Lucknow became the state capital. Meerut retained its supremacy due to its strategic significance. Agra, Lucknow and Bareilly were also selected from strategic point of view. Kanpur was identified as a military town with the establishment of a cantonment of the British army. The cotton textile mills of Kanpur were additional pull factors on account of which it gradually developed in the form of an industrial centre. Thus in Uttar Pradesh, the effective urbanization started from 1921 with nearly 51 per cent of total urban population settled in cities of more than 20,000 population along with Moradabad adding into the list of new class I towns.

The decade of 1931-41 was a turning point in the history of urbanization of Uttar Pradesh. There was a considerable rise in the degree of urbanization form 11.2 per cent in 1931 to 12.4 per cent in 1941. Four new cities of Shahjahanpur, Saharanpur, Aligarh and Jhansi were added up. Thus the class I city growth rate was recorded as 71.2 per cent, the highest in the country. The promotion of only one city in thirty years during 1901-31 and four cities in ten years during 1931-41, explains the underlying trend and mechanism of urban-economic development of Uttar Pradesh.

The economy of Uttar Pradesh was predominantly an agrarian with only small-scale handicraft industries at the beginning of 20th century. Gradually a large-scale industrialization aided by efficient transport network started attracting migrants from rural areas. The simple market towns were also giving way to small-scale industries. Under this changing economic scenario, the emergence of Moradabad as a centre of brass works, Jhansi, Shahjahanpur and Saharanpur as trade and commerce centres; Aligarh as a centre of higher learning due to the establishment of Aligarh Muslim University besides a flourishing small scale lock industry, became significant. During the same period several districts located mostly in Great Plain in the vicinity of transport arteries, recorded a distinctive growth rate in urban population. However, the political milieu had a negative impact in which the call for non-cooperation and the economic depression had a limiting effect on the growth pattern of urban population. Therefore, during 1931 and 1941, 18 district recorded a decline in the percentage of urban population among them Faizabad, Moradabad, Meerut, Varanasi, Azamgarh, and Nainital are significant.

During 1941-1951, the percentage of urban population in Uttar Pradesh increased from 12.4 per cent to 13.6 per cent as against a national average of 13.9 per cent and 17.3 per cent in the corresponding period. This decade also proved to be critical in the urbanization history. The initial lead in urbanization in the beginning of the century was finally lost. Although Uttar Pradesh recorded a consistently increasing pace of urbanization but maintained a low profile far below the national average.

In 1947, following the partition of India, Uttar Pradesh, recorded only 13.6 per cent of urban population compared to 17.3 per cent of the national average. The general increase in urban population was recorded all over India as a consequence of rural to urban migration specifically to large cities. According to Kingsley Davis (1962) after partition nearly six million Muslims and almost same number of Hindus migrated between India and Pakistan, most of these immigrant refugees settled mainly in large cities. Consequently, in 1941, the concentration of urban population increased from 48.07 per cent in 1941 to 54.23 per cent in 1951. The medium towns recorded a decline from 29.98 per cent in 1941 to 25.83 per cent in 1951. Small towns remained almost stagnant. Thus, the twin streams of migrants both from rural and small urban centres were directed towards large cities under the impact of political instability in the sub-continent and economic compulsion from rural areas under deteriorating agricultural scenario. The graduation of four towns of Dehradun, Rampur, Mathura and Gorakhpur can be explained in the above context. Under the impact of immigration of refugees from Pakistan the cities of Kanpur, Agra, Rampur, Varanasi, Meerut and Lucknow recorded a substantial growth in urban population.

Urbanization in India after independence, has shown a steady rise in industrial employment, therefore, role of urbanization as a concomitant of economic growth was recognized for effective urban economic planning. The need was also realised to make the census definition of 'urban' at par with other countries for international comparison of urbanization. In 1961, two important improvements upon the previous census definitions of urban places were incorporated. Firstly, the inclusion of economic aspect of urbanization through setting a limit of definition of urban place as having 75 per cent of more population in non-agricultural activity; secondly, 'Town Group' concept in which the urban sprawl was need not to be continuous spatially.

Since the definition showed a sensitivity towards small settlements particularly those with less than 20,000 population, there was a deceleration in the number of towns from 486 in 1951 to 267 in 1961 resulting in a reduction of 219 or 45.06 per cent of small towns in Uttar Pradesh which accounted for 45.81 per cent of total declassified towns of India during 1951-61. This drastic reduction in number of towns, however, is not properly reflected in the percentage of urban population to total population, which also registered a marginal decline from 13.6 per cent in 1951 to 12.9 per cent in 1961.

Considering the population size class distribution of towns, between 1951 and 1961, the percentage of population with less than 20,000 declined from 32.0 per cent in 1951 to 23.4 per cent in 1961 compared to the places with more than 20,000 population which recorded a considerable increase in proportion of urban population from 68 per cent in 1951 to 77 per cent in 1961. Thus, Uttar Pradesh, which was already having a disproportionate growth of large cities, maintained the same trend towards metropolitanization even during 1951-61.

The other point of concern is the disproportionate share of population concentrated in large and medium cities due to the decrease in absolute urban population of small towns as well as increased percentage share of large and medium cities. However, the net effect of metropolitan growth as denoted by the percentage figures is rather more apparent than real. This was basically a misinterpretation of 1961 census definition as most of the declassified towns were included in the Town Group. Out of 222 towns, 9 belonged to class IV, 85 to class V and 128 to class VI category. The next notable feature of 1961 census was the criterion of designating an area as urban which itself was highly controversial. In case of Uttar Pradesh, 192 urban places were omitted from the list of urban areas though these places were continued to be considered as urban by local government agencies.

The inter-censual comparability of data for 1951 and 1961 was also affected due to the definitional changes of 'urban'. Thus, 1961 onward was taken as a more stable and reliable decade for all comparison purposes of the data analysis and interpretation. In 1971 the concept of 'Urban Agglomeration' was incorporated which was an improvement upon the 'Town Group' concept of 1961. It defines urban agglomeration as a continuous urban spread, which contains at least more than one town physically within its extended municipal limits.

Thus, a significant rise in the degree of urbanization from

12.9 per cent in 1961 to 14.0 per cent in 1971 was recorded. The total number of class I towns increased from 17 in 1961 to 22 in 1971 with five towns of Faizabad, Ghaziabad, Muzaffarnagar, Farrukkhabad and Firozabad having attended the class I status in 1971. The impact of industrial development was becoming prominent. Delhi exerted considerable urban influence on the pattern of industrial development and more so in case of cities located nearby like Ghaziabad, Meerut and Muzaffarnagar. Traditional handicrafts like glass works of Firozabad also found a market and consequently its status was upgraded. However, industrialization was mostly confined to large urban areas due to economies of scale. There was a heavy in-migration to upcoming industrial centres. Consequently by 1971, the size of urban population residing in class I cities reached a level of 53.03 per cent. The small towns were either stagnating or rapidly loosing their population more in favour of large cities. In western part of Uttar Pradesh, 1966 onward, Green Revolution brought about an agricultural prosperity that ensured a more integrated economic development. Thus, the districts like Muzaffarnagar, Saharanpur, Meerut, Ghaziabad, Shahjahanpur, Barielly, Aligarh, all recorded above the state average decadal growth rate of urban population. However, the districts like Varanasi and Lucknow, recorded below the state average. A marginal rise in the percentage of urban population was contributed by 22 small towns; however, their impact on the pace of urbanization cannot be taken as decisive.

During 1971-1981, urbanization continued with an all time increasing pace. Majority of the districts experienced highest urban growth rate, which was responsible for the share of urban population from 14 per cent to 18 per cent in 1981. The number of towns was doubled from 325 in 1971 to 704 in 1981. In 1981 the concept of urban agglomeration took into account one town with similar outgrowth compared to 1971 criteria in which an urban agglomeration had two or more adjoining towns with their outgrowths. As a result more emphasis was laid on areal expansion of each town, which in turn was a reflective of the concept of increasing functional specialization attached to a town. In 1981, there were 30 class I towns which included 26 urban agglomerations containing 47.23 per cent of urban population. There was an increase in the percentage of urban population in every class of cities in sharp contrast to class III cities where the percentage declined to 14.48 per cent in 1981 compared to 17.49 per cent in 1971.

The sharp increase in pace of urbanization was partly brought about by re-classification of most of 1961 declassified towns. These towns kept up their economic base expanding. There was resurgence in the industrial growth of towns in western Uttar Pradesh. It was a trend that had already set in due to the twin impacts of agricultural prosperity through green revolution and industrial development promoted by proximity to National Capital Region (NCR) of Delhi. There was an emergence of a large number of entirely new towns not only in the fast developing western part of Uttar Pradesh but also in the hilly districts of the state.

In 1981, eight other towns of the state were upgraded to Class I city status raising the figure of total number of cities to 30, which included 26 urban agglomerations. The most remarkable feature was reclassification of 200 towns along with more than 1 million population cities. Besides, 198 new towns were included in the category of urban, in small town category. This phenomena had a negative impact on the percentage of population recorded in class I cities which came down to 47.23 compared to 53.0 per cent in 1971.

In 1991, the Directors of Census Operations in consultation with concerned state government/Union territory administration, have included places with major projects, colonies, areas of intensive industrial development, railway colonies, important tourist centres etc., though the places might not lie under (b) category of minimum population of 5000, with 75 per cent of non-agricultural workers and density of 400 persons per sq. km., to be treated as urban.

The outgrowths (OGs) of cities and towns also treated as urban as part of Urban Agglomeration (U.A.). For this purpose all villages near urban areas were revised under the new definition of urban, formerly classified as villages as per 1981 census. This demographic criterion was applied to those towns that were designated as census towns for the first time in 1981 and those towns, which were denotified by concerned authorities after 1981 census. Thus, the continuity of a town from 1981 to 1991 was tested after applying this criterion.

Table 1.6 : Trends of Urbanization in Uttar Pradesh 1901-1991

Census Year	*Total Population*	*Urban Population*	*Decadal Variation (%)*	*Urban Population (%)*
1901	48,627,655	5,390,611	-	11.09
1911	48,154,908	4,906,673	-8.98	10.19
1921	46,672,398	4,936,416	+0.61	10.57
1931	49,779,538	5,568,789	+12.81	11.19
1941	56,535,154	7,016,490	+26.00	12.41
1951	63,219,655	8,625,699	+22.93	13.64
1961	73,754,554	9,479,895	+9.90	12.85
1971	88,341,144	12,388,596	+30.68	14.02
1981	110,862,013	19,899,115	+60.62	17.95
1991	139,112,640	27,605,915	+38.72	19.84

Compared to the national average of 25.71 per cent, Uttar Pradesh ranks sixteenth out of 25 states in India with 19.84 per cent of urban population. In 1991, there were 753 urban centres in Uttar Pradesh as against 705 in 1981, with 62 new towns were added up contributing 2.83 per cent of total urban population in 1991. Ghaziabad recorded a rise and moved to class I category with 9 more towns added to it, followed by Dehradun with 7 more towns, Nainital with 7 towns. Only 31 districts have recorded an increase in number of towns.

Considering class-wise break up of cities only one city was added to class I list, NOIDA in Ghaziabad. A maximum of 39 towns were added to the list of class V towns. However, between 1981 and 1991 only class I, and class III towns recorded an increase, while below class III towns recorded a decline. With additional 49 urban units to the 1981 total of 507, makes it as 753 urban centres in 1991. Out of the above urban units, the following break up shows the administrative status of all town, 8 were under Municipal corporation (MCs), 227 Municipal Board (M.Bs), 22 cantonment board (C.Bs), 33 Notified Areas (N.As), 420 Town Areas (T.As) and 43 Census Town (C.Ts). The number of statutory towns or municipal towns reached up to 710 in 1991 as against 678 of 1981.

In 1991, there were only two metropolitan cities of Kanpur U.A. with a population of 1.89 million and Lucknow U.A. with 1.62 million population. Together these two metropolitan centres had 3.5 million or 12.67 per cent of the states total urban population. There

Table 1.7 : Class-wise Distribution of Urban Settlements 1991

Cities/Town groups	*Cities/Town Population range*	*Total Urban Population*	*Percentage to state's total*	*Number of cities/ Towns*
Metro cities	10,00,000-49.99,999	3,498,535	12.67	2
Large cities	5,00,000-9,99,999	4,480,680	16.23	6
Medium cities	3,00,000-4,99,999	2,052,326	07.43	5
Small cities	1,00,000-2,99,999	4,387,968	15.90	28
Large Towns	50,000-99,999	3,318,010	12.02	47
Medium towns	20,000-49,999	4,353,412	15.77	145
Small towns	Less than 19,999	5,514,994	19.98	520
Total		27,605,925	100.00	753

were six large cities with in 1 million to 0.50 million of Varanasi U.A., Agra U.A., Allahabad U.A., Meerut U.A., Bareilly U.A. and Gorakhpur U.A. which accounted for 16.23% of the total urban population of Uttar Pradesh. Within 0.50 million to 0.30 million, 5 cities of Aligarh M.B., Ghaziabad U.A., Moradabad U.A., Saharanpur U.A., Jhansi U.A., combinedly contribute 7.43 per cent of state's total urban population. Within 0.30 million to 0.10 million, 28 cities are included under the category of small cities contributing 15.90 per cent of the total urban population of Uttar Pradesh. Thus, 52.03 per cent of the total urban population is shared by class I cities in 1991.

Considering the degree of effective urbanization, out of 753 cities and towns, 520 or 70 per cent of the total towns were less than 20,000 in population size which sustained only 20 per cent (5.51 million) of total urban population of Uttar Pradesh. While 1,00,000 to 20,000 category is represented by 198 large and medium towns or 26.30 per cent of the total towns that contribute 27.79 per cent (7.66 million) of total urban population. However, the degree of metropolitan development is represented by above 1,00,000 population in which 41 cities or 5.50 per cent of the total towns and cities account for 52.23 per cent (14.42 million) of the total urban population of Uttar Pradesh.

Though the absolute urban growth in Uttar Pradesh from 1971 onward has been significantly high but an equally fast expanding rural population has certainly pulled down its status on urbanization in low category. Regarding decadal variation of towns in various size categories, it is again the class I cities recording an increase in growth rate of 4.03 per cent, in which Kanpur U.A. has recorded a decline by -4.10 per cent, Lucknow U.A. has recorded a sharp increase by +41.87 per cent from 1981 to 1991. The class II towns have recorded a decline by -0.60 per cent, class III towns a marginal rise by +1.22 per cent, the class IV towns have recorded a decline by -1.12 per cent during 1981 to 1991. The class V towns recorded a decline by -2.61 per cent, the class VI towns have recorded a decline by -0.90 per cent, from 1981 to 1991. Thus, a definite gain in the percentage of urban population is recorded by class I cities in the last decade.

An attempt is made to study the growth rate of urban population in various districts of Uttar Pradesh taking base year as 1901. As against a national average of nearly 500 percent increase in urban population from 1901 to 1991, the districts then existed in 1901, have shown an increase are, Dehradun (13056.1%), Nainital (1149.4%) Sultanpur (1195.5%) all are very high in growth rate of urban population. Next in order are Kanpur (934.52%) followed by Kheri (768.29%), Pratapgarh (643.14%), Lucknow (591.59%), Banda (588.95%), Varanasi (587.4%), Jalaun (544.1%). Rai Barelli (533.14%), Hamirpur (526.4%), Jhansi (520.8%) Muzaffarnagar (519.2%), Rest of the district recorded growth rate of urban population below the state average.

During 1981 to 1991, a definite trend towards metro-politanization is noticed. There is a considerable shift of towns from medium and small group to large cities. Partly it can be ascribed to the definitional changes during 1991 as a result nearly 200 town areas were declassified. Consequently urban population base reduced in less than 20,000 population size towns and a rise in percentage of urban population in class I cities is noticed. However, the absolute rise in number of class I cities does not support the above view. It seems rather a contradictory situation. That on one hand, the number of class I cities is increasing along with increasing population size of cities, on the other hand, the total urban population of Uttar Pradesh has recorded a sharp decline in terms of decadal growth rate.

Table 1.8 : Uttar Pradesh: Classwise Growth of Urban Population (%) 1901-1991

Year	*Class I*	*Class II*	*Class III*	*Class IV*	*Class V*	*Class VI*
1901	24.20	13.97	11.42	18.28	21.22	10.91
1911	25.66	13.49	11.00	18.47	19.64	11.74
1921	25.71	15.34	10.68	15.73	19.60	12.93
1931	27.89	14.25	15.82	15.29	16.78	09.97
1941	37.77	10.81	16.99	12.89	15.21	06.32
1951	45.70	09.04	14.40	11.42	13.51	05.94
1961	54.88	11.76	16.65	10.85	05.65	00.22
1971	57.66	10.93	16.87	09.83	04.54	00.18
1981	51.48	12.43	12.82	13.39	08.46	01.42
1991	55.51	11.83	14.04	12.27	05.85	00.51

However, the 1991 census results were below the projected urban population. This difference between estimated population and actual population was surprising. Thus, an alternate explanation can be offered by attributing this lessening attraction of urban places to an increasing economic viability in rural area. During 1980's many rural development programmers were instituted by the government like Rural Labour Employment Guarantee Program (RLEGP), the Integrated Rural Development Programme (IRDP) and Jawahar Rozgar Yojna (JRY). Another point of concern is the rate of rural population growth in Uttar Pradesh. The generally held view is that the share of rural population growth falls as the share of agriculture in the economy decreases with increase in urbanization. It is rather observed that the rural population growth continued unabated 1960 onwards in Uttar Pradesh.

After Independence the thrust on industrialization apparently failed to achieve the desired results of sectoral development and transfer of economy from rural-based to urban-based. In Indian economic history, 1980 marks the beginning of modern industrialization. Yet the large-scale industrialization in India could not lessen the dependency on traditional economic sector that is agriculture and its allied activities.

In case of Uttar Pradesh, the impact of above phenomena is well marked. Urban economics of scale have operated along with its colonial history of urbanization. An increase of 11 class I cities from 30 in 1981 to 41 in 1991, is an obvious indication of the preferences of industries to locate themselves near large cities. The government apathy to control growing concentration of industries in few selected locations resulted in sharp rise of the percentage of urban population in class I cities from 47.23 per cent in 1981 to 52.23 per cent in 1991. The National Capital Region (NCR) of Delhi has been delineated with a view to integrate the interdependence that exists between various metropolitan areas of the extended metropolises, its effects on Uttar Pradesh urbanization scenario is posing queries.

2

DEMOGRAPHIC ASPECTS OF URBANIZATION

Urbanization in a strict demographic sense is the percentage increase of urban population to total population (Davis and Hertz: 1957). Customarily, the degree of urbanization of any place is defined as the proportion of urban population above a specified minimum population size residing in an urban area for a particular point of time.

Implicit within this definition of urbanization, is a multitude of underlying processes that bring about the concentration of population in cities and towns of various sizes. Popeno, D. (1965) has drawn a distinction between urbanization and urban processes. Urbanization is defined as the aggregation of people into relatively large, dense and heterogeneous settlements of various sizes. This process itself, according to him, is an outcome of the spatial manifestation of urban process which defines economic functionalities of various population groups. The concept of ecological analysis to explain the demographic aspect of urbanization was suggested by Lampard, E. (1965) as an organizational component of a population achieved capacity for adaptation to a given socio-economic environment to attain a certain minimum level of security and sustenance.

In a statistical sense, the percentage increase of urban to total population is a function of the underlying processes like the rate of net migration, natural increase and reclassification of cities. With rural and urban natural growth rates being almost the same, migration from rural to urban areas contributes effectively in the increase of the degree of urbanization.

The interplay of factors to bring about the change in demographic components are varied in case of developed and developing countries. Urbanization in the western world was a gradual and sequential transformation of population from agricultural to non-agricultural occupations. The mechanization of agriculture was accompanied by a rising demand of labor in the steadily expanding industrial sector of economy. Consequently there was a decline in percentage of rural or farm population with a corresponding rise in the percentage of urban or non-farm population.

In developing world, urbanization is progressing mainly from a lack of demand for agricultural workers due mainly to increasing man-land ratio in rural areas along with a slow expanding industrial sector in urban areas. India has also availed to itself the modern agricultural technology developed in western world which is rather labor saving than labor absorbing. This adds more pressure of population to the already stressed agricultural lands resulting in increasing proportions of marginal and non-workers in rural areas, thus generating destitute stream of rural out-migrants in search of employment towards urban places.

At comparable levels of urbanization with the western world, India is already suffering from a rapidly expanding base of its both rural and urban population. In rural areas, the medical facilities and family welfare clinics have helped in reducing the mortality rates to a great extent due to which a high rate of natural increase of population in the countryside is recorded. Therefore, the immediate problem faced by India is the absolute urban growth of population rather than urbanization itself since level of urbanization is low, only 25.72 per cent in 1991.

Percentage of Urban Population

The percentage of urban population to total population for all practical purposes forms the basis to assess the levels of urbanization. At any given point of time, it is a reflective of on-going process of technological development, pace of industrialization and changes in the agrarian structure of the economy over a considerable period of time. Thus, it is a cumulative and causative index of recording all pull and push factors operative in urban and rural areas respectively. This indicator, although suffering from various constraints, is still considered to be one of the basic indicators to reflect the underlying dynamics of urbanization. However, it is highly sensitive to what constitutes 'urban'.

Spatial Process

In Uttar Pradesh, during 1991, the percentage of urban population was 19.84%, which in itself denotes a very low level of urbanization. The underlying mechanism for the state as a whole during 1991 is reflected by the correlation matrix, according to which the process of urbanization is occurring through in-migration from outside the state particularly from urban areas (+0.61). It further corresponds to the effective urbanization (+0.54) suggesting that migration is generally aimed at large cities. Males with metric but below graduate degree (+0.49) especially in working age group (+0.52) also explain the underlying occupational mechanism. The female workers more than graduate (+0.47) and large family size (+0.47) also corresponds along with dependency ratio of youths (+0.48) highlighting the characteristics of urbanization.

Spatial Patterns

The interplay of factors operative on state at an aggregate level is manifested in spatial perspective with varying degree of intensity resulting in definite spatial patterns (Fig.3).

Between 51-84 per cent lies very high category with only two districts of Kanpur Nagar (84.0%) and Lucknow (62.6%) with very high effective urbanization rates. Lucknow being an administrative center shows preponderance of highly educated workers both males and females while in Kanpur Nagar, the workers belong to educated category only up to graduation mainly due to the industrial base of economy. Female work participation in high paid services is a characteristic phenomenon of both the places. In general, Kanpur Nagar records lower in-migration and lower decadal growth rates while Lucknow records a higher decadal variation with more in-migrants mainly from urban areas.

The high category lies between 34-50 per cent in which 4 districts including Dehradun in Kumaon Himalayas and Ghaziabad,

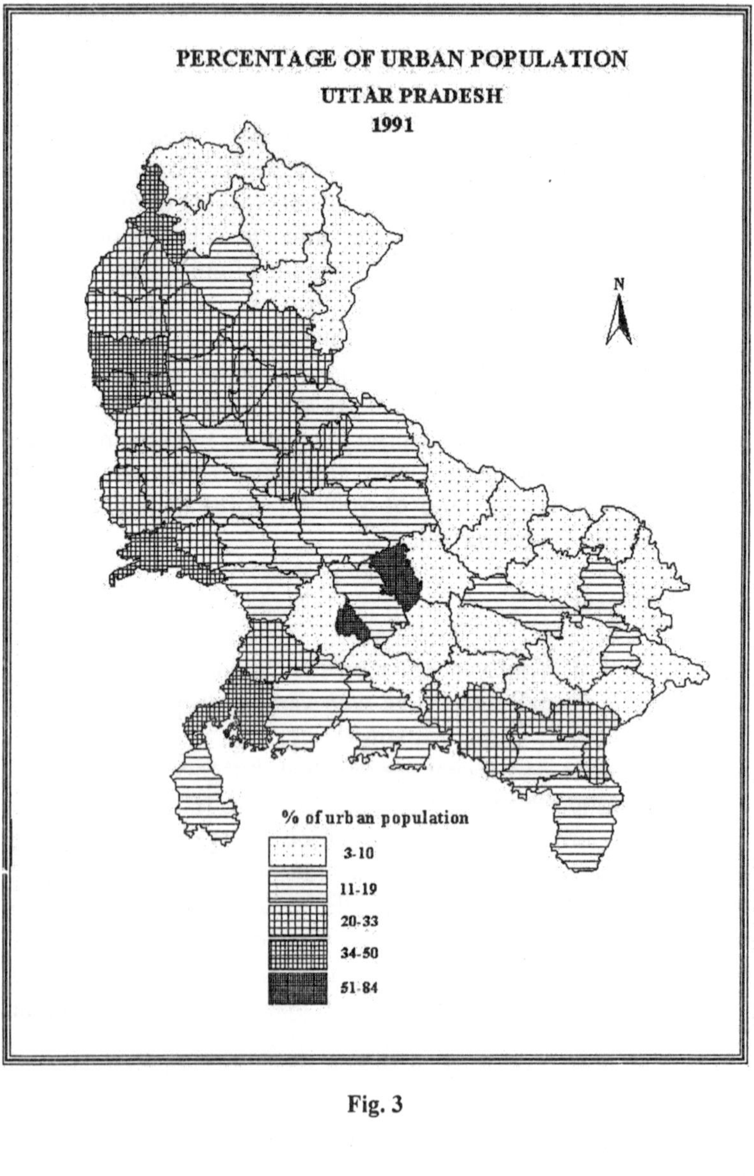
PERCENTAGE OF URBAN POPULATION
UTTAR PRADESH
1991
N
% of urban population
3-10
11-19
20-33
34-50
51-84

Fig. 3

Meerut, Agra in Upper Ganga Plain lie. All these except Dehradun, are centers of industrial importance showing almost the same mechanism underlying urbanization as discussed in case of very high category. However, these areas except Agra are low in urban density with effective urbanization. The decadal variation rate for 1981-91 is very high in case of Ghaziabad and Meerut due to the impact of National Capital Region of Delhi.

Between 20-33 per cent lie the medium category under which 17 districts cover almost the entire Upper Ganga Plain in the north and part of it in the south. The agricultural economy of this area is sound and a balanced development of towns is noticed as in Muzaffarnagar, Saharanpur, Mathura and Aligarh. The effective urbanization is also well marked in this region. Another concentration comprising of Varanasi and Allahabad, though has effective urbanization, the percentage of main workers is low suggesting the dominance of service sector with more seasonal workers.

Between 11-19 per cent lies the low category, with 19 districts showing a heavy concentration towards the east and south of the previous category in southern Upper Ganga Plain and parts of eastern Middle Ganga Plain. Budaun, Etah, Mainpuri, Pilibhit, Mau, Faizabad and Gorakhpur are basically areas of poor base of urban economy. The whole of the Southern Plateau region is covered by this category excluding Jhansi and Etawah. In general, it is a low productive area with little economic resources for industrial development; therefore, low degree of urbanization prevails.

The very low category lies between 3-10 per cent in which 21 districts cover the whole of Middle Ganga Plain and the whole of Uttar Pradesh Himalaya. The Northern hill districts, apart from Dehradun, are fast urbanizing despite its very low percentage of urban population. In Ganga Plain region, the limited economic opportunities with mounting pressure of population upon existing agricultural lands has promoted out-migration of active age group males. This area is prone to urban environmental problems like malnutrition, poverty, congestion and crowding as suggested by very high dependency ratio of both young and old population.

In general, the spatial pattern of urbanization has shown a close affinity with the regional pattern of economy. The thriving agricultural base has introduced a more balanced urban economic development and an integrated hierarchy of towns as noticed in case of western Uttar Pradesh while stagnant economy of central part has promoted pockets of polarized urban development like Kanpur Nagar and Lucknow. The agricultural backwardness as in case of eastern Uttar Pradesh has lead to the lopsided development of urban hierarchy in which one or two cities dominate the area with general low to very low level of urbanization in the district as a whole. The role of migration in the urbanization process in general, is highly localized.

Density of Urban Population

Urban density, basically a function of area and population, reflects the control of many official changes in the delimitation of district that affects the consistency and continuity of tracing the course and directions of urbanization in Uttar Pradesh. The areal units rather act as an interaction fields in which the cities serve as fixed nodes for the interplay of forces behind urbanization process. The city-hinterland functional relation defines the urban population density on an aggregate level for the urban territory. It is an on going process which determines the level of concentration of urban population under the influence of either a sustained polarization effect of urban economy or spurious incidences of insurgence of urban growth. Both these processes are active in case of Uttar Pradesh. While the former process has led to a "push back" operative system due to a snag in industrial policy noticed recently resulting in lessening of urban density, the latter in face of over population and deteriorating agricultural scenario has expressed itself in areas of high urban density through the process of in-migration and rate of natural increase.

Spatial Process

As per 1991 census, the urban density in Uttar Pradesh is 4927 persons per square kilometre. The density corresponds with rising pressure of population on large cities as is shown by the density of households more than 5 persons with 2-room facility (+0.66) and a corresponding association with total tertiary workers (+0.53) with short distance migration from urban to urban areas (+0.50) in places of more than 20,000 population (+0.48) and rising sex ratio (+0.49) as a result of female non-agricultural workers (+0.42).

Spatial Patterns

However, the combination of factor identified through correlation matrix might not be operative on same magnitude all over Uttar Pradesh. Regional variations exist considerably, perpetuated by local or regional factors (Fig. 4).

Between 8265-11653 persons per sq. km. very high category lies which covers only 5 districts in Upper Ganga Plain. Incidentally all these areas are medium to low on percentage of urban population but have high to medium level of effective urbanization. Lying within an agriculturally highly productive region, the area is under immense population pressure receiving migrants from both rural and urban areas mainly directed towards towns of more than 20,000 population. Historically important on urbanization scene is Muzaffarnagar with highest density followed by Saharanpur, Bijnor, Etah and Shahjahanpur.

Between 5789-8264 persons per sq. km. lies high category under which 11 districts cover the highly urbanized parts of the Upper Ganga Plain and Middle Ganga Plain. Kanpur Nagar with highest degree of urbanization, followed by Mathura, Agra, Moradabad, Rampur, Varanasi, Allahabad with high to medium percentage of urban population as well as effective urbanization. The highly diversified base of economy has attracted migrants from various socio-economic strata resulting in high density of urban population.

Between 4396-5788 persons per sq. km. is medium category which occupies 18 districts covering areas widely scattered all over the Ganga Plain including districts with high percentage of urban population and developed sector of economy like Lucknow, Varanasi, Meerut, Aligarh, Bulandshahr, Nainital, Jhansi along with a zone of low urbanized region in central part of Ganga Plain in Unnao, Barabanki, Kheri along with the districts of Jaunpur, Azamgarh, Sonbhadra. This category identifies areas of both

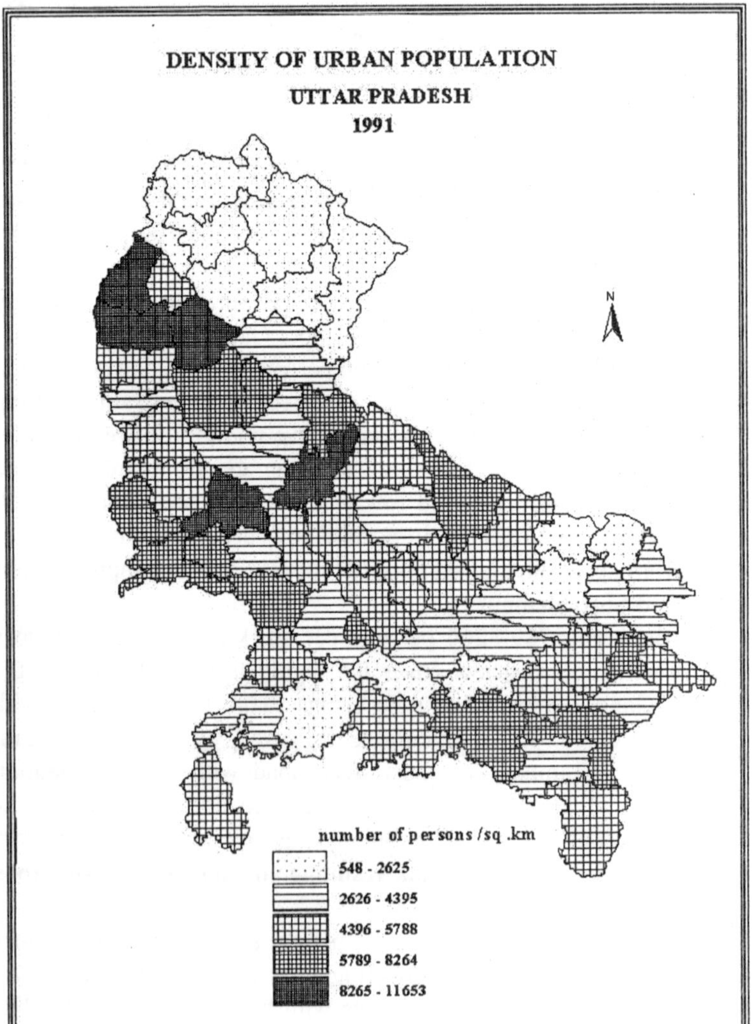
DENSITY OF URBAN POPULATION
UTTAR PRADESH
1991
N
number of persons /sq .km
548 - 2625
2626 - 4395
4396 - 5788
5789 - 8264
8265 - 11653

Fig. 4

affluence and poverty like Lucknow and Unnao lying almost at par regarding urban density.

Between 2626–4395 persons per sq. km. lies low category, which includes 16 districts mainly in the eastern Middle Ganga Plain in which Faizabad, Sultanpur, Gorakhpur, Deoria and Ghazipur are significant. Ghaziabad in the Western Uttar Pradesh and Varanasi in the southern Uttar Pradesh along with Jhansi is also included in this category. In general the decrease in the level of urbanization seems to be related with the decrease in urban density within this category.

Very low category lies between 548-2625 persons per sq .kms. in which 13 districts cover the whole of northern hill districts of Uttar Pradesh for obvious reason of more land in relation to population. Hamirpur, Fatehpur, Pratapgarh, Basti, Siddarthnagar and Maharajganj also lie in this category as a result of lesser economic opportunities to attract migrants, consequently with lesser density of urban population.

Thus, the spatial pattern of distribution of urban density seems to arise from basically the economic forces responsible for concentration of urban population especially in cities of more than 20,000 at two levels. The first level concerns with the areas of high level of urbanization and high effective urbanization in which the work participation rates in both secondary and tertiary sectors are defined by majority of educated workers with more in-migration at inter-district level from urban areas in places like Kanpur Nagar, Lucknow, Allahabad, and others. The second aspect concerns with places of less degree of urbanization with effective urbanization in which there is more concentration of less educated secondary workers with intra-district migration like in Rampur, Shahjahanpur, and Pilibhit. However, the inclusion of districts like Unnao, Barabanki, and Kheri with a very low level of urbanization within medium density category foretells a deteriorating scenario of urban living environment.

Decadal Variation of Urban Population (1981-1991)

Urbanization is leading to concentration of population in cities and towns of various size groups. The economic disparities in the region manifest itself in functional disparities within the urban centers influencing the rate of in migration. As a result of concentration of active age group population, the urban growth through natural increase competes with the rate of migration especially for large urban centers, which are able to sustain the growing streams of migrants at one level or other. In case of Uttar Pradesh, an obvious low level of urbanization curtails the absolute growth of urban population because both rural and urban population growth rates through natural increase are almost the same.

Spatial Process

During 1981-91 the spatial process to bring about decadal variation in urban population of 38.73 per cent seems not to be influenced by any particular variable as suggested by the correlation matrix. A very weak correlation exists with urban density (+0.23) suggesting that already densely populated areas are experiencing decadal variation of urban population during 1981-91.

Spatial Patterns

Although, on aggregate level, the process was not revealing itself in any particular mechanism, on regional level variations exist (Fig 5).

Between 57-98 per cent lies very high category with 7 districts in scattered and isolated pockets of urban population increase. The two notable groups are highly urbanized Ghaziabad, Nainital, Lucknow along with the low urbanized Tehri Garhwal, Sultanpur, Gorakhpur and Maharajganj. Thus, emergence of industrial activities and development of tertiary sector seem to have determined decadal variation rate.

Between 45-56 per cent lies the high category in which 8 districts with low urbanization levels have recorded high percentage increase of urban population in which Pithoragarh, Pilibhit, Siddharthnagar, Mainpuri, Mau and Sonbhadra are experiencing an increase in the tertiary sector of economy. Meerut in the vicinity of Ghaziabad is able to attract migrants as a result of its industrial base of economy. A healthy sign is the corresponding rise in secondary workers in the other than household industry and female work participation in active age group is one of the highest in these districts.

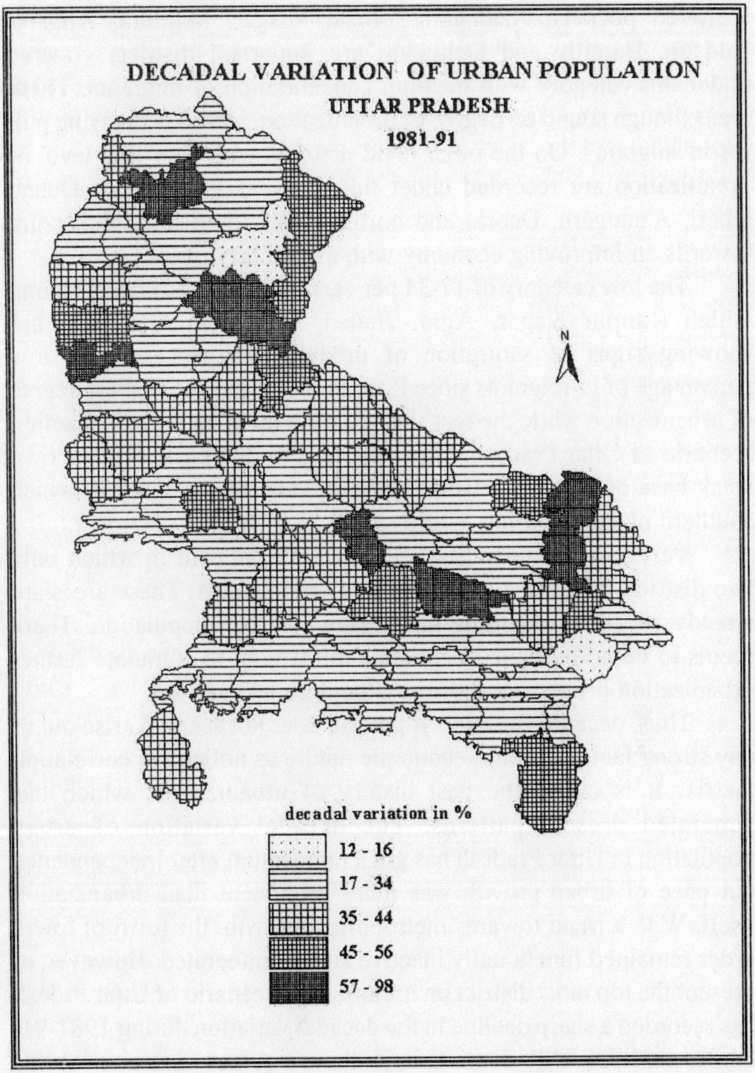
DECADAL VARIATION OF URBAN POPULATION
UTTAR PRADESH
1981-91
N
decadal variation in %
12 - 16
17 - 34
35 - 44
45 - 56
57 - 98

Fig. 5

Medium category is formed by 35-44 per cent of decadal variation under which 16 districts in the whole of Ganga Plain lie in scattered pockets. Azamgarh, Muzaffarnagar, Mathura, Aligarh, Budaun, Bareilly and Dehradun are important districts covered under this category with medium concentration of migrants. These areas though sound on degree of urbanization, record decreasing pull for in migrants. On the other hand districts with very low level of urbanization are recorded under this category like Kanpur Dehat, Kheri, Azamgarh, Deoria and northern Hill districts, which point towards an improving economy with availability of jobs.

The low category of 17-34 per cent includes 30 districts among which Kanpur Nagar, Agra, Jhansi, Varanasi, Allahabad are showing signs of saturation of urbanization process with low percentage of in-migrants since Kanpur Nagar has the highest degree of urbanization while the rest also are prominent on the urbanization scenario of Uttar Pradesh. Other districts on the basis of their own weak base of urban economy are occupying this category in which southern plateau and few northern hill districts are prominent.

Very low category lies between 3-10 per cent in which only two districts of Ghazipur and Almora are included. These areas are already very low regarding percentage of urban population. There seems to be no particular economic motivation to stimulate further urbanization process as shown by the decadal variation.

Thus, decadal variation at present does not seem to arise out of any strong factor of socio-economic nature as noticed in correlation matrix. It is rather the past history of urbanization, which has generated present patterns. The decadal variation of urban population in Uttar Pradesh has got a momentum after independence but pace of urban growth was more prominent than urbanization itself. With a trend towards metropolitan growth, the town of lower order remained functionally inactive and un-integrated. However, at present the top most district on urbanization scenario of Uttar Prdesh has recorded a sharp decline in the decadal variation during 1981-91, while northern Hill districts and the very less urbanized parts especially along Tarai region and around Kanpur Nagar-Lucknow have recorded a rise. In face of a slowly expanding industrial base of economy both spatially and sectorally, under employment and unemployment have resulted. This acted as a deterrent to the flow of in migrants, therefore, bringing down the urban growth rates in highly urbanized areas, while less urbanized areas continued to record urban growth.

Effective Urbanization

Indian urbanization is marked by a definite trend towards metropolitan growth due to its colonial heritage of few large cities, which continues to grow and expand even after independence. The economies of scale preferred concentration of productive forces in few large cities of colonial era which with due course of time became catalyst for a balanced regional urban economic system. In this process small cities, which were usually handicraft and marketing centers and even medium towns suffered loosing their population base in favor of large cities.

The weakening economic base of small and medium towns could not support the emerging urban occupation structure. Therefore, in Indian context, places less than 20,000 can better be termed as urban villages or quasi-urbanized, and places with more than 20,000 population are considered to measure the degree of urbanization in a more effective way.

Spatial Process

Uttar Pradesh has a very high degree of effective urbanization with 80.09 per cent of urban population in places of more than 20,000, which correlates well with the degree of urbanization (+0.54) suggesting it to be a phenomenon of highly urbanized areas. It also recognizes the workforce structure of females engaged in non-agricultural activities (+0.59) along with secondary workers (+0.47) especially in other than household industry (+0.45).

Spatial Patterns

At district level certain spatial regularities are noticed in the distribution pattern of the degree of effective urbanization with varying set of forces (Fig.6).

Between 81-99 per cent of urban population in places of 20,000 or more, the very high category lies under which 18 districts cover most of Upper Ganga Plain and part of Middle Ganga Plain particularly in the east. Though varying on the degree of

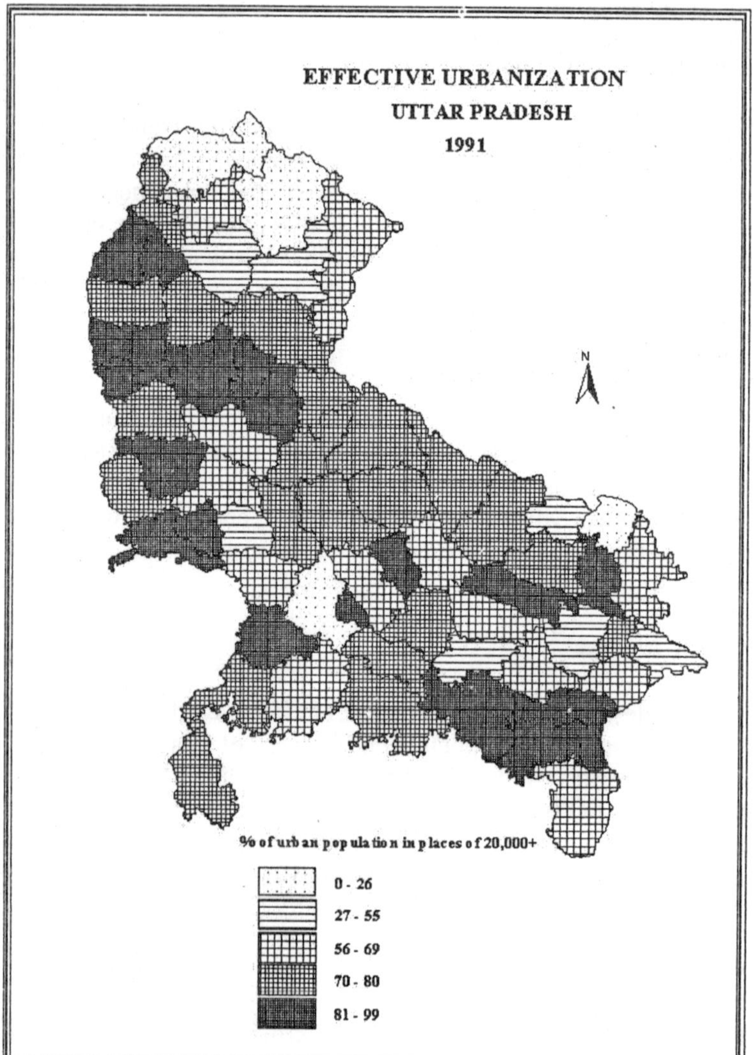
EFFECTIVE URBANIZATION
UTTAR PRADESH
1991
N
% of urban population in places of 20,000+
0 - 26
27 - 55
56 - 69
70 - 80
81 - 99

Fig. 6

urbanization, majority of the districts have a history of urban-economic and socio-political changes. Within very high to high degree of urbanization, Kanpur Nagar, Lucknow, Mathura, Agra, Varanasi, Allahabad and Meerut and low urbanized areas like Aligarh, Jalaun, Faizabad, Gorakhpur and Mirzapur have an old urbanization base except the newly industrialized district of Ghaziabad.

Between 70-80 per cent lies the high category with 22 districts cover almost the whole of Tarai and western Middle Ganga Plain, western Upper Ganga Plain and Southern Mirzapur Plateau. Dehradun, Muzaffarnagar, Mathura, Jhansi are areas with high degree of urbanization and a sound economic base. The group of district along Tarai region suffers from a weak base of economy, thus only selected towns or cities are significant on urbanization scenario like in Pilibhit, Kheri, Bahraich, Gonda. Similar situation prevails in the interior and southern part where Banda, Fatehpur, Rae Bareili, Mau, Bijnor, Nainital show same phenomenon.

Between 56-69 per cent lies medium category, which occupies 13 districts covering mainly eastern Middle Ganga Plain with mainly low to very low degree of urbanization and only one or two cities of dominance. These districts are occupying generally areas with stagnant agricultural activities and disproportionate concentration of urban economic activities in few cities. The areas with upcoming economic opportunities like Tehri Garhwal and Sonbhadra lie at par with Hamirpur, Sitapur, Deoria and Jaunpur.

Between 27-55 per cent lies low category in which 7 districts are widely distributed. In the foothills of the Himalayas the districts of Almora and Garhwal have insignificant percentage of urban population. In eastern Uttar Prdesh the districts of Pratapgarh, Azamgarh and Ballia are important though the base of urban economy is weak.

Very low category lies between 0-26 per cent in which 4 districts including Uttar Kashi, Chamoli, Maharajgang and Kanpur Dehat reflect the functional limitations or monofunctionality of towns discouraging effective urbanization.

Thus, effective urbanization in Uttar Pradesh, is arising out of either multi-functional character of selected cities, encouraging in migration as in case Upper Ganga Plain or functional stagnation of regional economy as in case of most of Ganga Plain especially in the central part where Kanpur Nagar and Lucknow dominate the scene of effective urbanization. The selectivity of population concentration in places of more than 20,000 is a reflective of the functional dominance of few cities in the absence of a diversified economic base of the study area. Since the policies of industrial decentralization could not be implemented very effectively, no systematic hierarchical evolution of towns for whole of Uttar Pradesh could be evolved.

Urban Sex Ratio

Apart from the differentials in the rate of natural increase of male and female population, the age and sex selectivity of migrants also tends to accentuate the difference between numbers of females per thousand males. In Indian case, females are considered less mobile and generally accompany their husband after the settling down of the male counterpart in the place of destination. Consequently, in the early stage of the cycle of migration, the birth rates tend to decline both at the place of origin and destination of migrants. At a later stage females accompany and urban sex ratio tend to equalize again till a new incentive in the form of upcoming opportunities in urban areas sets in motion a fresh cycle of migration flow and destabilization in urban sex ratio.

Spatial Process

Urban sex ratio in Uttar Pradesh is low with 860 females/1000 males. It correlates strongly with large family size of more than five persons (+0.85) and also the household density with more than 6 persons with 2 room facilities (+0.67) suggesting it to be a feature of congested and densely populated urban places. Since the variables do not show any relation with percentage of urban population or in places with effective urbanization, it points out to be a feature of stagnant or socially backward area.

Spatial Patterns

At local level, certain other factors apart from those mentioned above might interact to influence the ratio of females to males. In general the sex ratio shows almost uniform spatial distribution (Fig. 7).

Between 885-932 lies the very high category covering 9 districts in which Bijnor, Rampur, Lalitpur, Barabanki and eastern parts of Middle Ganga Plain are included. All these districts stand low to very low except Rampur with medium degree of urbanization. It represents basically areas with economic backwardness and out migration of males as shown by very low percentage of workers in active age group which has increased sex ratio in districts like Barabanki, Azamgarh, Ghazipur, Mau and Ballia.

Between 850-884 lies high category under which almost whole of the Ganga Plain lies. It is the most prevalent category covering 36 districts including Lucknow. This whole belt is characterized by low percentage of population of males within active age group, which is a suggestive of out-migrating male population. In case of Upper Ganga Plain especially in Lucknow, Mathura Aligarh, Muzaffarnagar and Etah, short distance migration of females along with males has changed the demographic character of this area in favor of females while the rest of area hints at out-migrating males.

Between 754-849 lies the medium category, which 10 districts including high-urbanized parts like Kanpur Nagar, Ghaziabad, Allahabad, Dehradun along with Faizabad, Etawah, Hardwar. All these areas have incidentally a sound level of urbanization except Hamirpur and Hardwar. Sex selectivity of male in-migrants seems to be the prime cause of disturbed sex ratio in these areas.

Between 625-753 lies low category in which 4 districts of Uttar kashi, Almora, Garhwal and Sonbhadra are included. Incidentally, all these areas are undergoing rapid urbanization and attracting male migrants in active age group, thus disbalancing the sex ratio.

Between 563-624 lies the very low category in which 2 districts of Chamoli and Tehri Garhwal are included. In these two districts the migration is solely by males for economic reasons and family migration is discouraged due to hostile climatic conditions.

Thus, urban sex ratio seems to be basically an outcome of out-migration of males in active age group for reasons mainly economic from areas of economic stagnation like eastern Uttar Pradesh or in migration of males in active age group in areas of active economy like in western Uttar Pradesh. However, all throughout the Ganga

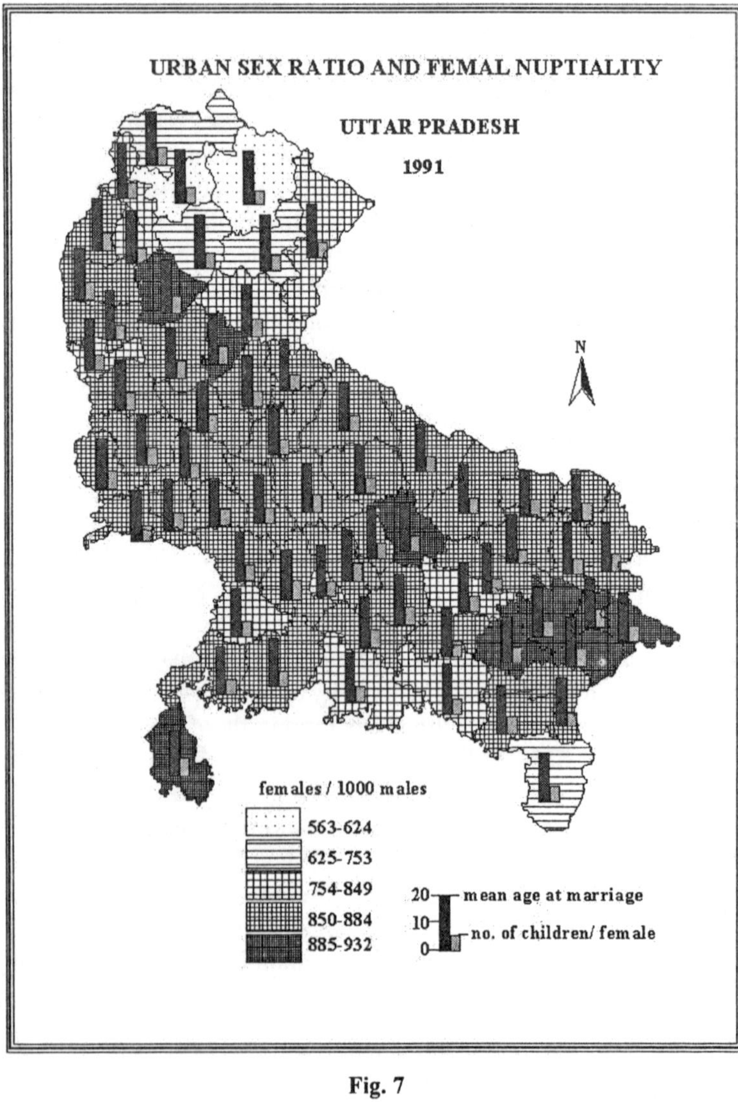
URBAN SEX RATIO AND FEMAL NUPTIALITY
UTTAR PRADESH
1991
N
females / 1000 males
563-624
625-753
754-849
850-884
885-932
20
10
0
mean age at marriage
no. of children/ female

Fig. 7

Plain the high urban sex ratio compared to state average, signifies both the out migrating males as well as the relative mobility of females especially from short distances from rural to urban either for economic or social reasons. In areas of hostile climate or difficult terrain like the Northern Hill districts, the relatively more mobility of males had a deciding effect on the sex composition of population.

Female Nuptiality

Female nuptiality is a character of marital status of women at a specific age. The influence of urbanism is most strongly reflected in the changing life styles of females. The desire for higher education and career building generally delays the age at marriage. The impact of urbanism also manifests itself in the decision-making power of an urban female compared to her rural counter part.

Spatial Process

In Uttar Pradesh, in 1991 the female mean age at marriage in urban area records 19 years. A number of factors might have influenced the females' marriageable age, as is indicated by correlation values. The female educational level, more than graduate correlates very strongly (+0.82) with the age at marriage. The female workers with more than graduate (+0.80), workers in tertiary sector (+0.60) and better living conditions with basic amenities (+0.80). However, households with medium family of 3-5 persons with 2 rooms suggest the joint family system and a traditional setup of the society to which these educated and working females belong to.

Spatial Patterns

Regional variation exists regarding the combination of factors influencing age at marriage. A clear pattern emerges in which the role of socio-cultural and economic set up of the society seems to be more important than just the degree of urbanization (Fig.7).

Only 11 or 17.5 per cent of the districts lie in high category within 21 above years of mean age of marriage of females. In general the whole of northern Hill districts by virtue of their socio-cultural distinction either as institutional area or tourism centers, have established a culture of female education, economic independency and late marriage like in Dehra Dun, Almora and Nainital. Even less developed districts like Pithoragarh, Garhwal also show higher mean age at marriage. While in Ganga Plain, apart from Lucknow, only Saharanpur and Bijnor have recorded values in high category. Lucknow being a highly urbanized area understandably shows impact of modernizing society. Though Saharanpur and Bijnor seem to suffer from the socio-economic backwardness, still show a satisfactory level of female education with graduate and above degree. The whole of northern Upper Ganga Plain though records medium to low on percentage of urban population, represents medium age around 19 years of female at marriage. Even Kanpur Nagar and Allahabad along with Kanpur Dehat, Fatehpur, Rae Bareli and Unnao record medium age of around 19 years. In general, the whole of Ganga Plain with 27 or 42.9 per cent of the districts lying below average, irrespective of its degree of urbanization, is dominated by a traditional society. It still attaches values to its own custom and tradition where despite female education and economic independency, marriage is generally at an early age around 18.

However, a combination of higher education of females and more specifically their working status in tertiary sector seem to have determined the mean age at marriage at local levels. Thus, it is both the impact of modernization and inherent poverty levels of the families, which is pushing up mean age at marriage of females in Uttar Pradesh.

Number of Children Per Female

Though a demographic criteria, this indictor is more oriented towards the social aspects of urbanization. The culture of city dwellers is markedly different from their rural counterparts. The high cost of living in urban areas in face of aspirations for a respectable life style, tries to restrict number of children in a family. Still in India, the decision to determine the size of the family, is generally taken by males however, rising educational levels in females and economic independency have given them liberty to exercise their own choice for number of children. The more number of children seems to be also a character of high-density areas where the traditional societies try to stick to their own family norms. Thus, to reflect upon the present transformations in the urban society in Uttar Pradesh, only the child bearing age group (15-49) of females is considered with number of children per female.

Spatial Process

In 1991, urban female within age group 15-49 have on an average 4 children, which in itself indicates an excess of children in the demographic scenario of urban Uttar Pradesh compared to the rest of India. Regarding number of children, there is no well-established link with any social or economic indicator. A weak correlation exists with the migrants from outside the state from rural areas (+0.40) with a corresponding weak correlation with sex ratio (+0.35). It suggest that the existing scenario is a character of rural migrants mainly those accompanied by their wives and children as is also suggested by a weak positive relation with density of households of more than 5 person with 2 rooms facility.

Spatial Patterns

The spatial distribution of the number of children per female within 15 to 49 age group shows a definite pattern (Fig.7).

In general large family norms are common in Uttar Pradesh as it is basically an agricultural state with deep-rooted cultural ethos, which favour large family size. Nearly 30 or 47.2 per cent of the districts record high values of more than 5 children per female. Even places like Kanpur Nagar, Lucknow and Dehradun have recorded 3-4 numbers of children per female within childbearing age group of 15-49 years. The high category coincides with medium level of urbanization in Saharanpur, Muzaffarnagar, Bareilly, Moradabad, Aligarh, Bulandshahar and Mathura, which though economically stabilized but seems to be inhabited by traditional urban society with large family norms. In central and eastern Uttar Pradesh Deoria, Ghazipur,Mau, Mirzapur, Hardoi, Unnao, Rai Bareli and Fatehpur all have very low degree of urbanization with high number of children.

However, away from the Kanpur Nagar and lucknow especially along Tarai and southern margins of the state, the low values of 4 to 3 number of children per female are recorded.

Despite of female education and work participation rates, the desired impact of urbanism in determining the size of family seems not to be working very effectively in Uttar Pradesh. The reason partly lies in the role of rural migrants to urban areas with their large family size, which pushes up the figures at an aggregate level for even in high urbanized areas.

ACTIVE AGE GROUP

The age composition of population between 15-59 is generally defined as active age-group in demographic and working age group in economic terms. The relative proportion of population in this age group in any urban area is a function of fertility, mortality and most significantly the age selectivity of migrants.

Active Age Group: Total

India is passing through the second stage of demographic transition, which is characterized by a falling death rate without a corresponding decline in birth rates. Therefore, growth of population approximately at the rate of 2.1 per cent per annum is going to continue in near future as well. For urban areas the rate of population increase is variable, roughly around 3.2 per cent per annum, which is likely to rise further in near future.

In Indian scenario of urbanization, the urban areas are recording an increase in the active age group population mainly due to in migration of economically active population basically from rural to urban areas as well as from small urban places to large urban places in response to changing socio-economic stimulus between the place of origin and destination. The net effect is a disproportionate concentration of active age group in urban places specifically in large cities that can continue to record urban growth through natural increase itself even if the migration streams are abated.

Spatial Process

The percentage of active urban population within 15-59 is only 55 per cent in 1991 in Uttar Pradesh suggesting a high dependency ratio of both old and young age group of population. The correlation matrix suggest that concentration of active age group relates very strongly with in-migration of male population (+0.76), with educational level of males of above graduate (+0.72). It also relates with females more than graduate (+0.63) especially female workers more than graduate (+0.66), with tertiary sector development (+0.59) and rising household densities (+0.79).

Spatial Patterns

The selectivity of the process in spatial perspective is well marked giving rise to well defined distributional patterns (Fig. 8).

Between 63-66 per cent lies very high category covering only 2 districts of Almora and Tehri Garhwal, which are attracting migrants in active age group of both sexes from various educational backgrounds due to the industrial and tourism development. However, the small base of urban population results in very high proportion though the volume of active age group population itself is very low.

Between 60-62 per cent lies high category covering 6 districts in which Kanpur Nagar emerges significant followed by Dehradun. The causes favoring the concentration of active age population are the existing potential job markets in these urban areas. The remaining districts lie in the Northern Hill region, though very low on the scene of urbanization are attracting migrants from active age group due to economic reasons like Pithoragarh and Garhwal.

Between 56-59 per cent lies the medium category in which 10 districts cover scattered pockets mainly to the south western margins of Ganga Plain in Agra, Etawah, Jalaun and in eastern part of Uttar Pradesh in Faizabad, Sultanpur and Allahabad along with Sonbhadra. The position of Lucknow which is the second highest on urbanization is significant. Allahabad, Agra, Ghaziabad and Hardwar are areas already highly urbanized but now show lesser concentration of active age group. There seems to be a decreasing attraction in the already high-urbanized areas for potential migrants.

Between 53-55 per cent lies low category having 33 districts, which include the whole of southern Upper Ganga Plain and western

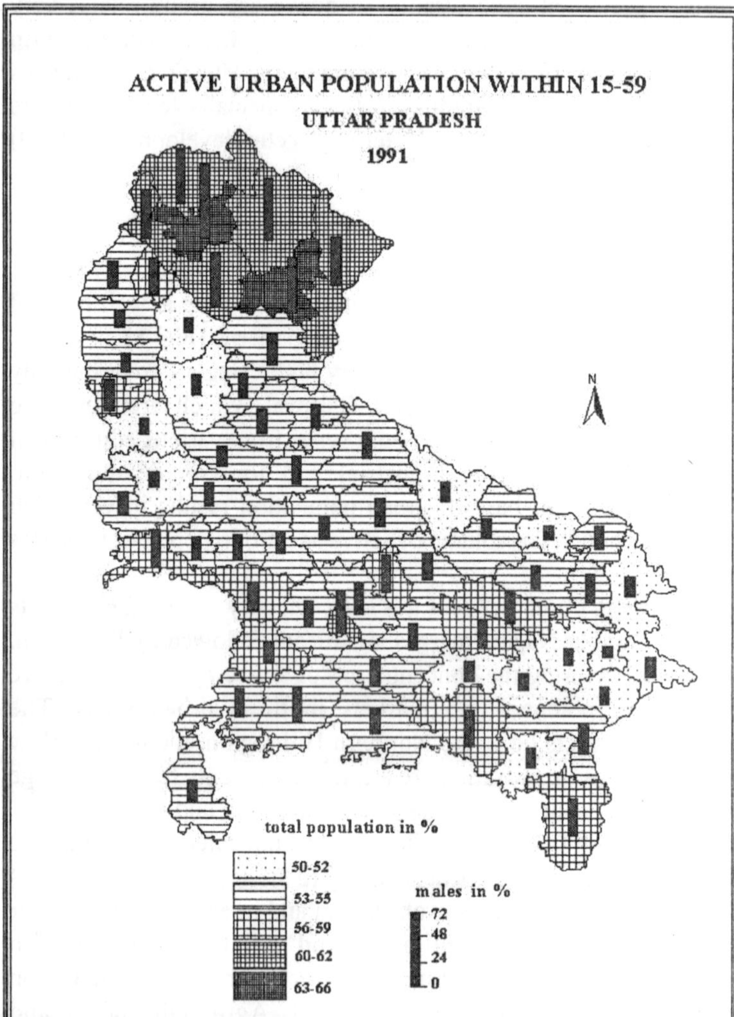
ACTIVE URBAN POPULATION WITHIN 15-59
UTTAR PRADESH
1991
N
total population in %
50-52
53-55
56-59
60-62
63-66
males in %
72
48
24
0

Fig. 8

Middle Ganga Plain excluding Lucknow and Kanpur Nagar. It covers areas with medium to low level of urbanization with a general degree of economic backwardness except Varanasi and Mathura.

Between 50-52 per cent lies very low category in which 15 districts lie covering margins of eastern Uttar Pradesh or western Uttar Pradesh with low to very low degree of urbanization. The inclusion of Aligarh and Moradabad in this category is signifying lesser desirability of this area by migrants mainly due to decreasing job opportunities.

Apart from combination of factors identified for Uttar Pradesh aggregately, the concentration of active age group seems to be determined by migration as noticed in case of northern hilly regions for upcoming new opportunities and also to large cities, which due to multifunctional base of economy are supportive of in-migrants. In case of highly urbanized service centers, the proportion of population in active age group is high as in Kanpur Nagar and Dehradun. The position of Lucknow on medium category presents a contrast, as it is second on scene of urbanization. Similarly, the areas with both small and large-scale industries like Agra, Aligarh and Ghaziabad are already showing signs of economic saturation as reflected in decreasing proportion of active age population. The low to very low level of percentage of population in active age group in the whole of Ganga Plain is more a function of vast base of urban population in as size of the family and dependency ratio especially for juvenile is high.

Active Age Group: Males

In any urban society, the age group of males especially in the active (15-59 years) is a sign of both demographic and economic change. This age group determines the rate of natural increase in population as well as economic prosperity of the area. The economic contribution through remittances by the migrants is also coming through this age group, which can also be a measure to equalize the inter-regional especially rural-urban wage differentials and inequalities in standards of living.

Industries and services requiring skilled labor generally opt for young workers. However, at any given point of time the proportion of males in active age group can be taken as a sign of a progressing economy.

Spatial Process

In Uttar Pradesh in 1991, the percentage of urban males in active age group of 15-59 is 55.90 per cent. It is strongly correlated with the total main workers (+0.83), below graduate (+0.67) and above graduate (+0.67) males suggesting it to be a character of workers in productive sector of economy. Females with above graduate (+0.62) and below graduate (+0.67) are also strongly correlated along with nucleated households with less than 3 members (+0.83). It further correlates with levels of amenities (+0.55). Thus, the process identifies itself with positive aspects of urbanization.

Spatial Patterns

The combination of factors has not been operative all over geographical space uniformly. Deviations result in percentage distribution pattern of urban males in active age group (Fig. 8).

On a broader scale of generalization, the same forces operative for Uttar Pradesh as a whole for total active population are causing concentration of males in active age group in spatial perspective. In case of Hill districts, the immediate family members are not accompanying males, giving rise to the proportion of males in active age group. Thus, only 6 or 9.5 per cent of the Hill districts lie above average within a range of 72-66 per cent of males in active age group.

However, in case of industrial city of Kanpur, or service-dominated places of Lucknow and Allahabad, either accompanying families or educated females through in-migration process in tertiary sector have lowered down the percentage of males in active age group. Thus 44 or 69.5 per cent of the districts lying mainly in the Upper and Middle Ganga Plains have recorded a value around 56 to 50 per cent of males in active age group. All throughout Ganga Plains, the low proportion indicates that the region has already exhausted its economic opportunities for migrants rather it represent an area of out migration of males in active age group. However, in comparison to total active population, this variable has shown selectivity in spatial pattern within districts with low to medium level of urbanization. While Saharanpur, Muzaffarnagar, Aligarh, Nainital and Etawah have recorded very low rates, the districts with very low level of urbanization are recording medium degree of concentration like Unnao and Banda.

MIGRATION

The increasing concentration of population in cities and towns of various sizes can best be explained in terms of migration specifically for India where both rural and urban population growth differential through natural increase remains almost the same.

The approach to the study of migration is generally through spatial analysis in which distances, directional bias and information flows can be comprehended through the application of gravity models (Shaw: 1975). To analyze the dynamics of aggregate flow, Ravienstein's model (1885) forms a base for the explanation of interactions and intervening opportunities between places of potential migration streams. Lee's theory of migration (1969) is an extension of Ravienstein's model which identifies the role of push and pull factors in defining the selectivity of migrants for personal preferences.

The notions of equilibrium derived from neo-classical economies suggested that in any region characterized by the wage differentials between rural and urban areas, labor would migrate from low to high-income areas. A corresponding equilibrium will try to maintain itself, through the transfer of labor from labor surplus to labor deficit regions till the rate of expansion of demand for labor in urban areas outstrips the growth rate of population in rural areas (Lewis: 1954).

Sjaastad's Human Investment Theory (1962) treats the decision to migrate as an investment decision involving costs and returns distributed over time. The 'returns' are divided into 'money' and 'non-money' components but 'decision' remains unaccounted in money terms.

Todaro (1976) presented a model of rural-urban migration in which he identified the concept of an 'expected income' at the place of destination, which was basically a function of both the prevailing urban wage structure and a subjective probability of obtaining employment in the urban modern sector. However, the modal lacks in the consideration, of non-economic factors in mobility decision, and also the assumptions abstract from the structural aspect of economy.

In-Migration: Total

In Indian conditions, no model can fully explain the mechanism of migration process. The socio-political conditions along with economic disparities are also a cause of concern. Indian society is also tradition bound and less mobile compared to the west. The under-currents promoting both in and out-migration in urban places are the interplay of a number of factors in which religion, caste, language, ethnicity need a special mention. The unpredictability in defining migration aggregate model calls for simulating migration process in which a disaggregated behavioral approach can explain migration mechanism in spatial diffusion (Hagerstrand: 1966; Dorigo and Tobler: 1983).

In Uttar Pradesh, with a rich cultural and historical background there exists diversity in physical, economic and socio-political scenario. The process of urbanization aided by migration is a reflective of the on going socio-cultural, economic and political changes. For the present study, only in migration is considered since out migration is a process of de-urbanization.

Spatial Process

In 1991, Uttar Pradesh recorded 22.17 per cent of urban population as in-migrants. Migration as a process in Uttar Pradesh is accompanied by corresponding in-migration rates of males (+0.94) followed by female in-migration (+0.79). The undergraduate male workers are migrating more to urban areas of Uttar Pradesh (+0.71). The concentration of males within the age group of 15-59 is also positively related (+0.69) and the literacy levels of total, male and female ranging from +0.60 to + 0.65 show significant relationship with the process of in-migration.

Spatial Patterns

At local level, the process of in-migration to Uttar Pradesh is influenced by a combination of factors resulting in spatial patterns (Fig.9).

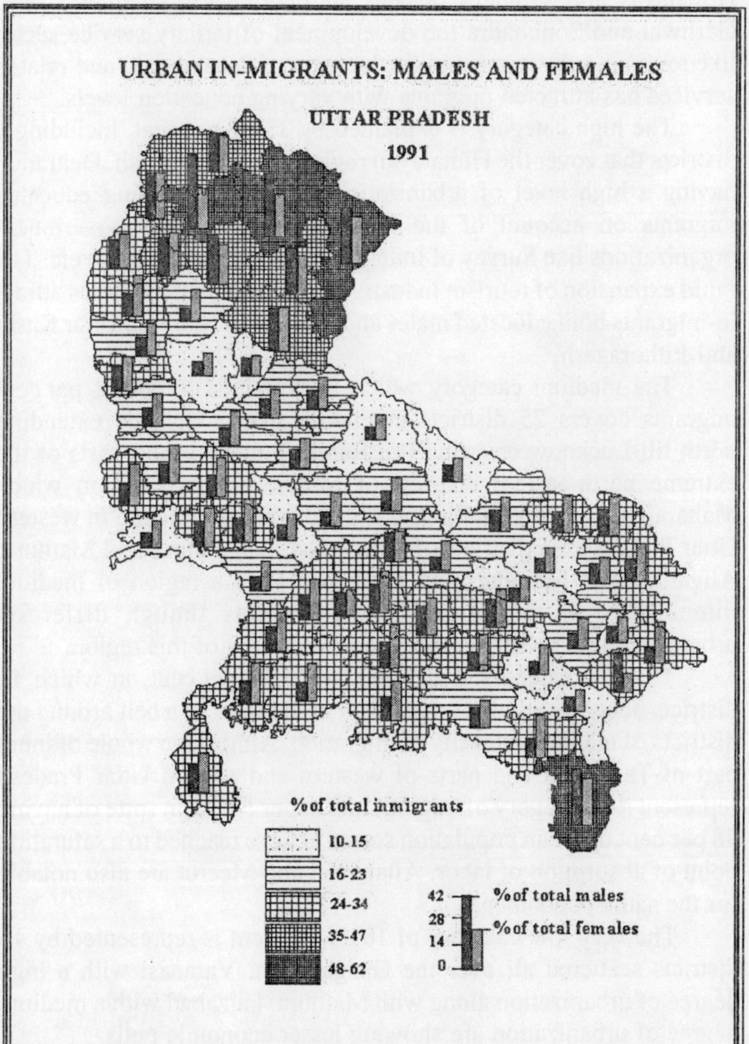
URBAN IN-MIGRANTS: MALES AND FEMALES
UTTAR PRADESH
1991
% of total immigrants
10-15
16-23
24-34
35-47
48-62
42
28
14
0
% of total males
% of total females

Fig. 9

The very high category lies within 48-62 per cent in which 4 districts are from very low urbanized parts of Uttar Pradesh Himalayas and southern plateau. In Pithoragarh, Chamoli, Tehri Garhwal and Sonbhadra the development of tertiary service sector like tourism, pilgrimage and the location of Rihand dam and related services has attracted migrants with varying education levels.

The high category is explained by 35-47 per cent, including 6 districts that cover the Himalayan region of Uttar Pradesh. Dehradun having a high level of urbanization is further attracting educated migrants on account of the location of prestigious government organizations like Survey of India, Forest Research Institute etc. The rapid expansion of tourism industry and educational institutes attract in-migrants both educated males and females in Nainital, Uttar Kashi and Pithoragarh.

The medium category which is explained by 24-34 per cent migrants covers 25 districts mainly in Jhansi Uplands extending north till Lucknow covering Rai Bareli, Sultanpur and parts of the extreme north-eastern districts of Middle Ganga Plain in which Maharajganj, Deoria, Ballia and Mirzapur are significant. In western Uttar Pradesh, the districts of Ghaziabad, Saharanpur and Mathura, Aligarh, Etah, Mainpuri and Firozabad form a region of medium intensity of in-migration. These districts though differ on urbanization level, reflect the role of economy of this region.

The low category is defined by 16-23 per cent, in which 16 districts occur mostly in Ganga Plain in the form of a belt around the districts of medium intensity of migration. Almost the whole of inner part of Tarai belt and parts of western and eastern Uttar Pradesh represent this category of migration. Kanpur Nagar in spite of having 98 per cent of urban population seems to have reached to a saturation point of absorption of labor. Allahabad and Meerut are also notable for the same phenomena.

The very low category of 10-15 per cent is represented by 16 districts scattered all over the Ganga Plain. Varanasi with a high degree of urbanization along with Mathura, Faizabad with a medium degree of urbanization are showing lesser economic pulls.

In Uttar Pradesh, the regional variation in percentage of in migration rates are reflecting the urbanization dynamics in which large urban centers are loosing their attraction or in other words multiplier effect of urban economy is on decline. In comparison to it, upcoming areas on the scene of economy like northern hill districts and southern plateau exhibit a good potential for further in-migration. However, the small base of urban population in Hill districts results in higher proportion of in migrants, though the volume of migrants is less. In general, there seems to be a decline in percentage of migrants with increasing urbanization levels. If absolute volume of migrants is considered, the highly urbanized areas will remain the prime choice for in-migrants.

In-Migration: Males

Sex selectivity of migrants especially in favour of males is firmly established in case of developing countries. In India, it generally takes place through stages of migration where males migrate first then females follow at different stages of the migrant cycles (Bogue and Zacharia: 1962). In the early stage of male out-migration from place of origin and in-migration to place of destination, a disbalancing effect on sex ratio of both places is noticed especially in case of rural to urban. The existing percentage of male migrants in total male population at any point of time reflects the previous history of socio-economic push and pulls exerted by the place of origin and destination respectively.

Spatial Process

In Uttar Pradesh, in 1991 out of 22.17 per cent total in migrants only 7.84 per cent were males. The process understandably is strongly positive correlated with 15-59 age group of total population (+0.76) specifically males (+0.77) along with the size of the family with less than 3 persons with 2 rooms (+0.89). The males with less than graduate (+0.73) are more strongly correlated than males with graduate (+0.56) and above degree. The total male literacy within age group of 60+ for males (+0.70) shows a concentration of literate population in senile age group through migration process. This suggests that the mobility of males is more within the less educated group generally in the form of a nucleated family.

Spatial Patterns

The process identified for concentration of male in-migrants may not be operative on the same magnitude all over the state. Considerable variations manifest themselves in definite spatial patterns (Fig.9).

In general, the spatial distribution pattern of male in migrants to Uttar Pradesh closely follows that of the total in migrants. Only 11 or 17.5 per cent of the districts lie in high and very high category within a range of 42-26 per cent of male in migrants in the Hill districts. While 43 or 68.3 per cent of the districts lie within low to very low category within a range of 10-2 per cent of in migrant males covering nearly the entire Ganga Plain especially all along the Tarai region. Even Kanpur Nagar and Lucknow, the two most urbanized districts of Uttar Pradesh, record low to very low values of 9.59 per cent and 13.8 per cent respectively. All significantly urbanized districts like Varanasi, Agra, Mathura, Meerut, Allahabad jhansi record within 9-2 per cent. It clearly reflects the decreasing mobility of male population towards large urban centres due obviously to the lessened economic benefits involved in this process. It is rather away from the heavily populated Ganga Plain, places with either medium or small-scale industries along with the development of tertiary sector like the northern hill region or the south eastern plateau that seem to be more potential for attracting male migrants.

In-Migration: Females

The cohort and life cycle aggregate approaches favor the deterministic point of view under which migration process is seen as an outcome of social and environmental pressures. In case of female migration in India, the cause is more social than economic on the broader scale of generalization. There seems to be no strong motive in rural areas except after marriage migration to accompany their spouse. However, economic motives like job or education seems to be more operative in case of small urban centers sending migrant females to large cities. Thus, female migration rate does not confirm any functional mechanism underlying migration process in India, and females are generally thought to be less mobile compared to males.

Spatial Process

In 1991, 14.33 per cent of the total in-migrants in Uttar Pradesh were females. Thus, contrary to the common belief of lesser mobility of females, percentage wise seem to be more mobile than males. In Uttar Pradesh, the process is closely linked with the rate of total in-migrants (+0.79) suggesting it to be a prevalent phenomenon. No well-defined relationship could be observed with other indicators except with educational levels of males less than graduate (+0.38) and male workers less than graduate (+0.44), which are a suggestive of after marriage migration of females within Lees educated category. However, short distance migration from urban areas (+0.45) correlates suggesting it to be also a voluntary move for marriage, educational or economic reasons.

Spatial Patterns

The factors affecting female mobility though recognized above through correlation values show considerable spatial variations in response to the regional socio-economic setup (Fig.9).

Although the percentage of female in-migrants to total urban population is negligible, it is within the total migrants that the percentage of female in-migrants is more than the males. It is the rise in educational levels and work participation in non-agricultural sector particularly tertiary sector, which has brought about this welcoming change. The spatial pattern of female in migration rates in general corresponds more to the pattern of total in-migration rates again highlighting the role of female migration in the changing urbanization scenario of Uttar Pradesh. Nearly 29 or 46% of the districts have recorded high to very high within a range of 17-24% of female in migrants. Apart from Dehra Dun and Almora, even Pithoragarh and Chamoli have shown very high concentration of female migrants. Mathura, Unnao, Rae Bareili, Ballia, Mirzapur and Sonbhadra are highlighting a mix of socio-economic factors that need further probe.

INTRA-DISTRICT MIGRATION

To analyze the overall patterns of migration in terms of total volume of migrants associated with a particular place, distance and direction, it is imperative to define a specified distance zone. Thus, any in-migration field is a functional and nodal region that delineates the origin of in-migrants while the out-migration field defines the destination of migrants; both can be represented formally and abstractly through vector flows and linkage analysis (Slater: 1984). General field theory provides a framework to define interplay between characteristics of places and flow of migrants between them (Schwind: 1975; Slater: 1989). The empirical approach to define migration fields is based on Pareto-curve and analysis of distance decay model for a point location in space.

In India, the educational levels and socio-economic aspirations also define migration behavior and associated field of interaction. Mobility for economic causes is certainly related with educational and functional competency of migrants with no considerations for intervening distances if the returns are handsome although Lee's model suggest that distances are negatively related with volume of migrants. The short distance migration is not as such motivated by any particular cause. A multitude of factors affect it particularly seasonal unemployment in rural areas. Females with low literacy levels generally opt for short distance migration for economic causes.

Intra-District Migration: Rural To Urban

Though the rural to urban migration model of Todaro, (1976) favors the role of income differentials as perceived by the potential migrants, the short distance migration-taking place within the district itself unfolds a different mechanism. For short distance migration it is generally an ad hoc decision taken by the rural migrants generally during the post-harvesting season, rural workers move to the nearby urban areas to compensate for the loss of earning during no work period. The census of India in 1981 has identified them as marginal workers, as those working for less than 180 days in a year. Apart from marginal workers there may be quasi-permanent or permanent migration streams generated from surrounding rural areas under conditions of economic compulsion. Thus short distance rural to urban migration does not highlight any specific purpose. It is rather a more prevalent form of migration in case of females who aim for large cities for getting absorbed in generally informed sector of economy.

Spatial Process

In Uttar Pradesh 24.16% of urban migrants are from rural areas. There seems to be a loosely defined relation between intra-district migration from rural area with total literacy of males in 60 + age group (+0.30) and female workers within 15-59 age group (+0.27). Therefore, this migration stream from rural areas within the district fails to define any specific mechanism related with urbanization in Uttar Pradesh as was argued before.

Spatial Patterns

There seems to be no particular mechanism promoting intra-district rural to urban migration still the spatial distribution of this phenomenon shows certain regularity (Fig.10).

Between 43-57% lies the very high category in which 13 districts cover in general the very low urbanized parts of Uttar Pradesh, in the eastern Himalaya and in the eastern Middle Ganga Plain in which Fatehpur, Pithoragarh, Chamoli, Unnao, Kanpur Dehat, Hamirpur, Banda, Pratapgarh, Deoria and Ballia are significant. All these areas are agriculturally backward with no specific industries to provide employment all through out the year.

Between 34-42 per cent, lies the high category in which 19 districts cover extensive areas of eastern Middle Ganga Plain and few scattered pockets in Upper Ganga Plain. The districts of Muzaffarnagar, Bijnor, Etawah, Jaunpur, Gorakhpur, Azamgarh, Faizabad are important with a sound degree of urbanization. The rest of the districts lie in economically backward areas like Kheri, Baraich, Rae Bareli, and Pratapgarh.

Between 27-33 per cent lies medium category in which 10 districts mostly fall within high to medium urbanized parts of upper Ganga Plain in which Aligarh, Meerut,Etawah, Siddharthnagar and Sahjahanpur are significant.

Between 13-26 per cent lies the low category in which 14 districts cover scattered areas in Varanasi, Allahabad, Jhansi, Agra, Mathura, Muzaffarnagar, Rampu, Mau and Gorakhpur are significant.

Between 4-12 per cent lies very low category in which 7 districts cover the very highly urbanized parts like Kanpur Nagar,

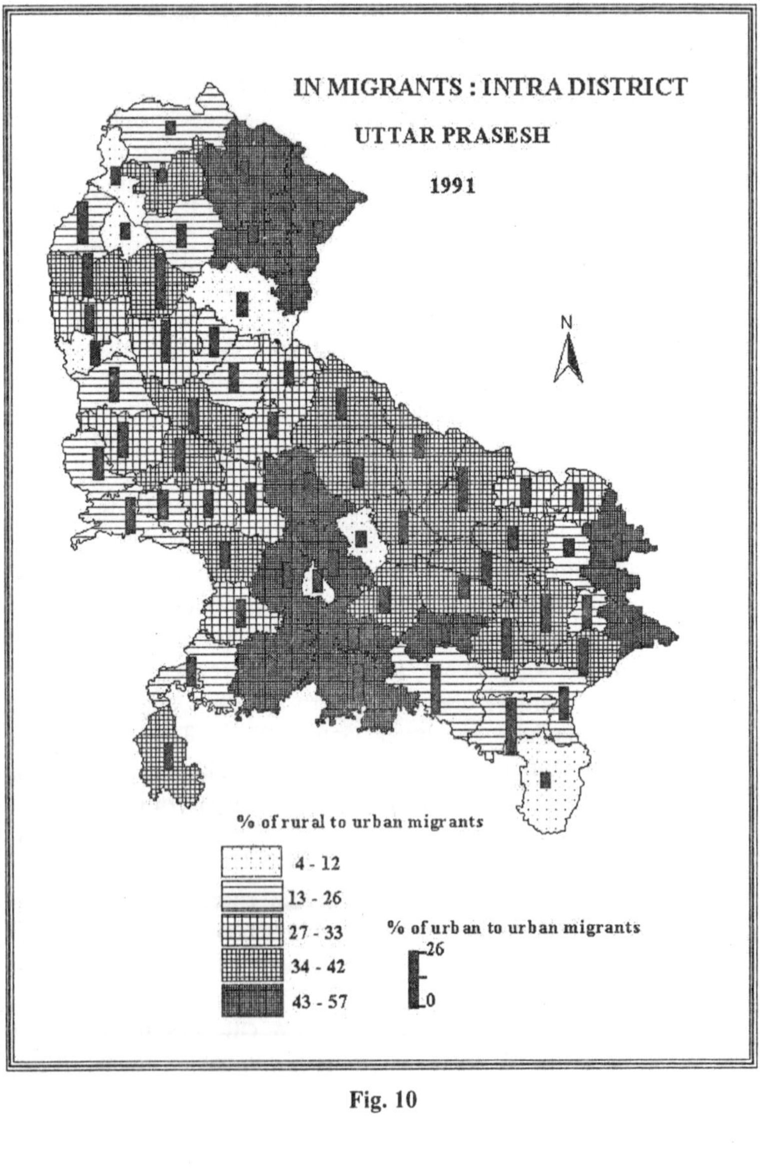
IN MIGRANTS : INTRA DISTRICT
UTTAR PRASESH
1991
N
% of rural to urban migrants
4 - 12
13 - 26
27 - 33
34 - 42
43 - 57
% of urban to urban migrants
26
0

Fig. 10

Lucknow, Ghaziabad, Dehradun, Haridwar and Sonbhadra. These entire region since has a well-established base of economy, with a defined nature of job market, which seems to discourage short distance migrants from rural areas.

In Uttar Pardesh, it seems that the rural to urban migration is influenced by the consideration of both distance and economic cost incurred during the process of migration. The rural migrants, since lack initiatives, prefer short distance migration for a temporary period since these migrants generally like to go back once the remittance to their place of origin has been paid and their future requirements have been partially secured. Therefore, this migration stream bespeak of an urban economy, which in case of districts with large cities are unable to attract any more marginal workers as is noticed in case of highly urbanized areas of Kanpur Nagar and Lucknow with effective degree of urbanization. The spatial pattern certainly has shown a reverse relation with degree of urbanization. This migration stream is rather signifying female migration for socio-economic causes particularly after marriage migration.

Intra-District Migration: Urban To Urban

Migration within the district from urban areas may be a both voluntary and involuntary move. For short distance urban migration, weakening economic base at the place of origin generally causes the free flow of population. The cost involved in short distance migration since is less, the migrants move frequently to maximize their economic returns. Female mobility is also recorded high due to advantage of lesser economic cost incurred in migration process. Since Indian society has a close bond of family ties thus, this migration streams also symbolize the benefits of frequent trip to their place of origin.

Spatial Process

In 1991, 10.78 per cent of migration is intra-district from urban to urban for Uttar Pradesh. The indicator shows highest correlation in household size of more than 5 persons (+0.61), dependency ratio for both juvenile (+ 0.52) and senile (+0.56). It hints at rising density of urban areas, which is quite expected in case of a congested small urban place or a large city. The negative correlation with places of 20,000 population (-0.54) suggests that in-migration within the district is occurring in places of lower size of urban population.

Spatial Patterns

Within the district urban to urban movement of population is clearly defined by some driving force, which might not be very strong. However, the spatial distribution of this process expresses itself with certain regularity (Fig. 10).

Only 13 or 20.6 per cent of the districts are recording high values within 15-26 per cent covering the medium urbanized areas of Allahabad, Mirzapur and Bijnor. The developments of service sector of Allahabad and secondary activities of other two districts perhaps are the main causes. While Ballia, Ghazipur, Azamgarh and Jaunpur in eastern Uttar Pradesh and Agra, Moradabad, Saharanpur and Muzaffarnagar in western Uttar Pradesh are sound on the scene of urbanization. All the districts lying in this category have sufficiently developed tertiary and secondary sectors with high concentration of female workers within the age group of 15-59. It further suggests a female-based migration stream both for economic and social causes.

The rest of Ganga Plain especially the whole of Upper Ganga Plain and selected pockets in eastern Middle Ganga Plain including Mathura, Aligarh, Bulandshahr, Budaun, Farrukhabad, Hardoi, Faizabad and Varanasi show only a moderate intensity of migration stream generated from urban area within the district. A corresponding increase in other than household industries and tertiary services in these districts seem to have attracted both male and female urban migrants from within the district.

Almost the entire western Middle Ganga Plain as well as the districts in the interior Upper Ganga Plain including Kanpur Nagar, Ghaziabad and Meerut fall within 6-10 per cent, suggesting a decreasing pull for short distance migration despite high level of urbanization.

While Lucknow and Dehradun along with the mountainous region especially Almora and Pithoragarh record a value around 5 per cent or less suggesting that the short-term economic opportunities are exhausted there.

Analyzing the regional variation in pattern of short distance migration, the highly urbanized places seem not to be providing temporary or seasonal job facilities except in other than households or service sector where females are generally absorbed. In general, the central part of Ganga Plain irrespective of its degree of urbanization seems to have exhausted its economic hold.

INTER-DISTRICT MIGRATION

The universality of the concept that migration occurs within young age group (15-29 years) with relatively better educational levels than their counterparts in place of origin holds very much true in India. The self-evaluation attached in expected income levels enable the educated migrants, though mostly under-graduate, to move to comparatively longer distances across the district boundary. The social values attached to a white-collar job instead of traditional farming are basic considerations for intra-state or inter-district migration from rural to urban areas. Female migration also forms a major part.

Inter-District Migration: Rural To Urban

The agricultural scenario in rural Uttar Pradesh is dominated by increasing man-land ratio and deteriorating agricultural conditions, which initiate the process of rural to urban migration. The increased literacy rates also dissuade the rural youth from agricultural occupations. Further more, the seasonal unemployment during post harvesting season sets out streams of short-duration migrants towards the nearby urban centers to compensate the loss of earnings. The nature of jobs for such migrants can be in both formal and informal sector of economy.

Spatial Process

In 1991 with 27.41 per cent of urban migrants originated from rural areas within the state, Uttar Pradesh shows the effect of increased literacy levels. Under the educational category of both male workers less than graduate (+0.37) and female workers less than graduate

(+0.31), along with total literacy of females (+0.40) describe and define a pattern of movement of population from rural to urban area at inter district level.

Spatial Patterns

The manifestation of above process in spatial perspective has shown variability in response to a combination of local factors (Fig. 11).

Between 40-49 per cent lies the very high category, which covers only 3 districts of Kanpur Nagar, Sonbhadra and Uttar Kashi. The strong economic motives and the nature of manufacturing and tertiary sectors of Kanpur Nagar seem to have attracted migrants from an agriculturally stagnating surrounding area. Sonbhadra with its hydel-power projects and Uttar Kashi with its upcoming economic attractions are attracting migrants belonging to lower educational levels.

Between 30-39 per cent lies the high category in which 13 districts cover scattered pockets with varying degree of urbanization. The highly urbanized Lucknow, Dehradun, Ghaziabad have a job market in either secondary or tertiary sector. On the other hand, the low urbanized districts like Pratapgarh, Etawah, Mainpuri and Etah have a concentration of migrant workers with below graduate education in mainly service sector and secondary especially other than household industry.

Between 23-29 per cent lies medium category in which 19 districts cover considerable portion of medium or less urbanized parts of eastern Middle Ganga Plain like Rae Bareilli, Sutanpur, Jaunpur, Mau or inner Middle Ganga Plain along Tarai region with Bahraich, Kheri, Sitapur, Pilibhit, Shahjahanpur and in northern Upper Ganga Plain in Bulandshahr, Aligarh.

Between 18-22 per cent lies the low category in which 17 districts cover areas with generally low to very low degree of urbanization. In this group Varanasi, Agra, Allahabad and Shahjahanpur have shown definite signs of decreasing economic pull for rural migrants from medium distances. The group of districts especially around Lucknow and Kanpur Nagar like Kanpur Dehat, Unnao, Fatehpur, Banda, which are already low on urbanization level, are not registering any change on economic scenario to attract further rural migrants.

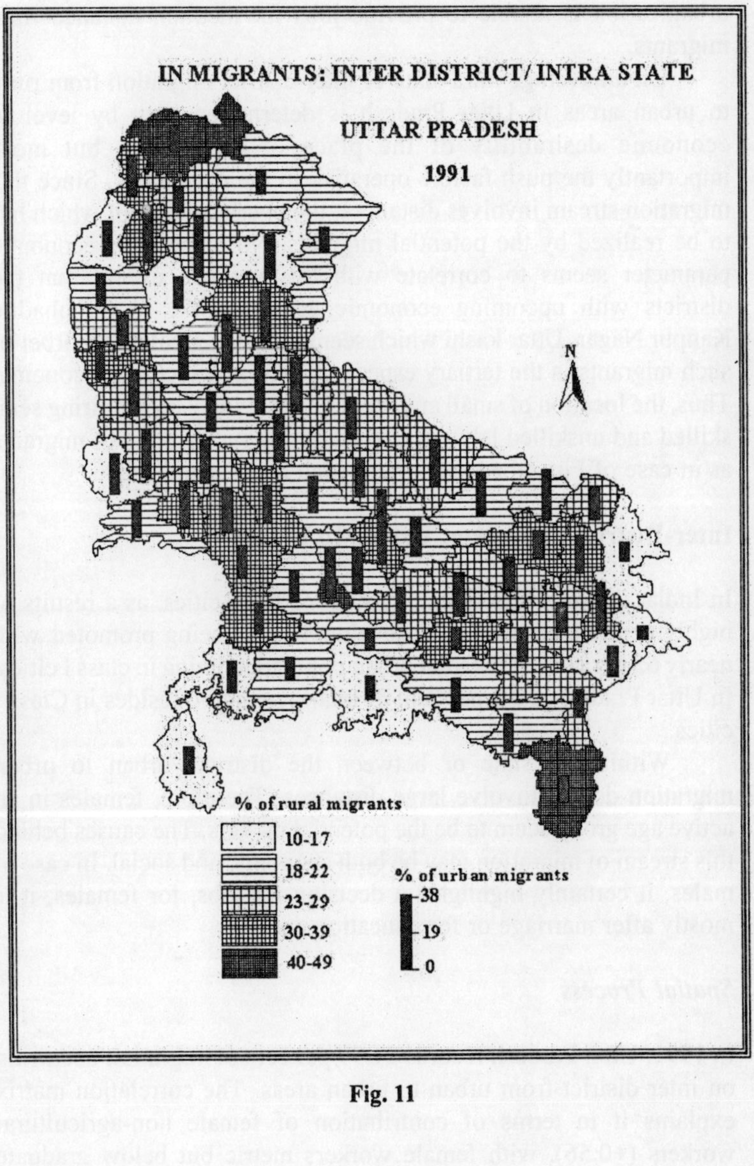
IN MIGRANTS: INTER DISTRICT/ INTRA STATE
UTTAR PRADESH
1991
N
% of rural migrants
10-17
18-22
23-29
30-39
40-49
% of urban migrants
38
19
0

Fig. 11

Very low category is formed by 10-17% in which 10 districts cover in general the plateau area of the south in which Jhansi and Lalitpur are significant. Even Mathura with very high degree of urbanization is unable to provide jobs for medium distance rural migrants.

On an average intra-state or inter-district migration from rural to urban areas in Uttar Pradesh is determined both by level of economic desirability of the place of destination but more importantly the push factors operative in the rural areas. Since this migration stream involves distances, the overhead cost of which has to be realized by the potential migrants. No remarkable economic parameter seems to correlate with this variable except that the districts with upcoming economic activities like in Sonbhadra, Kanpur Nagar, Uttar kashi which seem to be the greatest absorber of such migrants in the tertiary especially informal sector of economy. Thus, the location of small and medium scale industry requiring semi skilled and unskilled labor is also attracting such stream of migrants as in case of Firozabad, Mainpuri, Mau and Farrukhabad.

Inter-District Migration: Urban To Urban

In India, the disproportionate growth of large cities, as a results of highly centralized economic development, is being promoted with nearly 65 per cent of the total urban population living in class I cities. In Uttar Pradesh, 52.5 per cent of total population resides in Class I cities.

Within the state or between the districts urban to urban migration do not involve large distances. Therefore, females in an active age group seem to be the potential movers. The causes behind this stream of migration may be both economic and social. In case of males, it certainly highlights a decision for jobs, for females, it is mostly after marriage or for education and job.

Spatial Process

In 1991, Uttar Pradesh records 21.99 per cent of migration occurring on inter district from urban to urban areas. The correlation matrix explains it in terms of contribution of female non-agricultural workers (+0.56), with female workers metric but below graduate (+0.47), total literacy in 60+ age group (+0.43). The density household of 3-5 persons (+0.42) and density household of more than 6 persons (+0.45) suggest it to be a phenomenon of generally female migration with low educational level belonging to high-density houses, most probably for economic reasons. However, no well-defined mechanism could be found behind this migration stream.

Spatial Patterns

Though the process of urban to urban migration is ill defined, it shows certain spatial regularity in the distribution pattern (Fig.11).

Between 23-38 per cent lies high category in which 21 or 33.3 per cent of the districts of varying economic development and urbanization levels are included. Lucknow with its highly developed tertiary sector, Rampur, Moradabad and Pilibhit with almost a saturated economy, Hardwar with a fast expanding pilgrim activity and Tehri Garhwal with hydal power projects are areas supportive of both female in migration and male in economically active age group. While rest of the districts have generally medium levels of urbanization as in Aligarh, Firozabad, Mainpuri, Bulandshahr and with low level of urbanization like Kheri, Gonda. Since dominated by medium and small-scale industries, urban in migrants from different educational backgrounds are getting absorbed in productive sector of economy.

Between 19-22 per cent the medium category includes 13 districts in which Varnasi, Mathura, Agra, Dehradun and Almora along with very low urbanized districts of Sitapur, Hardoi, Budaun are notable.

Below 18 per cent are recorded the low and very low values covering 34 or 46.1 per cent of the districts in which Allahabad, Ghaziabad, Saharanpur, Meerut along with Jaunpur, Azamgarh, Ghazipur are notabe. The industrial districts of Meerut and Ghaziabad suggest exhausted economic opportunities in discouraging in-migrants.The Hill districts of north, parts of Southern Plateau, and extreme eastern Middle Ganga Plain including Pithoragah, Deoria, Ballia, Lalitpur and Banda show decreasing economic pull for medium distance migrants.

As a whole, in Uttar Pradesh, within the state migration from urban areas does not seem to be a preferable move as suggested by the low values recorded by all highly urbanized areas except

Lucknow. The multiplier effect of large cities seems to have declined even in economically sound areas like Kanpur Nagar, Ghaziabad, Dehadun, Varanasi, Mathura and Agra. Since the industrial base of economy is weak and the specialized job requirement by the industries are less, the intra-state migration of both educated males and females seems to be on decline. However, the service sector inclusive of both formal and informal sector of economy is able to sustain migrants. The female migration, however, remains unaffected as both social and economic mobility is noticed behind their migration patterns.

INTER-STATE MIGRATION

The decision to take up migration out side the state from one urban area to another reflects a condition in which the migration is not occurring necessarily out of economic compulsion, it is rather voluntary. As proposed by Sjaastad(1962) in human investment theory, the decision to migrate has an investment component involving costs and returns distributed over time. The cost includes both money or expenditure and non-money or psychological cost. The returns are also realized in the same terms. Thus urban to urban migration reflects the above mechanism. However, the realization of respected income by a potential migrant, as suggested by Todaro (1976), basically determines the selection of place for 'promised' income. Thus the migration stream distributes the labor force between the highly developed modern sector whether large or small and the traditional sector of urban economy.

Inter-State Migration: Rural To Urban

In case of India, the impact of unequal land ownership, ineffective application of agricultural reforms and disparities in income levels has affected adoption levels of new agricultural technology. The failure of policies to redistribute land had an impact on the agricultural efficiency and carrying capacity of land. Application of modern technologies afforded by large landowners has replaced manpower. The increased productivity of land as a result of adoption of new agricultural technology brought down crop prices, which affected small farmers who depend upon traditional system of farming. It has further sharpened the rural income differentials causing a rise in the proportion of landless laborers and promoting out-migration for towns and cities of various sizes. The consideration for distances is of lesser importance. Generally, better-educated active age population tends to opt for longer distance migration.

Spatial Process

In Uttar Pradesh, outside the state migration from rural areas accounts for 5.15 per cent of total migration under conditions of economic pull, males less than graduate (+0.41) generally within age group of 15-59 years show a weak positive correlation with other than household secondary workers (+0.38).

Spatial Patterns

Though from out side Uttar Pradesh, rural migration is insignificant at state level, at district level it presents an influence of regional economy (Fig. 12).

Between 14-19 per cent lies the very high category in which Sonbhadra, Lalitpur and Jhansi cover the southern plateau region. It shows the deteriorating agricultural scenario of Rajasthan, Madhya Pradesh and Bihar which are sending out rural migrants.

Between 8-13 per cent lies the high category in which 7 districts cover either the western part of Uttar Pradesh where Agra, Mathura, and Ghaziabad are significant on account of their economy. Dehradun and Tehri Garhwal are attracting migrants from across the state. Varanasi is significant as the handloom industry is able to sustain the semi-skilled and skilled labour.

Between 5-7 per cent lies medium category in which 9 district cover mainly southern and eastern parts of the state suggesting the directional preferences of rural migrants to urban areas. Kanpur Nagar is significant along with Ballia, Ghazipur, Hamirpr, and Banda.

Between 3-4 per cent lies the low category under which 16 districts cover inner parts of Ganga Plain. Lucknow, Aligarh

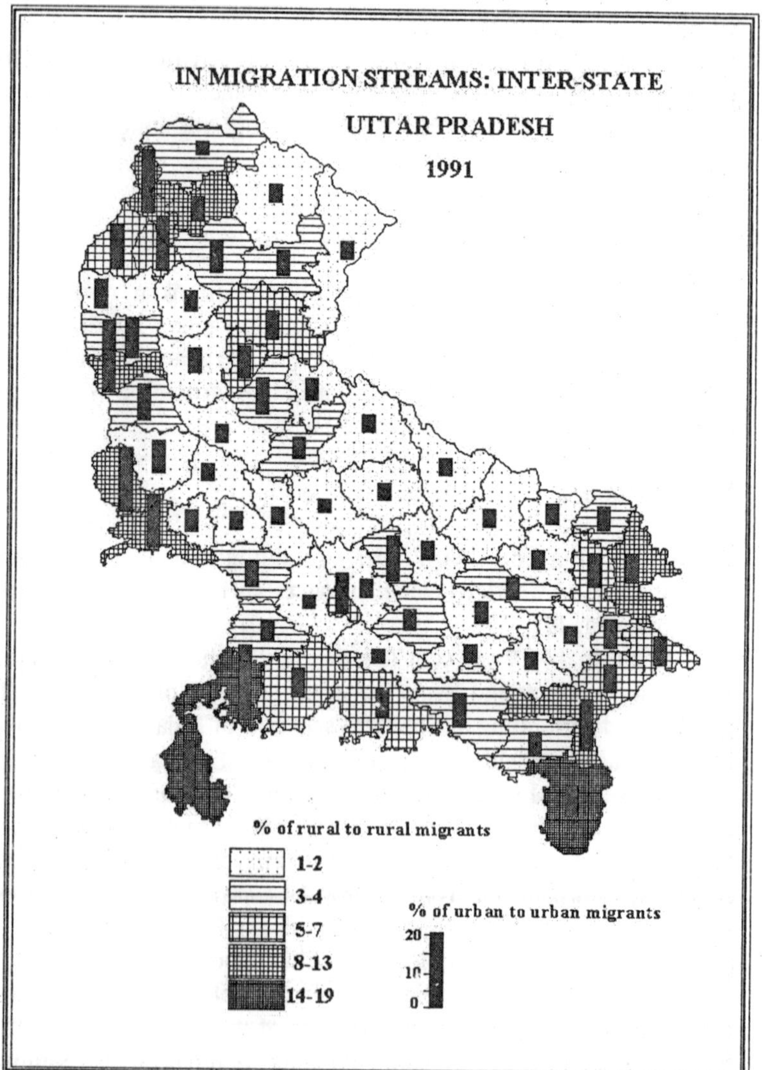
IN MIGRATION STREAMS: INTER-STATE
UTTAR PRADESH
1991
% of rural to rural migrants
1-2
3-4
5-7
8-13
14-19
% of urban to urban migrants
20
0

Fig. 12

Bulandshahr and Muzaffarnagar are areas that have lesser attraction for rural migrants. Other distracts in this category since low on urbanization scene, are unable to attract rural migrants.

The very low category includes 1-2 per cent of the migrants coming from rural areas of other states covering 28 districts mainly in interior parts of Middle Ganga Plain where no significant urban economic activity seems to be attracting migrants except in Moradabad and Aligarh.

In general, the rural to urban migration on inter state level seems to be insignificant. It is highly localized in space especially in areas bordering the eastern margins of the state and southern plateau as it is backed by an undulating terrain not much suitable for agriculture in states like Madhya Pradesh, Bihar and Rajasthan. While Ghaziabad, Agra and Mathura on the basis of industry and manufacturing are attracting rural migrants with generally below graduate degree.

Inter-State Migration: Urban To Urban

The motivation underlying migration from urban to urban are variable depending upon the history and nature of urbanization. In general, the long distance mobility of urban migrants is deeply rooted in environmental or socio-economic factor that determine the direction of migration streams. The identification of linkage processes through which macro-stimuli are translated into considerations for individual decision-making is important. The maximization of profits of expected economic returns are associated with long distance migration (Jong and Fawcett: 1979). Such information of economic avenues and residential preference are gathered through or passed on by earlier migrants both relatives and friends. The maintenance of community links based on social ties seems to be relatively unimportant. In case of India, the ethnic ties, religion, caste and language has also a prominent role to play. The role of education for promoting long distance migration is highly significant.

Spatial Process

In Uttar Pradesh 7.11 per cent migrants from outside the state from urban areas are unable to be defined in terms of any specific set of forces. The destination of urban migrants outside Uttar Pradesh seems to be places of higher order population size (+0.61). A noteworthy feature is the association of females with graduate and above degree (+0.46). The absence of correlation of any variable related with work force structure of population suggests that long distance migration in Uttar Pradesh is not necessarily resulting in structural mobility of occupation of the migrant population

Spatial Patterns

The process of setting up migration streams from outside urban areas of the state has been influenced locally by other factors resulting in a well defined spatial pattern of distribution of percentage of migrants (Fig.12).

Only 10 or 15.9 per cent of the districts record a value within 9-17 per cent in which 5 districts cover the western part of the state with Dehradun, Ghaziabad, Mathura, Jhansi and Lalitpur. High degree of effective urbanization except Lalitpur along with high urban sex ratio, high educational levels of female and male workers in working age group mark this category. The location of Lalitpur at northern part of Madhya Pradesh defines its degree of desirability by the migrants. The rest of the 5 districts cover Lucknow, Varanasi and Agra having very high percentage of urban population and effective urbanization. Hardwar and Saharanpur have medium degree of urbanization. In these areas, manufacturing industry and tertiary service are attracting migrants with below and above graduate degree especially females.

Between 6-8 per cent the medium category contains 10 districts that cover mainly Upper Ganga Plain in which Muzaffarnagar, Aligarh, Bulandshahar and Allahabad are significant on the scene of urbanization. Kanpur Nagar is also recording medium level of migrant inflow although it tops on urbanization scenario of Uttar Pradesh.

Between 1-5 per cent lies the low category in which 40 or 63.5 per cent of the districts cover extreme eastern margins of the state, the southern plateau region barring Jhansi and Lalitpur, and parts of northern hill region. The lesser desirability of Varanasi lying in this category is striking. The whole of the Ganga Plain including mainly the central part including Lucknow is also showing signs of stagnant urbanization. Other districts have already weak urban base, therefore, are less attractive for migrants from across the state.

On an average, Uttar Pradesh presents a unique feature regarding long distance migration from urban areas in terms of its selectivity over space. Without going into the intricacies of the internal industrial and commercial development mechanism triggering off multiplier effect, as noticed in some areas, it is the exogenous economy also which counts. Uttar Pradesh is bounded by the underdeveloped state of Bihar, Madhya Pradesh and Rajasthan, which are potential areas for sending out-migration streams. The impact of National Capital Region of Delhi, in case of western Uttar Pradesh partly explains rising proportions of long distance migrants. The degree of effective urbanization seems to be a determining factor with or without a high degree of urbanization. The position of Lucknow with a limited base of urban economy, mainly service sector while Kanpur Nagar though most urbanized district with a multi functional economy are showing signs of saturation in economy. A hidden dimension of this aspect could also be the inability of urban places to absorb and provide employment in productive sectors of economy to migrants. In other words, diseconomies of large urban places have started up.

International Migration

The conceptualization of migration across the natural boundary is better analyzed in terms of both spatial and vertical mobility of a set of population. It is a voluntary move of rather a free migrant, the mechanism of which is better be explained in terms of the dynamic environmental set of the place of destination. The interaction space of migrant is thus, not simply geographic but socio-economically explorable space influenced by a distance decay of information flow. Urban hierarchy strongly influences the direction and volume of such flows.

In developing world it is mostly the influence of non-economic factors like inter-personal communication ties that tend to cut across this distance decay model. There seems to be clarity of objectives behind oprationalization of this process ranging from factors inducing partial displacement leading to reverse migration. The values and goals associated with international migration in case of India can easily be summarized in terms of either explicit migration chain effect in which migrants tend to follow the path and directions of associates or a 'resource push' expressed as paucity of resources in the place of origin (Connell: 1976). In this development paradigm, movements from traditional to modern localities are motivated by wage and jobs availability differentials, till modern sector sufficiently develops to transform the traditional sector or to absorb its excess labor.

Spatial Process

In Uttar Pradesh, international migration identifies itself with all the positive aspects of urban development. Females with mean age at marriage (+0.63) and an educational status of more than graduate (+0.64) show correlation with international migration. Males in the age group of 15-59 (+0.53), male main workers (+0.52) and in-migration (+0.56) all suggestive of educated and active proportion of males in the main category of workers are migrating rapidly. This again expresses itself in rising standard of living in terms of electricity (+0.54), safe drinking water (+0.50) cooking gas (+0.66) and Pucca houses (+0.46). There is no significant relation with percentage of urban population suggesting that international migration is not contributing much in degree of urbanization in Uttar Pradesh.

Spatial Patterns

Since the percentage of migrants under the category is itself very less and highly concentrated in space, no spatial mapping was required for analysis.

Uttar Pradesh, since an economically under developed state is unable to attract international migrants, therefore, only 2.21 per cent of the total migrants are from outside India. Though a meager figure in itself, it shows the desirability of certain districts on migration levels.

Out of 63 districts, only 17 districts are above the state average of 2.21 per cent. Dehradun 9.10 per cent, Nainital 6.4 per cent Saharanpur 6.04 per cent Haridwar 5.72 per cent, Tehri Garhwal 5.1 per cent, Almora 4.8 per cent are significant. Other lie between 4.7-2.2 per cent in which apart from Kanpur Nagar with 2.8 per cent all are low urbanized. It seems the government offices of Dehradun, the hydel-power stations and tourism cum religious activities of the hill district region are the prime areas selected by international migrants.

3

ECONCMIC ASPECTS OF URBANIZATION

Urbanization necessitates the specialization of economic activity to initiate the process of concentration of population in selected space. The link between urbanization and economic development is well established. Childe (1950) while discussing the forms of identification of phases of economic growth and development postulated a number of features distinguishing the new towns from older towns on the basis of specialization of economic activities.

Berry (1962) has also evaluated urbanization process in terms of economic growth and development. He observed the mechanism of city growth as a concentration of spatially differentiated but functionally integrated areal units.

Reismann (1964) has developed an extended critique of theories of urbanization and postulated his own organization theory on the same lines developed by Berry. However, his application model is limited to industrial city thereby excluding all other earlier cities.

In a neo-evolutionary approach, Gras (1965) has outlined the relationship between economic development and settlement or habitat pattern in his account of economic history. He has fused historical ways of making a living with technological development on one hand and with developments of human habitat on another.

Thus, urbanization is viewed as a product of increased economic specialization. The connection between urbanization and economic growth has closely defined itself over geographical space in which the most important centers of urbanization were those where manufacturing industry and other auxiliary services are performed.

During the process of urbanization, opposing centripetal and centrifugal forces operate within the space economy. With technological advancement, various theories of urban economic development have been put forward. The core periphery model by Myrdal (1957) and Hirchman (1958) explains the dominance of centripetal forces during early stages of economic development drawing the periphery towards core-region. With increasing growth and development over a considerable time period, diffusion or centrifugal force exert a spread or trickle down effect, manifesting itself in technological diffusion and new ideas. This process continues eventually it outweighs the centripetal forces leading to urban development across periphery till a state of equilibrium is attained.

This linear model of stages of economic development and urban growth was later on elaborated by Friedman (1966) as a model of spatial economic development, and Williamson (1965) as inverted U-thesis of regional inequality. This model by simple interpolation could be applied equally to developing countries.

The role of regional economy is considerably marked in deciding the location of particular industries. The pattern of urbanization reflects the role of urbanization economies in terms of availability of specialized skilled labor, quality transport at minimum of capital, which is mainly concentrated in selected large cities.

The role of multiplier effect (Pred: 1977) has, however, become questionable. The sectoral development of Indian economy along with its localization in geographical space has hampered the balanced urban economic development in regional perspective. The desired linkage provided by a both spatial and functionally activated regional system of cities is missing. The ratio between the basic and non-basic services in a city or region is also distorted in favor of a more pronounced tertiary sector of economy. At city level, urbanization economies have started giving way to urbanization diseconomies. At regional level, polarization of economic activities have produced core regions of development within regions demarcated as underdeveloped. The streams of migrant workers towards large cities have been originated under the twin impact of agrarian crisis in rural areas and stagnation of urban economy or slowing down of it in medium or small towns. Therefore, rising population pressure upon given urban facilities has resulted in congestion, crowding, shortage of basic infrastructural facilities which have had a manifold affect. On economic front at city level, it promoted sub-urbanization of industries, which moved to the peripheries of cities in face of legislations and various planned strategies, giving rise to urban sprawl. On demographic front, it promoted fringe development of cities through intra-city mobility and in migration through inter-city and inter-region mobility of population.

The urban economic system is not operating the way explained by circular and causation theory where any developmental change in economic system brings about a corresponding set of change in the whole system to reinforce its direction of growth. In Indian scenario, the opening up of any economic opportunity is generally a feature of large urban areas. These centers are acting as magnets to attract the population and resources from surrounding rural and urban areas. Thus, core cities and core region of urbanization are developing at a faster rate in demographic terms than their degree of economic development justifies.

In western world, economic development was a concomitant of urban growth and consequently of urbanization. In developing world, especially in India, economic development is not keeping at par with the high rate of urban population growth. Indian economy is still underdeveloped and inclined towards the use of high technology, which in itself is a labor saving device. During the last three decades, a definite rise in industrial and manufacturing factory employment is seen. But a corresponding rise in number of industrial centers is not recorded suggesting a localization aspect of India's industrial and manufacturing centers in space. Therefore, the role of agglomeration economies is not fully understood in case of India's urbanization. However, it is partly the economic policies that fail to diffuse technological innovations and capital accumulations in both sectoral and spatial perspectives. It also indicates the lack of desired linkage provided by a well-integrated system of cities of India.

Main Workers : Total

The cities are supposed to be both an employment generator and employment provider to the increasing base of its population during the process of urban economic change and development. The agglomeration of urban economies is not operative in general except selected cities of thriving industrial base especially the large metropolitan cities. There is a cyclic or seasonal order of availability of employment reflecting the inconsistency of job provisions to labor supply of a particular activity. Thus, there is a distinct class of main workers engaged all the year round i.e.183 days employed in a productive sectors of economy compared to the seasonal i.e. less than 183 days, or marginal workers engaged in both productive as well as self employed service sectors. Therefore, percentage of main workers forms a significant variable for the study of the degree of urbanization and consistency of the nature of job market in the study area.

Spatial Process

With 26.6 per cent, of the total males as main workers the underlying process is a reflective of the age and sex selectivity of migrants. The highest correlation is recorded by nucleated family (+0.87) with total male workers within 15-59 age group (+0.85), total population in age group within 15-59 (+0.76) especially of in migrant males (+0.74) in which female workers also contribute (+0.67). These workers are mainly literates (+0.52) and female literacy is also associated (+0.56).

Spatial patterns

In Uttar Pradesh regional variations exist that bring about spatial patterns of distribution of main workers at district level (Fig.13).

Between 36-40 per cent lies very high category under which only two districts of Chamoli and Tehri Garhwal lie. Due to very low base of urban population, the meager number of workers engaged in mostly tourism and pilgrimage activity has recorded very high.

Between 31-35 per cent the high category covers Uttar Kashi, Garhwal, Pithoragarh and Almorah. In this area cement and electrical equipment industries are located providing job all the year round to workers. Tourism and pilgrimage is also important.

Between 28-30 per cent lies the medium category in which 10

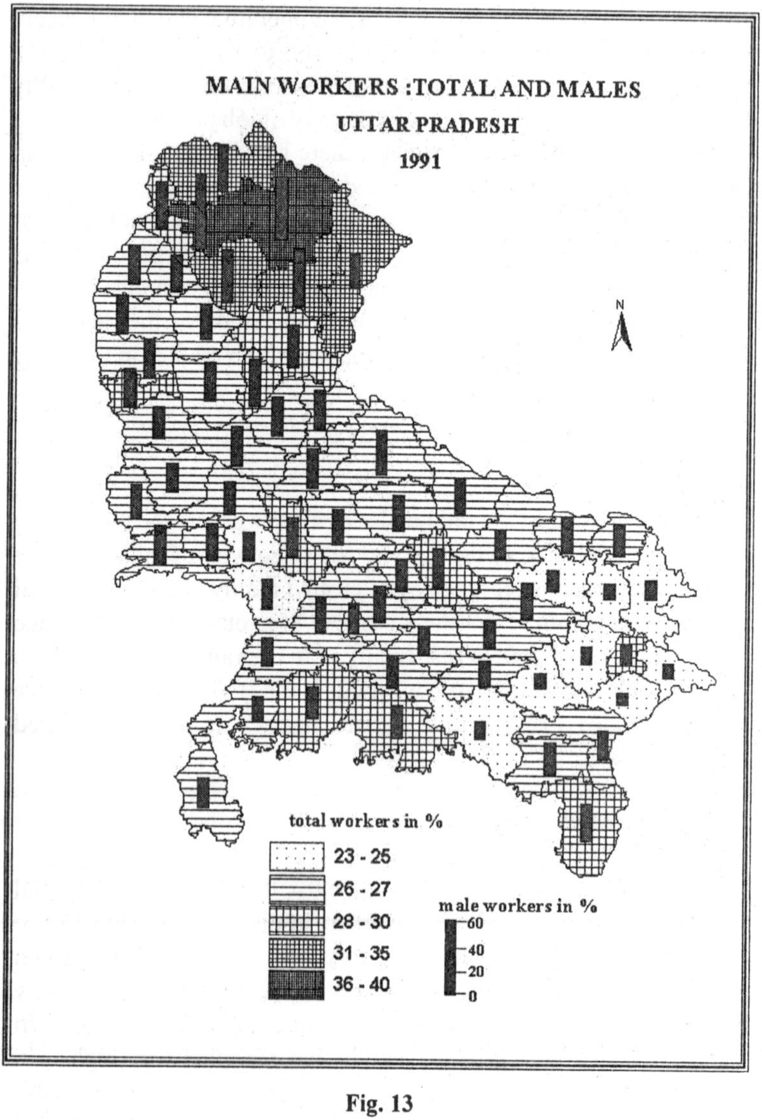
MAIN WORKERS :TOTAL AND MALES
UTTAR PRADESH
1991
N
total workers in %
23 - 25
26 - 27
28 - 30
31 - 35
36 - 40
male workers in %
60
40
20
0

Fig. 13

districts cover scattered pockets either along the foothill of Himalayan or the southern plateau. Dehradun with its prestigious government organization like Regional Remote Sensing Service Center and Survey of India besides others, Nainital with tourism and forest based industries, Ghaziabad with multiple industries of automobiles, electronics, Farrukhabad and Barabanki with traditional handicraft industries and Sonbhadra with its mega-power stations at Obra and Rihand, have all a sound base to provide jobs all throughout the year though the marginal workers are also found.

Between 26-27 per cent lies the low category in which 37 districts cover almost whole Ganga Plain and parts of Middle Ganga Plain. This area contains all major urbanized centers like Kanpur Nagar, Lucknow, Jhansi, Agra, Varanasi and many others with low level of urban economic development. The economy of these places is showing signs of saturation, as the jobs are not available all the year round.

Between 23-25 per cent is the very low category in which 10 districts mainly the underdeveloped parts of eastern Uttar Pradesh lie. Allahabad in this category with a dominant tertiary sector is noticeable. Other places by virtue of their unstable economic condition provide cyclic employment to labourers like Etawah, Ballia, Deoria.

In general, in 1991, the proportion of main workers in Uttar Pradesh seems to be determined by the nature of employment in mainly secondary activities and other than household industry. Administration-cum-service centers also ensure security for educated or trained personals. It is the informal sector of urban economy backed by a seasonal supply of labourers as in case of Ganga Plain, which causes lesser concentration of main worker even in large urban centers. The newly urbanizing areas like northern Himalayan region or southeastern plateau is able to sustain the main workers because of the lesser population concentration and an upcoming urban economy.

Main Workers : Males

The urban labor market is defined by the existing and potential job opportunities in response of which the spatial distribution of labor force exhibits itself both in geographical and economic space. The nature of the job in terms of physical labor sometimes defines sex selectivity of workers of both migrants and original residents and its availability all throughout the year. Therefore, the proportion of male main workers becomes a significant indicator for degree of urbanization.

Spatial Process

In 1991, this variable correlates very strongly to total main workers (+0.85), active age group population (+0.66) especially of males within age group of 15-59 (+0.59). It has also shown a corresponding rise in density of medium size of urban household of 3-5 persons having 2 rooms (+0.69).

Spatial Patterns

With 46.2 per cent of male main workers, the spatial pattern is certainly reflecting the role of sustaining economy through multiplier effects and brings out significant dimensions related with spatial distribution (Fig.13).

Only 8 or 12.7 per cent of the districts record high values within a range of 58-49 per cent of male workers in active age group in the very low urbanized Hill districts of Chamoli, Almora and Tehri although these areas recorded a very low concentration of total male workers in active age group. It is also suggestive of sex selectivity of migrants within active age group. The proportion of male main workers closely coincides with the distribution pattern of total main workers in Ganga Plains. From Himalayan foothills, the proportion decreases gradually eastward to the northern Upper Ganga Plain and districts around Lucknow and Kanpur Nagar. It also points out to the probability of opening up of economic opportunities in the southern Upper Ganga Plain especially along Tarai belt especially in and around Pilibhit. It seems that small-scale industries are basic cause of increasing concentration of male main workers in the low to very low urbanized areas like Firozabad and Sultanpur. Mathura is also recording moderate values. The urbanization pull of Lucknow and Kanpur Nagar in an agricultural set up seems to have declined. Thus seasonality of work and declining multiplier effect of urbanization economies is becoming a feature of metropolitan cities dominating regions which record around 40 per cent of male main like Kanpur Nagar, Lucknow, Dehradun, Ghaziabad, Aligarh, Varanasi and Agra.

Secondary Workers : Total

The secondary sector of urban economy consisting of industrial and manufacturing activities is synonymous with the concept of urban economic growth and development. The industrial transformation of urban economy after independence is conspicuous. Along with the historical cities of Varanasi and Delhi, there emerged series of industrial township based on metal and non-metal industries aided by the infrastructure development specifically transport and communication. The cottons and jute industry also got a spurt after independence. The majority of traditional industries also survived the initial impact of colonial era and stabilized their production after being recognized in the foreign market.

Spatial Process

In Uttar Pradesh, the process strongly associates itself with total secondary workers other than household (+0.63) which seem to be mostly concentrated in urban places of more than 20,000 population (+0.48).

Spatial Patterns

With 10 million people in household industries and 24.9 lakhs in large and medium scale industries, Uttar Pradesh lags far behind with only 25.8 per cent of main workers in secondary sector. In general, the secondary sector of economy has shown selectivity over geographic space (Fig.14).

Between 43-61 per cent lies the very high category in which only 2 districts of Mau and Firozabad lie with limited economic functions but a number of house hold industries.

Between 30-42 per cent lies high category in which 13 districts cover either the southern plateau of east including Varanasi,

Mirzapur and Sonbhadra or the western Upper Ganga Plain in which highly urbanized places like Ghaziabad, Agra are included along with Kanpur Nagar. Tehri Garhwal, Hardwar, Saharanpur, Aligarh, Moradaba and Rampur are other important districts.

Between 22-29 per cent lies the medium category in which 11 districts cover the highly urbanized districts like Mathura, Dehradun and Meerut along with districts with very low levels of urbanization like Rai Bareli, Barabanki and Jaunpur. Apart from the multi functional character of large urban areas, there is in general a dominance of small-scale units with household workers in this category.

Between 17-21 per cent lies the low category in which 18 district cover mainly the Tarai region, parts of northern Upper Ganga Plains and most significantly the highly urbanized districts of Lucknow, Jhansi, Allahabad. Although the size of industrial and manufacturing units remains significant in case of highly urbanized and low urbanized regions, the dominance of service sector in comparison to secondary is also noticeable as in case of Allahabad and Lucknow. The very low urbanized areas due to the level of economy are not supportive of concentration of secondary workers as in Bahraich, Gonda, Basti and others.

Between 8-16 per cent lies very low category in which 19 districts cover the whole of Uttar Pradesh Himalayas, and belt running along the western margins of Middle Ganga Plains, the Middle Ganga Plain of east. In this group of districts, mostly the districts have a very low level of urbanization except the districts in the southern Upper Ganga Plains.

The lack of functional diversity of urban areas along with dominance of service sector seems to be prime cause as noticed in case of Lucknow, Allahabad, Kanpur Nagar, Mathura and Agra. The more urbanized districts have the advantage of concentration of large industrial units in which the workers are employed in registered factories and large industrial establishments. While less urbanized areas in this group have high concentration of secondary workers in small-scale industrial units or even in household industries. The inclusion of both household and other than household industries accounts for the high value of this variable in many less urbanized districts especially in eastern Uttar Pradesh.

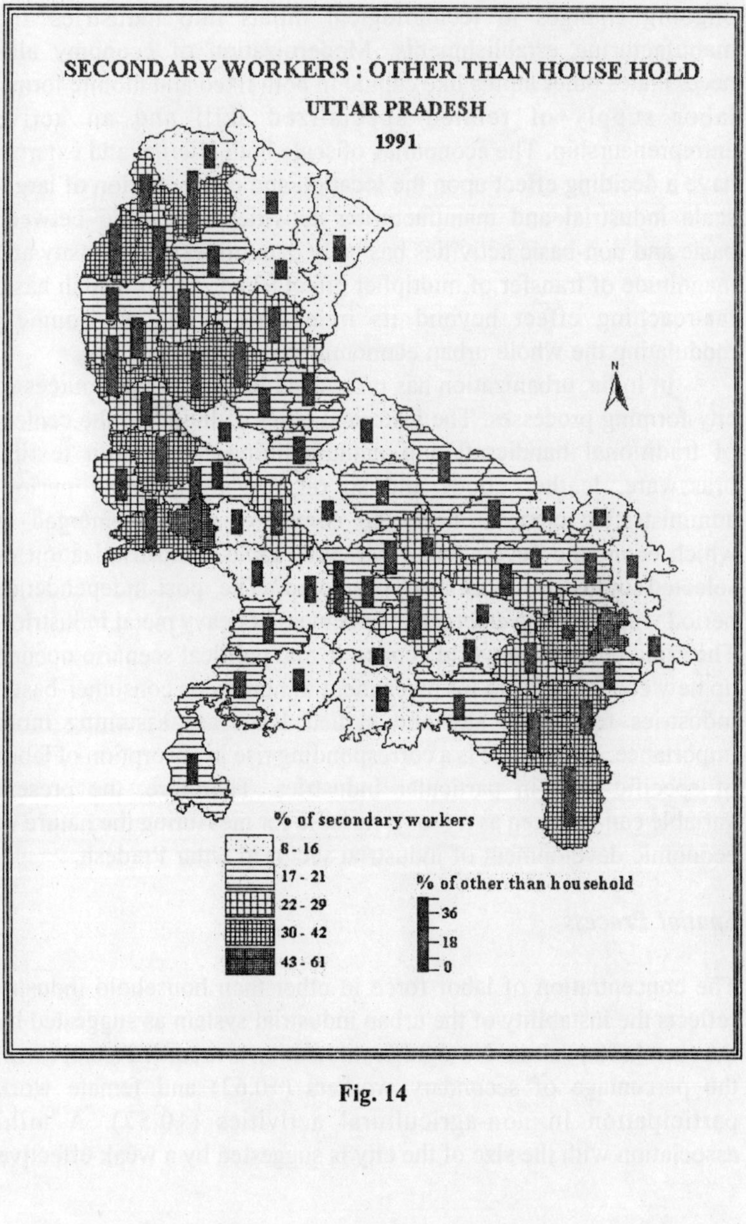
SECONDARY WORKERS : OTHER THAN HOUSE HOLD
UTTAR PRADESH
1991
N
% of secondary workers
6 - 16
17 - 21
22 - 29
30 - 42
43 - 61
% of other than household
36
18
0

Fig. 14

Secondary Workers : Other than Househose Industry

Urbanization accompanied by economic development reflects the ongoing changes in technological inputs into industries and manufacturing establishments. Modernization of economy also necessitates other inputs like capital in both fixed and mobile forms, labor supply of related specialized skill and an active entrepreneurship. The economies of scale both internal and external have a deciding effect upon the location and concentration of large-scale industrial and manufacturing activities. The ratio between basic and non-basic activities basically determines the intensity and magnitude of transfer of multiplier effect (Pred: 1977), which has a far-reaching effect beyond its immediate urban environment modulating the whole urban economic system.

In India, urbanization has proceeded from different sources of city forming processes. The historical cities of India are the centers of traditional handicraft and manufacturing like cotton textile, brassware, leather goods and so on. During colonial period, administrative cum business and commerce centers emerged in which economic development was very rapid. Industrialization of selected industries was also promoted. The post-independence period witnessed the emergence of centers of heavy metal industries. The rapid changes in world economic and political scenario opened up new economic vista for investment in numerous consumer-based industries for which site and skilled labor are assuming more importance. Thus, there is a corresponding rise in absorption of labor of specific skill in particular industries. Therefore, the present variable can be taken as a proxy variable for measuring the nature of economic development of industrial sector in Uttar Pradesh.

Spatial Process

The concentration of labor force in other than household industry reflects the instability of the urban industrial system as suggested by the correlation values. No significant relation is recorded except with the percentage of secondary workers (+0.63) and female work participation in non-agricultural activities (+0.52). A mild association with the size of the city is suggested by a weak effective urbanization (+0.46) and female workers more than graduate (+0.45) highlighting the role of female workers in this set up of economy.

Spatial Patterns

The spatial pattern of percentage distribution other than household industrial workers show variability over the geographical surface in response to the general size distribution of industrial units and level of economic development of the area (Fig.14).

Only 13 0r 21.2 per cent of the districts record a value within 24-45 per cent of workers engaged in other than household industry covering districts from varying urbanization levels both from the sparsely populated districts of Himalaya and congested parts of Ganga Plain. In general the distribution is closely related to the urbanization economies that attracts industries, especially those submitting returns and have a considerable per cent share of registered factories in net value added by industries. Thus, western region on an average is showing 58.87 per cent, central region 53.36 per cent, eastern region 38.83 per cent, and southern plateau region 37.14 per cent. However, the group of Hill districts tops with 72.63 per cent compared to state average of 50.48 per cent share of registered factories in net value added by industries (CMIE: 1997). Irrespective of the degree of urbanization, districts like Kanpur Nagar, Ghaziabad, Aligarh, and Agra lie at par with Sonbhadra, Tehri Garhwal, Faizabad, Hardwar. In case of multi functional economy, the service sector is also dominant as in case of Mathura, Kanpur Nagar and Ghaziabad. In addition, it is also the pressure of population upon existing job market which promotes a culture of allied occupations especially at house hold level thus bringing down the percentage of workers in other than household workers as is noticed in case of highly urbanized districts like Lucknow, Allahabad, Varnasi and Dehradun. The rest of the area is dominated by mono-functional towns.

Tertiary Workers : Total

The dynamism of any urban system is closely related with the degree of its city-forming sector or basic services and with its city-serving sector or non-basic services. The proper functioning of an urban economic system is closely linked with degree to which the service or tertiary sector of economy is able to supplement it. The various urban institutions need service personnel from different educational backgrounds to carry out organizational work. While the storage of products, its transport and marketing all involves labor both skilled and semi skilled, at one level or another. Research and development is also required to upgrade knowledge and compete with world market for quality product that absorbs job specific personnel.

In India, tertiary sector of economy sector does not reflect the control of demand and supply in the urban labor market. It is rather the saturation of job avenues, as institutes and organizations only require specialized skills while the in migrants belong to various educational or no education background who generally get absorbed in the informal sector of economy. Since all these activities are clubbed under services, this gives a false impression of the developed service sector, which in western world is synonymous with provision of specialized services, or an indicator of an advanced stage of tertiary urbanization.

Spatial Process

In Uttar Pradesh, with 56.5 per cent of the total work force as tertiary, the process shows a strong relation with educational levels of males especially percentage of male main workers with more than graduate degree (+0.77) within 15-59 age group (+0.70). The percentage of males with more than graduate degree (+0.66), the age specific literacy of total males (+0.58) and females (+0.67) are also important aspects of this process. Female workers with more than graduate degree also relate positively (+0.52) with this indicator.

Spatial Patterns

In 1991, in Uttar Pradesh, the process of tertiary sector development relates with positive and healthy signs of urbanization, however on regional levels, association of factors vary resulting in definite spatial patterns (Fig. 15).

Between 67-82 per cent lies very high degree in which 11

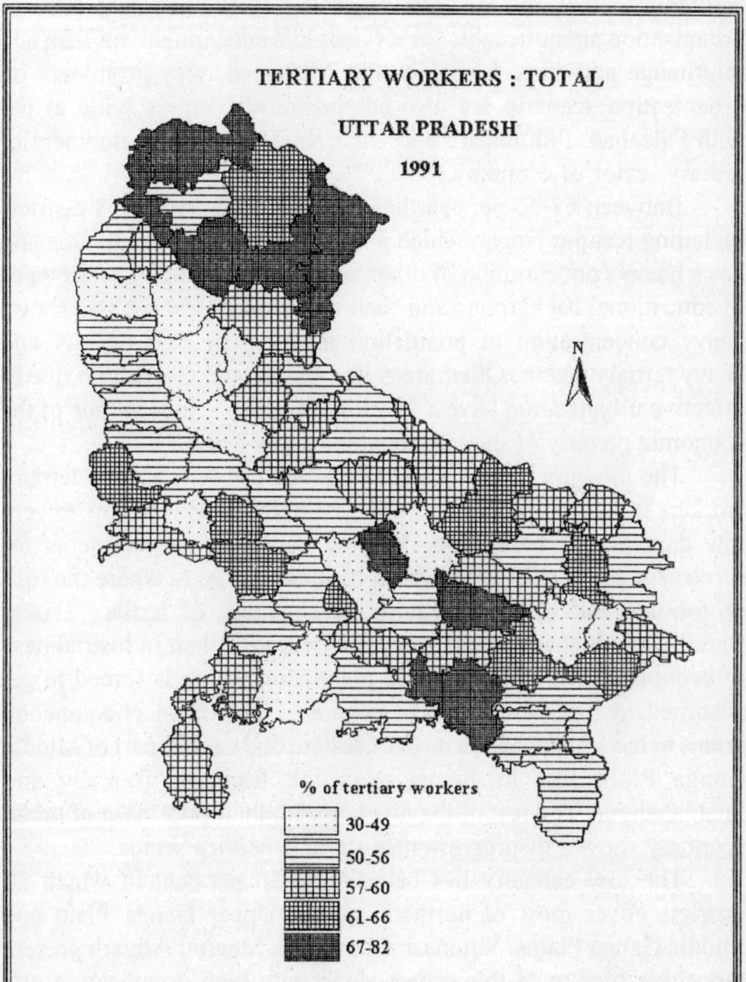
TERTIARY WORKERS : TOTAL
UTTAR PRADESH
1991
N
% of tertiary workers
30-49
50-56
57-60
61-66
67-82

Fig. 15

districts cover areas of varying degree of urbanization. Service sector is dominant in the hill region of Uttar Pradesh in which apart from Dehradun, other hill districts recording very low on degree of urbanization are noticeable for services like educational, tourism and pilgrimage activities. Lucknow and Allahabad, very prominent on urbanization scenario are also administrative centers lying at par with Faizabad, Pithoragarh and Uttar Kashi on the development of tertiary sector of economy.

Between 61-66 per cent lies the high category with 8 districts including Kanpur Nagar, which is a multi functional urban area and has a heavy concentration of urban population belonging to all types of educational background and economic strata. Mathura also shows heavy concentration of population resulting in high density and heavy tertiary sector. Other areas like Gonda and Gorakhpur due to effective urbanization have a developed tertiary sector in face of the economic poverty of their surrounding areas

The medium category includes 57-60 per cent of total tertiary workers in which 16 districts cover generally areas with low to very low degree of urbanization. Varying degree of requirements for services seem to exist in Hardwar, Nainital and Agra where the rush of tourists and pilgrims require development of tertiary sector. Bareilly, Shahjahanpur and Rampur by virtue of their industrial base of economy have attracted more population which is forced to get absorbed in informal sector of economy. The same phenomenon seems to have happened in most of eastern and central part of Middle Ganga Plain like in Jhansi, Nainital, Rampur, Bareilly and Shahjahanpur. The rest of the districts with their poor base of urban economy show a disproportionate share in service sector.

The low category lies between 50-56 per cent in which 20 districts cover most of northern part of Upper Ganga Plain and Middle Ganga Plains. Varanasi, Ghaziabad, Meerut, Aligarh present a positive picture of this aspect along with high urbanization and industrialization. The rest of the districts in this category do not reveal any attraction attached to cities in the form of job prospects in tertiary sector for either educated and uneducated population like Hardoi, Pilibhit, Kheri, Basti and Deoria.

The very low category lies between 30-49 per cent with 10 districts. A general lack of initiatives for the promotion of tertiary sector seems to characterize this area in which major parts of northern Upper Ganga Plains, scattered pockets in central eastern and southern plateau region like Hamirpur, Unnao, Bara Banki, Mainpuri, Mau, Moradabad and Budaun are included.

In general the development of tertiary sector, as identified through correlation analysis as well, seems to be occurring in the highly urbanized or medium urbanized districts where the requirement for services are part of city forming process like in Allahabad, Lucknow and northern hill areas. It is also dominant in areas with a considerable degree of effective urbanization despite low percentage of urban population. There seems to be a lack of demand of services in economically less developed area with mono-functional towns, which do not support much of tertiary activities as in Bahraich, Unnao, Bijnor and Budaun.

Total Workers : Active Age Group (15-59)

The urbanization economies of scale lead to the concentration of economic activities particularly the manufacturing industries in large urban centers. The middle and small towns on the contrary, due to weak infrastructural facilities generally fail to attract industrial location and manufacturing. The multiplier raises the demand for products and ancillary services keeps on increasing along with a healthy urbanization so that the growing population remains engaged in one or another type of economic activity in urban areas. In the economies of production, age is only significant in terms of working efficiency in the utilization of various technology levels in the work place. The rate of the migration of population in active age group is also the most significant factor for increasing percentage of total workers in the age group of 15-59 years. Thus, the percentage of economically active population is an indication of the existing potentials in the job market to absorb labor in the growing sector of economy whether secondary or tertiary. It further suggests the probable level of self-sufficiency amongst the earning group arising out of rising levels of income.

Spatial Process

In Uttar Pradesh in 1991 with 44.7 per cent total workers within the active age group of 15-59, there is a positive relation with the main male workers (+0.51) especially in active age group (+0.47). No other variable correlates with this aspect significantly.

Spatial Patterns

Uttar Pradesh shows regional variations perpetuated by local socio-economic factors in total workers within the active age group of 15-59, resulting in distinct spatial patterns (Fig.16).

Between 53-62 per cent lies very high category with 5 districts covering the northern mountain districts in which migration of active age group workers has been significant. Uttarkashi, Chamoli, Tehri Garhwal, Pithoragarh and Almora are areas of fast economic development and urbanization.

Between 50-52 per cent lies high category in which 4 districts, which are widely scattered, do not correspond to any pattern except that these are very low on degree of urbanization in which Garhwal, Mau, Hamirpur are important. Incidentally these areas are border districts of Uttar Pradesh experiencing in migration of active male workers across the state.

Between 47-49 per cent lies medium category with 14 districts in which Dehradun, Meerut, Ghaziabad are very high on degree of urbanization along with Nainital, Moradabad, Muzaffarnagar with medium degree of urbanization. In southern plateau region Sonhbadra, Mirzapur with medium category of urbanization presents economic pulls for active age population though mainly from rural areas.

Between 43-46 per cent lies low category with 29 districts in which Saharanpur, Agra, Bulandshahr, Mathura, Aligarh, Jhansi, are areas prominent on scene of urbanization but show a decrease in percentage of workers in active age group. The rest of the Upper and Middle Ganga Plain except Lucknow and Kanpur Nagar and a belt of districts on the eastern border of the state show decrease in percentage of urban population and low concentration of percentage of workers in active age group.

Between 40-42 per cent lies the very low category in which a belt of 11 districts cover districts on the eastern margin of the state extending till Allahabad like Mainpuri, Etawah and Jalaun. The most

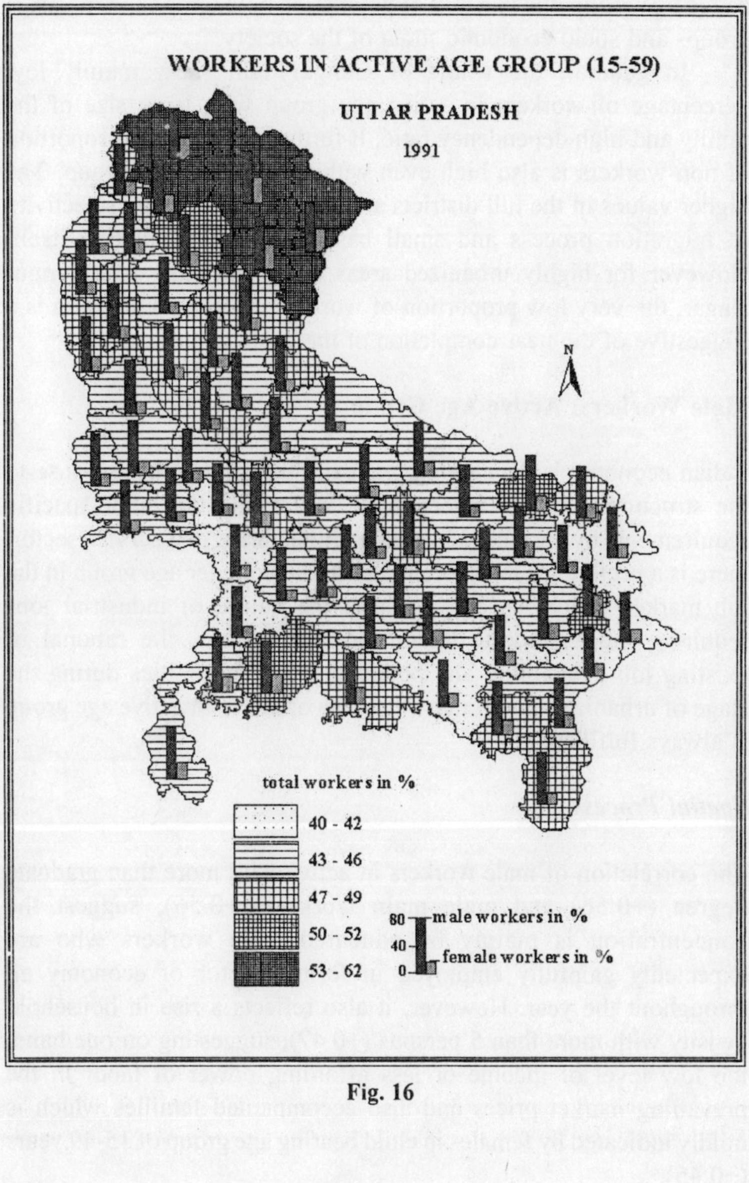
WORKERS IN ACTIVE AGE GROUP (15-59)
UTTAR PRADESH
1991
N
total workers in %
40 - 42
43 - 46
47 - 49
50 - 52
53 - 62
80
40
0
male workers in %
female workers in %

Fig. 16

striking is the position of two most urbanized districts of Lucknow and Kanpur Nagar which record very low percentage of workers on active age group due to a mix of population belonging to various age groups and socio economic strata of the society.

In general, the whole of Ganga Plain show mainly low percentage of workers in active age group with large size of the family and high dependency ratio. It further suggests the proportion of non-workers is also high even within the active age group. The higher values in the hill districts are only because of age selectivity of migration process and small base of urban population itself. However for highly urbanized areas as in Lucknow and Kanpur Nagar, the very low proportion of workers in active age group is a suggestive of the near completion of the cycle of migration.

Male Workers: Active Age Group

Indian economy is developing gradually but slowly. In response to the structural changes in economic sector and the labor specific requirements by various industrial manufacturing and service sector, there is a preference to absorb males in the younger age group in the job market which basically reflects the nature of industrial jobs requiring more working hours and labor. Thus, the rational of existing job availability and potential job opportunities during the stage of urbanization through migration of males in active age group is always fulfilled.

Spatial Process

The correlation of male workers in active with more than graduate degree (+0.56) and male main workers (+0.56), suggest the concentration is mainly by educated male workers who are expectedly gainfully employed in formal sector of economy all throughout the year. However, it also reflects a rise in household density with more than 5 persons (+0.47), suggesting on one hand, the low level of income or less affording power of labor in the prevailing market prices and also accompanied families which is mildly indicated by females in child bearing age group of 15-49 years (+0.45).

Spatial Patterns

In 1991, with 75.7 per cent of the total male work force, the male workers in active age group contributed significantly. In relation to the state average, the position of various districts shows significant spatial patterns (Fig.16).

In Uttar Pradesh, only 29 or 46 per cent of the districts record within 85-79 per cent of the male workers in active age group in areas with varying degree of urbanization. The very high concentration is found in the districts close to the National Capital Region of Delhi and records a decrease east and southward from the foothill of Himalaya. Thus, the degree of urbanization is not a sole determinant of percentage of males in active age group as is generally presumed. While Garhwal, Siddharthnagar, Banda, Budaun, Pilibhit and Mau are areas with very low degree of urbanization record higher values, the western most districts of Saharanpur, Muzaffarnagar, Meerut, Bareilly and Rampur also remain very high regarding the share of male workers in active age group despite medium degree of urbanization. This phenomenon suggests the role of mono functionality of urban centers as in case of Mau or Siddharthnagar. It further reflects the role of small and household industries in areas with long history of urbanization that provides subsistence urbanization to the inhabitants like in Jhansi, Faizabad, Sultanpur. However, the position of Kanpur Nagar, Lucknow, and Varanasi is posing queries. Kanpur Nagar is already urbanized to such an extent where multiplier effect of the economy seems to be decreasing thus discouraging the migrants within active age group. Lucknow in this regard has a slightly better position where the in migration rate are also of medium range and intensity. In case of less urbanized areas, the lack of economic opportunities is reinforcing out-migration of males in active age group as is noticed in Banda, Hamirpur, Deoria and Ghazipur. The Hill districts in general, present a better position as upcoming economic opportunities in the form of tourism and development of tertiary sector requires active age group male workers.

Female Workers: Active Age Group

The workforce structure of females in case of India still is ill defined.

The nature of industrial establishments is in demand of male workers except light manufacturing industry where supervision or office jobs absorb females in respective sections. However, in service sector, females are heavily demanded because of their lack of unionism and compromises on lower wage rates in low-grade jobs. In high-qualified field, both men and women are competing well. Under the economic scenario of Uttar Pradesh, it is the informal sector of economy in which there is a preponderance of female workforce especially those migrating from short distances after marriage, or in search of job. It is also the highly paid service sector where the migration of females is voluntarily; the basic aim is either job along with education, or job itself or job and marriage combined.

Spatial Process

In Uttar Pradesh, in 1991, the correlation with female workers less than graduate degree (+0.68), household density with less than 3 persons per room (+0.66) and in-migration of total males (+0.47). It suggests that the females in this age group are migrating to urban areas as a part of family after marriage or for economic reasons.

Spatial Patterns

In 1991 in Uttar Pradesh only 7.9 per cent workers in active age group were females. This proportion of female work participation though very low shows considerable variation over space under the influence of local socio-economic factors (Fig.16).

In Uttar Pradesh, only 8 or 12.7 per cent of the districts record within 32-19 per cent of the female workers in active age group mainly in the Hill districts. In general the distributional pattern of female workers in active age group fails to establish any relation with the levels of urbanization as even districts like Mau, Banda and Hamirpur have higher percentage of female workers in active age group. The whole Ganga Plain records the female workers in active group varying between 14-4 per cent. However, the northern Upper Ganga Plain and the whole middle Ganga Plain have shown a concentration around 10 per cent of the females in active age group. While Kanpur Nagar and Lucknow and the adjacent areas especially the districts comprising of the southern Upper Ganga Plains shows a remarkably low percentage of such female workers only around 5 per cent. It may be due to the concentration of females of all literacy level and educational background including in-migrants from the surrounding rural areas which increase the population base of such areas resulting in lower work participation rates of females in this category. However, the districts with medium to low level of urbanization due to the influence of concentration of economic activities in selected areas absorb females of all educational background, raising their work participation rate in active age group as in case of Hill districts. The areas dominated by traditional societies like in Budaun, Shahjahanpur, Sitapur, Mainpuri, Etawah also record around 4 per cent female workers in active age group.

Non-Agricultural Workers : Females

Female work participation in non-agricultural sector of economy is both an indicator of the economic participatory power of female folk of the society as well as the degree of modernization in a society. This indicator does also suggest sex specific labor demand in industries, manufacturing and related service sector of urban economy. A rising trend towards female literary has brought about a significant change in their outlook toward economic independency. In addition many consumer-based industries prefer female as workers due to their inherent sense of responsibility and hard work. The economic contributions made by females in household income have a positive impact on the life styles especially on child education and living standards as females have in general a strong bond with their family members. This indicator partly reflects the economic progress through an increase in work participation in non-agricultural occupations by females and partly reflects the rising impact of urbanism. Therefore, it serves both as an economic and social indicator.

Spatial Process

In Uttar Pradesh, 82.4 per cent of total working females were engaged in non-agricultural activities. The dynamics underlying this process are brought out by correlation coefficient in which the places of 20,000 or more urban population show strong correlation (+0.69), inter-state migration from urban areas (+0.57), and the level of education of females more than graduate (+0.59). There is also a mild relation with total secondary (+0.52) and tertiary sector (+0.47).

Spatial Patterns

In Uttar Pradesh, the forces of urbanism seem not to be operative at same level of intensity everywhere, which result in well-defined spatial patterns (Fig.17).

Between 89-97 per cent lies the very high category covering 19 districts with vaying degree of urbanization. Kanpur Nagar, Lucknow, Ghaziabad and Varanasi are included along with two significant concentrations: first in the Himalayan foothills with Dehradun, Tehri Garwal, Saharanpur, and second in the southern Upper Ganga Plain with Agra, Aligarh, Etah, Etawah, Firozabad, Farrukhabad, Shahjahanpur, Bareilly and others.

Between 81-88 per cent lies high category under which 12 districts cover the districts of Mathura, Bijnor, Moradabad, Budaun,Pilibhit, Hardoi, Sonbhadra, Allahabad, Jaunpur, Azamgarh, Faizabad with medium to low degree of urbanization.

Between 72-80 per cent is the medium category in which 14 districts cover scattered pockets all over Ganga Plain without any regular pattern except in Tarai and foothill districts of Uttar Pradesh Himalaya. All these areas show medium to low or even low as in eastern Uttar Pradesh, degree of urbanization with limited economic opportunities and are inhibited by traditional societies.

Between 55-79 per cent lies the low category in which 9 districts cover parts of eastern Tarai region in eastern Uttar Pradesh Himalayas and Muzaffarnagar. These areas are all low to very low on scene of urbanization except Jhansi and Muzaffarnagar

Between 33-54 per cent lies very low category consisting of 9 districts in areas of very low degree of urbanization and economic stagnation as in case of eastern Uttar Pradesh, central part of southern Plateau Region, and northern Uttar Pradesh Himalaya.

On the whole, female work participation in non-agricultural activities is a widely occurring phenomenon all over Ganga Plain

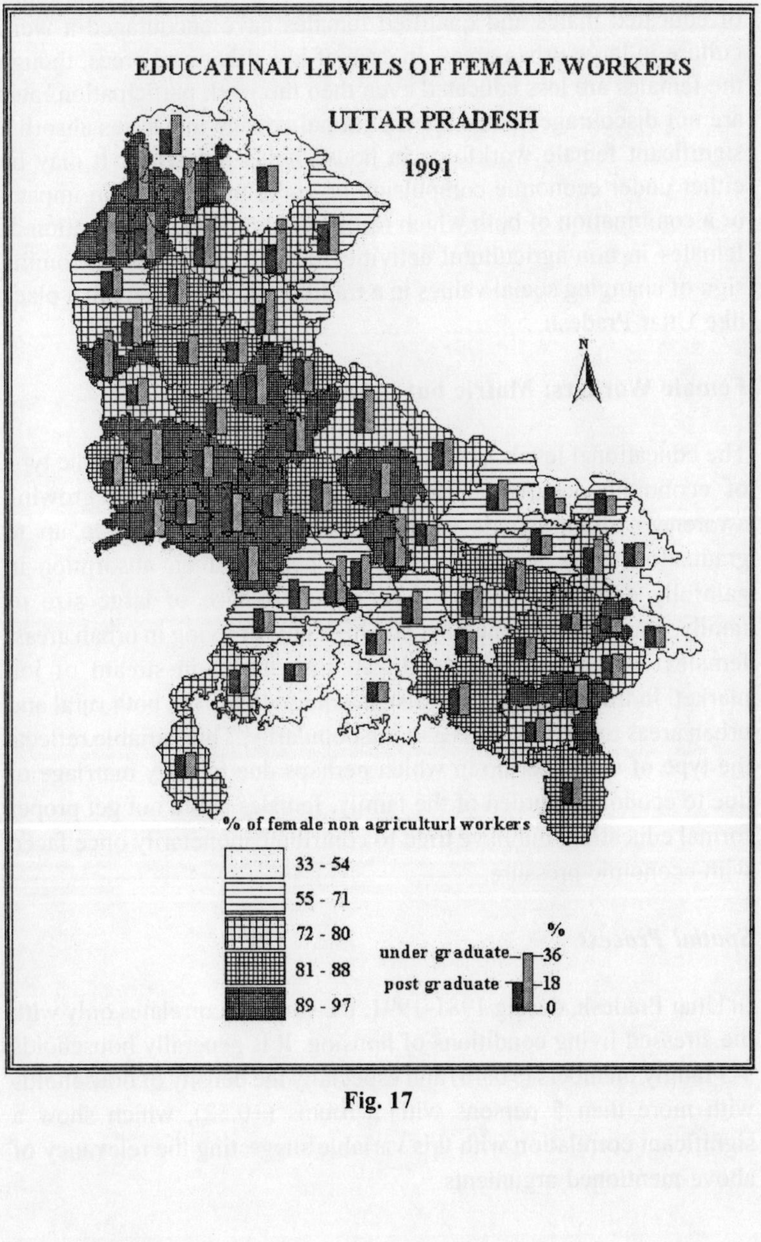
EDUCATINAL LEVELS OF FEMALE WORKERS
UTTAR PRADESH
1991
N
% of female non agriculturl workers
33 - 54
55 - 71
72 - 80
81 - 88
89 - 97
%
under graduate
post graduate
36
18
0

Fig. 17

and foothill region of Himalaya. Although Uttar Pradesh is an agricultural state, the growth of large cities promoting in-migrations of educated males and qualified females have encouraged a work culture in large urban areas. In case of low urbanized areas, though the females are less educated even then the work participation rates are not discouraged since the traditional cottage industries absorb a significant female workforce in house holds industries. It may be either under economic compulsion or under modernization impact, or a combination of both which results in high work participation of females in non-agricultural activities. However, it is a welcoming sign of changing social values in a tradition bound society in a place like Uttar Pradesh.

Female Workers: Matric but below Graduate

The educational levels of female workers assigns a value to the type of economic occupation they are attached with. With growing awareness about female education and literacy, a degree up to graduation either formal or technical helps in their absorption in gainfully employed sector of economy. In face of large size of family, single earning member and high cost of living in urban areas, females are gradually being drawn into the main stream of job market. In this process, short distance migration from both rural and urban areas to large cities is gaining popularity. This variable reflects the type of social set up in which perhaps due to early marriage or due to economic burden of the family, females could not get proper formal education, but have tried to contribute monetarily once faced with economic pressure.

Spatial Process

In Uttar Pradesh, during 1981-1991, the variable correlates only with the stressed living conditions of housing. It is generally households 3-5 family members (+0.45) and especially the density of households with more than 5 persons with 2 rooms (+0.52), which show a significant correlation with this variable suggesting the relevancy of above-mentioned arguments.

Spatial Patterns

In 1991, 12.9 per cent of female workers were metric but below the degree of graduation. However, this process does not manifest itself equally all over the geographical space. (Fig.17).

In 1991, only 18 or 28.6 per cent of the districts have high proportion female workers with metric up to graduation. Apart from Kanpur Nagar, Ghaziabad, Dehradun the area mostly coincides with medium to low level of urbanization in southern Upper Ganga Plain including Kanpur Dehat, Hardoi, Bahraich, Kheri, Bijnor, Budaun, and Pithoragarh. While eastern Uttar Pradesh shows lesser concentration of females in less educated category as the female work participation itself is less. This indicator brings out the role of local economy as areas with cottage and household industries seem to have employed less educated females irrespective of the degree of urbanization. In general, this indicator highlights the rapid changes in Indian society where even economically backward areas are recipient of modernization effects as reflected through the increase in work participation rates of middle class less educated females.

Female Workers: Graduate and Above

The relation between education, increasing work participation and high rate of urbanization is well established as far as female work participation in highly paid organized sector of economy is concerned. The levels of educational attainment of females of above post graduate including technical training and their levels of absorption in various economic fields are not just a measure of economic participation of educated female workers. It rather signifies an underlying process of modernization of society especially in India, which is still supposed to be backward regarding the recognition of educational status of female. For an under developed state like Uttar Pradesh, this indicator assumes special significance.

Spatial Process

In Uttar Pradesh, during 1981-1991, the underlying mechanism associated with this indicator is conspicuous. It identifies itself very strongly with the mean age of females at marriage (+0.80), internal in-migration (+0.63) and outside the state migration from urban areas (+0.49) suggest an increased mobility of female workers, may be after marriage or even before. A corresponding rise in the size of households with 3-5 persons per 2 rooms (+0.71) suggest that females even more than graduate degree belong to large family size and as such are a contributor to the family income.

Spatial Patterns

In 1991 Uttar Prdesh records 20.6 per cent of the total female workers with higher educational attainments of above graduate category. However, the percentage value in itself is not very high and shows a marked variation on district level (Fig.17).

The impact of urbanization also results in acceptance of role of females as either an economically independent working member of the family or a contributor to family income. Therefore, the proportion of females with graduation degree and above reflects the setup of the society as well. In Uttar Pradesh this phenomenon is supposedly associated with higher effective urbanization levels. However, only 17 or 26.9 per cent of the districts have high and very high concentration of female workers with graduate and above degree including the highly urbanized districts of Kanpur Nagar and Lucknow, Dehradun and Ghaziabad along with the northern hill districts of Almora, Tehri Garhwal, Garhwal as well as Hardwar, Saharanpur, Meerut, Aligarh, Agra, Bareilly and Nainital. Incidentally all these areas have better educational facilities and a dominant service sector that employ educated females. On the other hand, areas with low degree of urbanization also have a higher concentration of educated females in few selected towns encouraging their work participation rates as in Kheri, Gonda, Bahraich, Faizabad and Sultanpur. In Uttar Pradesh, this phenomenon signifies the acceptance of role of a middle class educated female as a contributor of the family income.

Male Workers: Matric but below Graduate

The job market in the urban areas varies with the occupation specific requirements. The industrial, manufacturing and service sector especially transport, marketing and other related aspects demand labor of varying specialization skills and levels of education. This encourages in-migrants from the surrounding region of males with varying technical and educational skills that contribute significantly both in formal and informal sector of economy. In rural areas, young males generally within 15-25 age group have a higher propensity to migrate for economic seasons. For them the relative wage differentials between rural and urban areas are as significant as the charm to get absorbed in a city based occupation. In general, the small-scale industrial sector and service or informal sector of economy attract the migrants with less than graduation degree. Thus, in Indian case this variable is the most important indicator of the development mechanism of urban economy operative within and outside any region.

Spatial Process

With 21.9 per cent in 1991, the male workers metric but below graduate results due to the interaction of many variables among which age selectivity of males within 15-59 (+0.68) along with varying literacy and educational levels are important. The total literacy (+0.89), male literacy (+0.88) and literacy of males in 60+ age group (+0.84) are significant. The next aspect is indicated by the migratory character of population in which male in migration (+0.73) especially from rural areas within the state (+0.51), outside state from rural areas (+0.43) and urban areas (+0.41) are significant. A corresponding rise in total tertiary workers (+0.58) is noticed along with increased household size of 3-5 (+0.55).

Spatial Patterns

A definite spatial pattern is noticed in the percentage distribution of male workers with low educational levels (Fig.18).

Between 28-33 per cent, 8 districts record very high category in which the whole of Uttar Pradesh Himalayas, Sonbhadra and Kanpur Nagar are included. Kanpur Nagar is an industrial-cum-service center due to which even semi-skilled workers are also

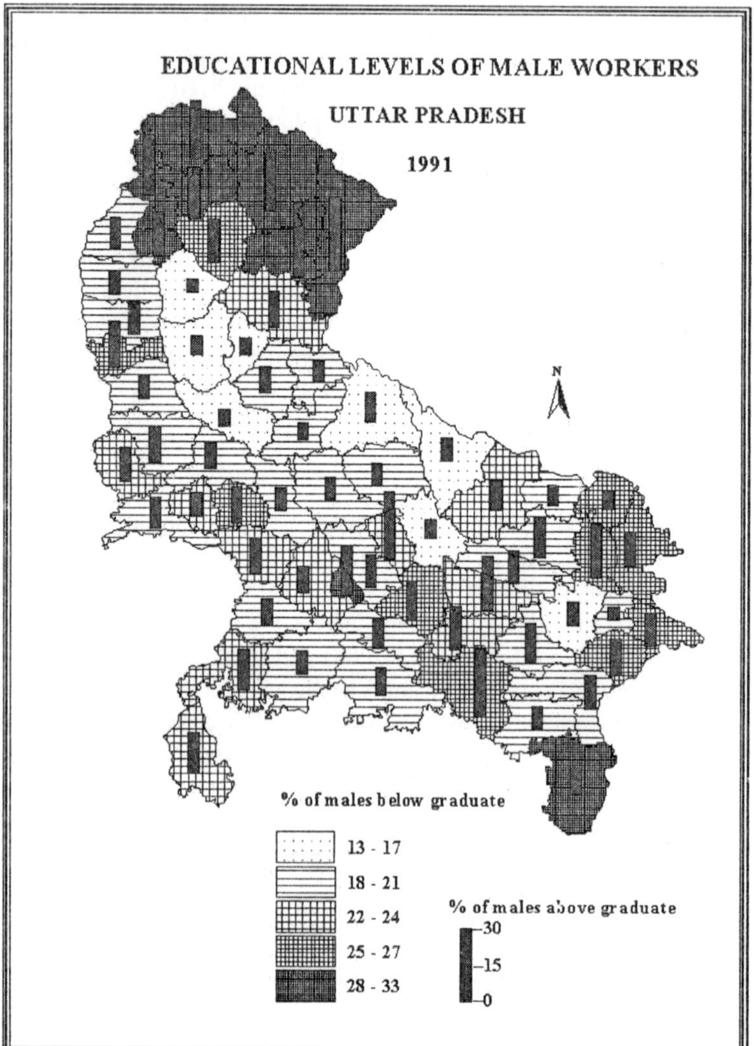
EDUCATIONAL LEVELS OF MALE WORKERS
UTTAR PRADESH
1991
N
% of males below graduate
13 - 17
18 - 21
22 - 24
25 - 27
28 - 33
% of males above graduate
30
15
0

Fig. 18

absorbed as marginal workers. In Uttar Pradesh Himalayas it is tourism industry with government establishment like in Dehradun that generally sustains even less educated workers in service sector.

Between 25-27 per cent lies high category in which 10 districts cover mainly eastern part of Uttar Pradesh. Allahabad and Ghaziabad are the two major centers with high urbanization and multifunctional character of cities that absorbs workers of lower educational background as well. In case of eastern Uttar Pradesh the districts of Maharajganj, Gorakhpur, and Ballia have the small-scale industrial set up which requires less educated workers.

Between 22-24 per cent lies medium category, covering 11 districts widely scattered all over Ganga Pain. Lucknow, Jhansi, Mathura have high degree of urbanization but medium concentration of workers with metric but below graduate workers. Sultanpur, Gonda, Nainital that do not have much functional diversity of towns, therefore, record medium values.

Between 18-21 per cent lies low category, which is the most prevalent including 25 districts widely distributed over almost the whole of Ganga Plain especially along river Ganga. Varanasi, Agra and Meerut, though high on degree of urbanization are mainly absorbing workers with low educational levels. The rest of the areas under this category have low to very low degree of urbanization and show a decrease in work avenues for low educated workers as a result of limited base of urban economy.

Between 13-17 per cent lies very low category covering 8 districts of Upper Ganga region, Tarai and eastern Uttar Pradesh including Bijnor, Rampur, Kheri. These districts are economically stagnated reflecting the lack of opportunities to absorb seasonal workers. Moradabad has brass work industry running on small-scale level as well.

In general, the functional diversity of towns and cities opens up new opportunities for the absorption level of workers even from lower educational strata like in case of Kanpur Nagar and Dehradun. A specialized service demand, on the other hand, results in a decline in the proportion of such workers as in case of Lucknow where the demand is more for highly educated administrative jobs. On the other, it is the upcoming areas on economic scene either large-scale industrial establishments like Ghaziabad, or small-scale industries backed by an underdeveloped regional economy like in Firozabad that absorbs even less educated workers. A set of exogenous factors in the regional economy also counts as in eastern most part of Uttar Pradesh where Ghazipur, Ballia, Deoria, Maharajganj are receiving labor generally low educated, migrating across the state.

Male Workers: Graduate and Above

In the economics of production, education has a significance in deciding the levels of adoption of new technological inputs upon which the progress of various economic sectors is dependent. A modern industrial unit or any knowledge-based organization recruits job seekers suiting to their own requirements. The role of education in deciding the nature of job availability reflects the direction of development towards which the economy is moving.

After Independence, India has made significant progress, though slow in the field of industrialization. The development of industrial economy has resulted in, on one hand, stagnation of cottage industries in small and medium towns and on the other polarization of capital-intensive economic activities in few selected regions of the country. Coupled with the increase in general literacy and higher education, the very nature of capital distribution has resulted in unemployed youth, which is one of the areas of concerns for affective urban planning strategies. Therefore, this variable measures the job provision aspect of more than graduate workers, which in itself is a sign of effective urban socio-economic development.

Spatial Process

In Uttar Pradesh, 13.6 per cent of male workers are with graduates and above degree in 1991.This indicator is very strongly correlated with the higher education level of males (+0.90) especially males within active age-group of 15-59 years (+0.59) which show again a strong degree of correspondence with the service or tertiary sector of employment for males (+0.77). The rates of the migration especially from outside the state from other urban areas are significant (+0.56) with international in migrants (+0.45).

Spatial Patterns

The distribution pattern of male workers with graduates and above degree at district level has shown definite spatial patterns (Fig.18).

In Uttar Pradesh, any direct link with the degree of effective urbanization and distribution of workers with higher education cannot be noticed. Only 11 or 17.5 per cent of the districts including the administrative cum service centers as in Lucknow, Allahabad, Kanpurnagar, Agra, Dehradun lie at par with Pithoragarh, Almora, Gorakhpur, Ghaziabad and Sultanpur. In general, it is the functional diversity of urban places especially in demand of specialized services like business, commerce, manufacturing, education and other institutional activities that determine the intake of educated workers like in Lucknow and Allahabad. Even the districts with small towns and a predominant service sector show workers with graduate or higher degree as noticed in case of Almora, Chamoli and Pithoragarh where the present high percentage is due to small base of urban population. In general, The Hill districts present a better picture compared to the Ganga Plains regarding male workers with graduate and above degree. However, eastern Middle Ganga Plain show a better scenario of educational levels of male workers as noticed in Gorakhpur, Sultanpur, Ghazipur, Jaunpur and Faizabad.

DEPENDENCY RATIO

With increase in urbanization the modern medical facilities are available which have a direct impacts on the longevity of life. Along with it, there are high birth rates even in urban areas since the rate of natural increase has not recorded any marked decline in India due to prevalence of culture for medium size family. In general, people are not concerned about the environmental implications of increasing population pressure until they themselves suffer serious economic constraint due to large family size. India has recorded a working population 15-59 as 60.8 per cent and Uttar Pradesh as only 44.7 per cent against the 66.8 per cent of developed market economies.

Dependency Ratio: Juvenile

It is a function of the proportion of non-working age group within 0-

15 years with the active age group (15-59 years) population. The higher ratio of juvenile dependency indicates the expending base of child population (0-15) that is supposed to be non-working. However, in Indian economic conditions, child labor is common despite the laws passed and imposed against it. Juvenile dependency is in one way an indicative of the freedom of the child from earning responsibility. It might also be concluded that this index measures better chances available for a child for education and development of his/her personality.

Spatial Process

In Uttar Pradesh in 1991 the juvenile dependency ratio is very strongly related with sex ratio (+0.80) as well as households of more than 5 persons per family (+0.86). It also shows mild correlation with inter-district urban to urban migration. The total literacy for 60+ group again shows a very strong relation (+0.72) with dependency ratio of youngs.

Spatial Patterns

In 1991, Uttar Pradesh recorded 702 juveniles as dependent on 1000 workers in active age group. On district level, variations exist leading to definite spatial patterns (Fig.19).

The emerging pattern of the dependency ratio of juvenile population states that between 792-865 per thousand lies the very high category in which 7 districts lie with medium degree of urbanization like Moradabad and Bijnor and very low degree of urbanization like Ballia and Azamgarh.

Within 743-791 lies high category in which 17 districts covering either the eastern Tarai belt of low degree of urbanization extending from Bahraich, Gonda till Deoria and the western part of Uttar Pradesh with high to medium degree of urbanization like Meerut, Muzaffarnagar, Rampur, Shahjahanpur.

Between 665-742 lies medium category in which 24 districts cover extensive areas of central Ganga Plain including Sonbhadra, Lalitpur, Unnao, which lie at par with Ghaziabad, Varanasi and Mathura.

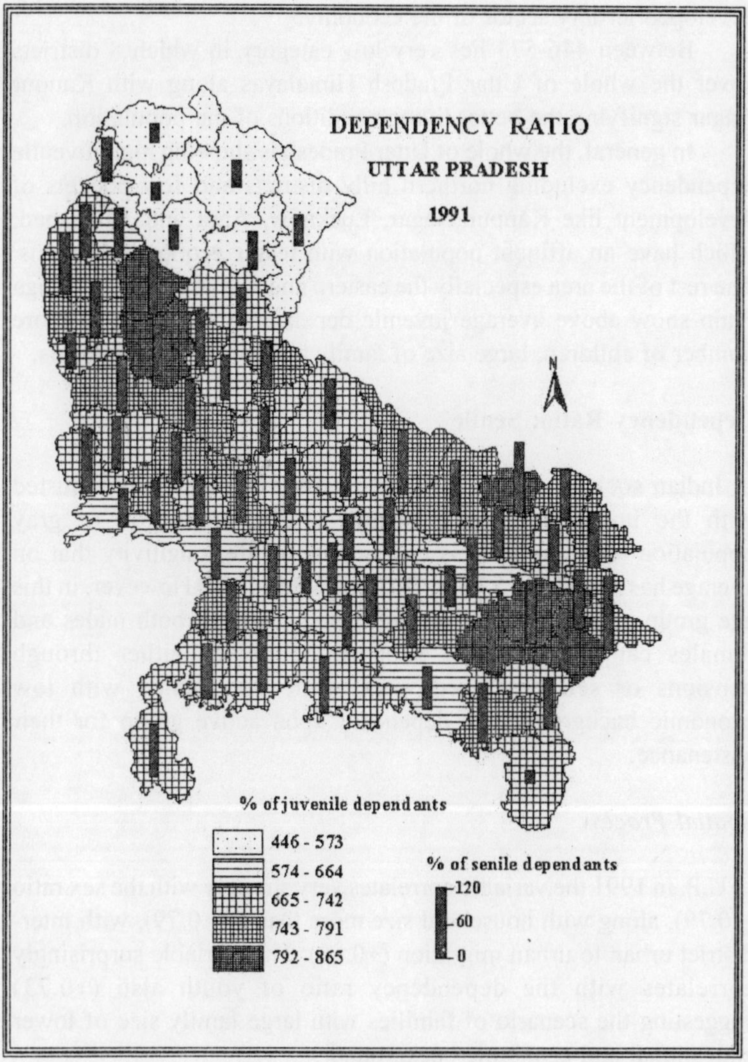
DEPENDENCY RATIO
UTTAR PRADESH
1991
N
% of juvenile dependants
446 - 573
574 - 664
665 - 742
743 - 791
792 - 865
% of senile dependants
120
60
0

Fig. 19

Between 574-664 lies low category in which 7 districts cover scattered areas like Allahabad Agra and Faizabad. The position of Lucknow in this category suggests an air of affluency due to the developed tertiary sector of the economy.

Between 446-573 lies very low category in which 8 districts cover the whole of Uttar Pradesh Himalayas along with Kanpur Nagar signifying the better living conditions of the population.

In general, the whole of Uttar Pradesh is showing high juvenile dependency excluding northern hilly districts and few pockets of development like Kanpur Nagar, Lucknow, Agra and Allahabad, which have an affluent population with lesser economic burdens. The rest of the area especially the eastern and western parts of Ganga Plain show above average juvenile dependency ratio due to more number of children, large size of family and lower income levels.

Dependency Ratio: Senile

In Indian society, old parents and relatives are generally adjusted with the immediate family members. The proportion of gray population (60+) in India is on rise due to life longitivity that on average has risen from 52.3 in 1980 to 58.3 in 1991. However, in this age group generally better educated population of both males and females can economically support themselves either through pensions or self employed work while uneducated with low economic background are dependent upon active group for their sustenance.

Spatial Process

In U.P. in 1991 the variable correlates very strongly with the sex ratio (+0.79), along with household size more than 5 (+0.79), with inter-district urban to urban migration (+0.56). This variable surprisingly correlates with the dependency ratio of youth also (+0.73) suggesting the scenario of families with large family size of lower educational and economic background.

Spatial Patterns

With 97 persons in senile age group dependent on 1000 workers in active age group, variations exist in the spatial pattern perpetuated by local factors (Fig.19).

There seem to be a close correspondence between the distribution pattern of juvenile and senile age group for eastern part of Ganga Plain where the senile dependency ratio is high due to large family size like in Siddharthnagar, Jaunpur, Ballia, Gonda, Bahraich Basti, Azamgarh, Deoria and Mirzapur. While In the parts of western Uttar Pradesh with more male workers in active age group, it seems that the family migration from short distance areas has pushed up senile dependency ratio. It seems to be a character of old urbanized areas inhibited by traditional societies as in case of Saharanpur, Muzaffarnagar, Bulandshahr, Jhansi, Jalaun, Hamirpur, Ballia, Siddharthnagar and Mirzapur. It further reflect the role of both more active age group and self sufficiency of old people as shown by low values recorded for Kanpur Nagar, Lucknow, Agra, Ghaziabad, Shajahanpur, Allahabad and Varanasi. In hill areas like Dehradun, Garhwal, Tehri-Garhwal, with a well-developed secondary and tertiary sector, senile dependency is lowest reflecting an increasing share of economically independent retired persons and more longitivity of life.

4

SOCIAL ASPECTS OF URBANIZATION

The city in itself provides both a formal and a functional space. The processes of functional interactions on geographical space characterize the patterns of human activity which is the determinant of spatial distribution of population. The role of urbanization in modifying the social patterns of life has a direct link with the level of economic changes. In general, the impact of urbanization leads to modernization. This phenomenon was identified as urbanism (Wirth, L.: 1938).

India has a great heterogeneity in the socio-cultural and economic composition of population. The impact of on going technological changes and innovations are not received equally by all sections of population due to variations in religion, believes, culture, customs and traditions that determine the level of acceptability of urban ways of life. It is an arduous task to translate them all into quantifiable variables to measure urbanism. However, in Uttar Pradesh, absolute measures of this aspect of urbanization though difficult, can be presented in the form of both direct and proxy variables.

Literacy and educational levels are considered to be an effective and reliable index of the social and economic transformations in the society. United Nations Development Programme has identified 'knowledge' as one of three basic indicators to calculate the Human Development Index. As per the index, the knowledge or educational attainment is defined under two sub-sets of variables. The first set is composed of combination of adult literacy with two third weight attached to it. The second set of variables is defined by combined primary, secondary and tertiary levels of education with one third of weight. Since the study under consideration refers to only spatial dimension in 1991, both literacy and educational level are considered equally significant.

LITERACY

The role of literacy to determine the nature of development of any particular urban economy is highly significant. Urbanization by its very nature necessitates the concentration of population of various skills and educational background to perform urban functions. In the absence of effective literacy it is generally the informal sector of economy, which develops.

The role of human beings in the formation of a sound human resource base can be achieved through literacy and education. The human beings or their potential skills as a productive source are recognized and equated with the notion of 'fixed capital'. However the economic cost of expenditure on formation of human capital base is realized through increased economic participation and maintenance of general level of well-being. Literacy and its role in the execution of health and related social welfare schemes have proved to be effective in cutting down the government budgetary expenditures on the related social service sector.

It is a crude and simple measure to calculate the population's achieved capacity to acquire a minimum skill of communication in both reading and writing. Therefore, it is a measure of overall level of development of the society. The Population Commission of the United Nations considers the ability to both read and write a simple message with a basic understanding in any language, a sufficient criteria to classify a person as literate. In 1991, the census of India has adopted this definition excluding the population up to the age of seven from the total population for calculating effective literacy rates.

The existing level of literacy at any given point of time acts an aggregate measure to evaluate the success of the various educational plans and its achieved targets. After independence, the average literacy rates in India has increased from 16.57 per cent in 1951 to 52.11 per cent in 1991. Though the progress of literacy seems to be satisfactory, it is the existing percentage of illiterates, 47.89 per cent that is disturbing.

Total Literates: Active Age Group (15-59 Years)

Within the working age group this index measures the efficacy of the various social targets to be achieved by the government. It foretells the possibility of workers to be absorbed in gainfully employed sector of economy. It is a further indication of the functional diversity of the urban area, which suggest a progressing economy.

Spatial Process

In Uttar Pradesh, for 1991, this variable correlates strongly with the active age group of total population (+0.79) specifically males in active age group (+0.76), the rate of total in-migration (+0.72) and total tertiary workers (+0.64) suggesting it to be a phenomena of male migrant workers in active age group, engaged in tertiary sector of economy.

Spatial Patterns

In 1991, Uttar Pradesh records 60.8 per cent of population within the age group of 15-59 as literates. However, the spatial pattern is variable in response to the given socio-economic set up of the area (Fig.20).

Between 74-86 per cent lies very high category in which 6 districts cover the northern part of Uttar Pradesh Himalaya including Dehradun, which has a large number of government organization promoting in migration of literates within active age group. Uttar Kashi, Chamoli, Pithoragarh, Tehri Garhwal and Almora are areas promoting in migration of literate males in active age group through varied economic activities.

Between 67-73 per cent lies high category that include 8 districts scattered widely over Ganga Plain and southern Plateau Region. It includes the highly urbanized areas of Kanpur Nagar, Lucknow, Allahabad, Jhansi, which understandably have more literate population within active age group as urbanism commensurate with increasing literacy. The position of Hardwar and Garhwal on this scenario is due to the pilgrim and tourism, which are attracting high proportions of literate migrants in active age groups. Sonbhadra also attracts literate persons due to the economic set up.

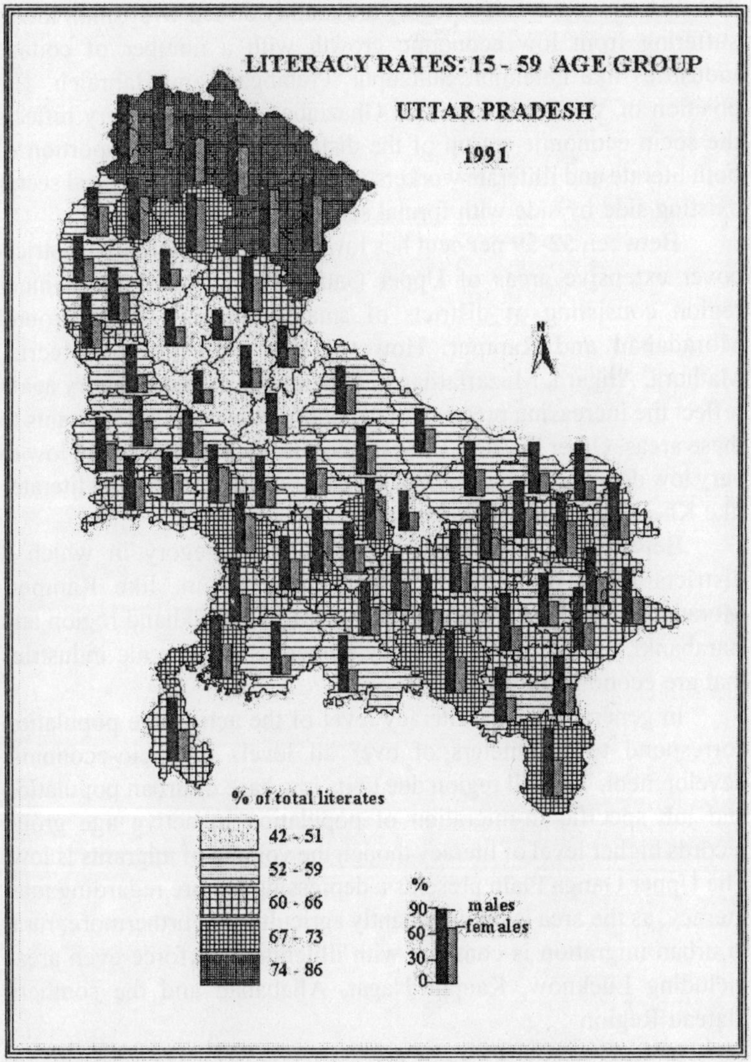
LITERACY RATES: 15 - 59 AGE GROUP
UTTAR PRADESH
1991
N
% of total literates
42 - 51
52 - 59
60 - 66
67 - 73
74 - 86
%
90
60
30
0
males
females

Fig. 20

Between 60-66 per cent lies the medium category in which 19 districts cover extensive areas in the eastern Middle Ganga Plain. The districts under this category are mainly dotted with small towns suffering from low economic growth with a number of cottage industries like Fatehpur, Sultanpur, Pratabgarh and Bahraich. The position of Varanasi, Agra and Ghaziabad in this category reflects the socio-economic set up of the districts where the proportion of both literate and illiterate workers is more as result of informal sector existing side by side with formal sector of economy.

Between 52-59 per cent lies low category in which 20 districts cover extensive areas of Upper Ganga Plain excluding an inner region consisting of districts of small industrial towns around Moradabad and Rampur. However, the inclusion of Meerut, Mathura, Aligarh, Muzaffarnagar, Saharanpur in this category again reflect the increasing pressure of generally illiterate rural migrants to these areas. Other districts since economically backward with low to very low degree of urbanization, have a low concentration of literates like Kheri, Sitapur and Budaun.

Between 42-51 per cent lie very low category in which 8 districts lying in northern Upper Ganga Plain, like Rampur, Moradabad, Budaun, Bijnor all form part of Rohilkhand region and Barabanki, are basically dotted by numerous small-scale industries that are economically stagnant.

In general the total literacy level of the active age population correspond to parameters of over all levels of socio-economic development. The hill region due to its low base of urban population and job specific in-migration of population in active age group records higher level of literacy though the volume of migrants is low. The Upper Ganga Plain presents a depressing picture regarding total literacy, as the area is predominantly agricultural. Furthermore, rural to urban migration is common with illiterate workforce even areas including Lucknow, Kanpur Nagar, Allahabad and the southern Plateau Region

Male Literates: Active Age Group

In Indian society, the literacy among males in active age group is a cumulative index of the over all measure of efficiency of various planned targets for the socio economic upliftment of the society. It also reflects as in case of male migrants, the level of development of the place of origin and the job specific educational qualification of the place of destination. In this age group, the male migrants are absorbed generally in industrial establishment or manufacturing as labor in tertiary sector of economy with varying levels of income.

Spatial Process

In Uttar Pradesh during 1981-91, this variable correlates strongly with both active age group of total in-migrants (+0.65) and male in-migrants (+0.62). There is a corresponding association with total tertiary workers (+0.64). The male workers both above (+0.86) and below graduate (+0.89) correlate strongly suggesting the deterministic role of literacy in urbanization of Uttar Pradesh.

Spatial Patterns

In Uttar Pradesh for 1991, 60.8 per cent of the total males within age group of 15-59 were literates. This age and sex specific effective literacy manifested itself with spatial variations (Fig.20).

Only 18 or 28.6 per cent of the districts record values in high and very high category within a range of 86-67 per cent literates. Incidentally all these districts show two important concentrations. The first occupies the Himalayan districts including Dehra Dun. The second occupies the border districts of southern plateau region in scattered pockets above Lalitpur and Allahabad respectively. The position of Kanpur Nagar and Lucknow is sound with high proportion of literates. In general, the spatial distribution pattern of male literates in active age group closely follows the spatial pattern of the total literates in active age group. The literacy as an index of modernization level, in case of Uttar Pradesh, seems to have been influenced by the type of economy prevalent all over the region. The agriculturally dominated areas in Ganga Plains show a low level of literacy around 55 per cent as noticed in Muzaffarnagar, Saharanpur. Even the industrial regions of Aligarh, Bulandshashr, Firozabad, Etah, Shahjahanpur, Rampur, Bareilly, and Moradabad though sound on level of urbanization, record low values reflecting an educational mix of working population required by the economy of these areas. Other districts like Kheri and Pilibhit have already a low level of urbanization, therefore, in face of economic backwardness, the low literacy levels of below 50% are prevalent. This further reflects the strainous conditions under which the economy is passing through as these areas are highly populated as well.

Female Literates: Active Age Group

Literacy of females is a reflection of social upliftment of the society as a whole more so in India where female literacy is already less. Compared to males, the role of females in the society especially in a rural set up is passive. After-marriage migration to urban areas enables them to take part in economic activities at various levels as per their literacy levels. Compared to male literates, female literates are generally in demand in the secondary sector of economy due to their compromises on low wage rates and abstaining from unionism. Small-scale industries generally prefer literate females as workers. In service sector also, the work participation rates of literate females are on rise. The market centers again like to employ females on account of their better sense of duty.

Spatial Process

In 1991, literate females in active age are strongly linked with in-migration (+0.65), tertiary sector of economy (+0.69), and with mean age at marriage (+0.62). It suggests that literacy affects the decision at the age of marriage and also encourages work participation rate through migration in mainly tertiary sector of economy.

Spatial Patterns

With 48.6 per cent of female literates in active age group, there exists a definite spatial pattern over the districts (Fig.20).

Only 15 or 23.8 per cent districts with female literates in active age group lie in high and very high category within 54-80 per cent, mainly in the north-eastern part of Uttar Pradesh Himalayas out of which Dehradun understandably stands very high. Kanpur Nagar, Lucknow and Allahabad since high on the scene of urbanization, are experiencing in-migration of literate females in active age group and stand very high regarding female literacy. However, the position of moderately urbanized districts with high values around 70 per cent like in Sonbhadra, Gorakhpur, Etawah and Hardwar are more significant revealing a mechanism of ongoing socio-economic changes in the urban society of Uttar Pradesh. Still the position of low urbanized districts like Lalitpur, Kanpur Dehat, Fatehpur, Rai Bareili, Sultanpur, Faizabad, Jalaun, and others definitely indicate a change being experienced in the urban society as reflected upon by moderate values of approximately 65 per cent female literacy in active age group. While Bulandshahr along with Pilibhit, Shahjahanpur, Budaun, Moradabad, Bijnor, Rampur and Bareilly with very low values of nearly 45 per cent present a contrast with the existing medium levels of urbanization. This region records short distance in-migration rates from the rural areas mainly and suffers from stagnating economy.

Thus, female literacy in Uttar Pradesh definitely unfolds a mechanism of socio-economic changes in areas below medium levels of urbanization with rising female literacy rates within active age group mainly through migratory females.

Total Literates : 60+ Age Group

The literacy level of an older generation is a strong indicator of the social changes that a society is recording. In an agriculture-based society, this indicator assumes a greater significance as urban areas in general receive migrants from surrounding region, bringing along with them their own set of values and culture. The role of literacy in the urbanization process becomes critical as it relates to the decisions taken by the migrants' way back in the various stages of migration process. The degree of social and functional desirability of the locality as perceived over time and space has led to concentration of literates in old age group in selected urban places. It also shows the late stage of in-migration cycle in which the older generation follows after the setting down of their children or near ones in urban areas. Further more, total literates in 60+ age group may also be the one left alone once the active age group members have settled somewhere else for job or for other reasons.

Spatial Process

In Uttar Pradesh, in 1991, the variable correlates strongly with places having more than 20,000 (+0.65), total tertiary workers (+0.69), medium household size of 3-5 persons (+0.60) per family and rate of in migration (+0.59). It seems it to be a phenomenon associated with a set of migrant population in large cities engaged in tertiary activities and adjusted with their family members in general.

Spatial Patterns

In 1991, Uttar Pradesh recorded 38.8 per cent of total literates in 60+ age group with variations over space resulting in definite spatial patterns (Fig.21).

Between 55-67 per cent lies very high category in which only 3 districts occupy the northern hill district of Uttar Pradesh. Dehradun is highly urbanized with an attraction for retired personnel from various prestigious organizations. Almora and Uttar Kashi have also received retired literates also through return back migration.

Between 44-54 per cent lies high category in which 11 districts cover mostly either the northern hill districts or in and around the highly urbanized areas of Ganga Plain. An assured economy through tourism and lesser preference of mobility of both males and females are main causes of 60+ literates population in hill districts. In very high-urbanized areas of Kanpur Nagar, Lucknow, Varanasi, Allahabad, Agra and Etawah, there is dominance of literates in +60 age group. All these areas have attracted mostly literate migrants due to economic reasons and most of them might have been permanently settled down even after retirement or moved away to their place of origin.

Between 37-43 per cent lies the medium category in which 18 districts cover marginal areas of the Ganga Plain towards north-east and south-west. Meerut, Ghaziabad, Mathura, Jhansi, are areas with higher urbanization levels, however, more migration of active males has lowered down the proportion of literates in 60+ age group. It may also be because of more number of illiterates in 60+ age group is much common through rural-urban channel of movement.

Within 32-36 per cent lies the low category in which 18 districts cover extensive areas in Middle Ganga Plain till Aligarh through Farrukhabad and Etah. This area is basically known for both agricultural and non-agricultural activities. In general, this area suffers from economic stagnation, which is reflected in lower literacy rates in 60+ age group.

Within 22-31 per cent lies the very low category in which 12 districts cover the northern part of Upper Ganga Plain including Bulandshahr, Budaun, Shahjahanpur, Kheri, Pilibhit, Muradabad, Rampur and Bijnor. This area is experiencing short distance migration especially from rural areas as the region is dotted by number of small scale and household industries that are capable of absorbing labour from all age groups even with low educational background. In addition, the dominance of business class population from middle income group is common which are generally simply literates.

In general, the 60+ age group literacy is more in either already highly urbanized areas or upcoming areas on urban economic scene like Dehradun where retired personnel or return back migration is heavy. In addition, the degree of effective urbanization also promotes the concentration of literates in this age group as noticed in case of Almora or Uttar Kashi, which have a very low degree of urbanization. It is, perhaps, the quality of life in such areas that define their degree of desirability by old age group in the literate category.

Male Literates: 60+ Age Group

Due to increasing life expectancy, the percentage of old members of the family is on rise. The percentage of literate males in 60+ age group signify their status as either retired or dependent on family members. However, in Indian conditions, especially in informal self-employed sector, the age does put a restriction on physical labor. Other self-employed activities not requiring physical labor, the participation of male literates in +60 age group is considerable. In low paid jobs, however, the working efficiency of such groups generally decreases due to low wages and high economic burdens.

Spatial Process

In Uttar Pradesh in 1991, 52.8 per cent males were literate in the 60+

age group. This indicator relates very strongly with the rate of migration (+0.71), the age group of 15-59 males (+0.76), with male workers above graduate degree (+0.80), better housing amenities (+0.73) and less size of households (+0.68).

Spatial Patterns

The dynamics associated with percentage of literates in 60+ age group males are manifested over spaces in varying proportion giving rise to specific spatial patterns (Fig.21).

Only 27 or 42.9 per cent of the districts record high and very high value within a range of 55-83 per cent of male literates in 60+age group, which mainly cover the Uttar Pradesh Himalayas, the south eastern margins of the state and the eastern Middle Ganga Plain. The northern Hill districts are incidentally areas of up-coming economic opportunities though at present with a low to very level of urbanization except Dehradun. This whole belt is experiencing rapid in-migration of both workers in active age group and retired government and military personnel due to its better economic opportunities and a respectable standard of living. While Mathura, Agra, Etawah, Jhansi, Lalitpur, Jalaun and Sonbhadra are experiencing in-migration from neighboring states and record high concentration of literate males in active age group. Other areas of eastern Middle Ganga Plain including Varanasi and Allahabad with a well developed tertiary sector in which the role of business and commerce for literate males even in 60+ group is crucial. Kanpur Nagar and Lucknow again are two very highly urbanized centers with high values representing a mix of economic and social opportunities sustaining literate male population in 60+ age group. A core group of districts with varying degree of urbanization forming a part of traditional Rohilkhand division, records low to very low values within 30-20 per cent of literate males in old age group like in Bijnor, Bareilly, Budaun, Rampur, Moradabad and Shahjahanpur.

In general, this indicator signifies a history of urban development through the process of literacy, occupational shift and locational shift of population. While an economically independent group of literate males in old age can exercise the will to select a place of residence after retirement as found in Dehradun, Allahabad, Kanpur Nagar, Lucknow; a financially dependent group on the other hand, has to be either on move or to stay back at their place of origin resulting in large family size and increasing senile dependency ratio as in case of nearly the whole Ganga Plain.

Female Literates: 60+ Age Group

Literacy of females in 60+ age group though a simple and crude measure of modernization impacts within an urbanizing society, is surely a sign of history of the socio-economic development of an area. Apart from measuring the impact of urbanism, this indicator also reflects upon the many decisions in economic and social directions in the urban society in which the females move. In urban areas at present, their economic contribution might be negligible as females in this age group are more vulnerable to physical and emotional disturbances than males with advancing age. However, in Indian society, particularly for the study area, this indicator is highly significant.

Spatial Process

In Uttar Pradesh in 1991, the percentage of urban population (+0.65) correlates strongly with percentage of literate females in +60 age group and shows strong association with pucca houses (+ 0.74) and basic amenities (+0.67). It also shows a correlation with total tertiary workers (+0.57) and the male workers more than graduate are also very strongly correlated (+0.86) with total literacy of females in 60+ age group. However, the medium size households with 3-5 persons (+0.54) suggest it to be a character of densely populated areas. Thus female literate in 60+ age group seem to be a phenomenon of a developed highly urbanized area.

Spatial Patterns

In 1991, Uttar Pradesh recorded only 21.6 per cent females as literate within the 60+ age group. However, certain regularities in the spatial distribution are noticed (Fig.21).

The existing percentage of female literates within old age group is a reflection of the past history of urbanization in Uttar Pradesh. Only 12 or 19.1 per cent of the districts record a high value

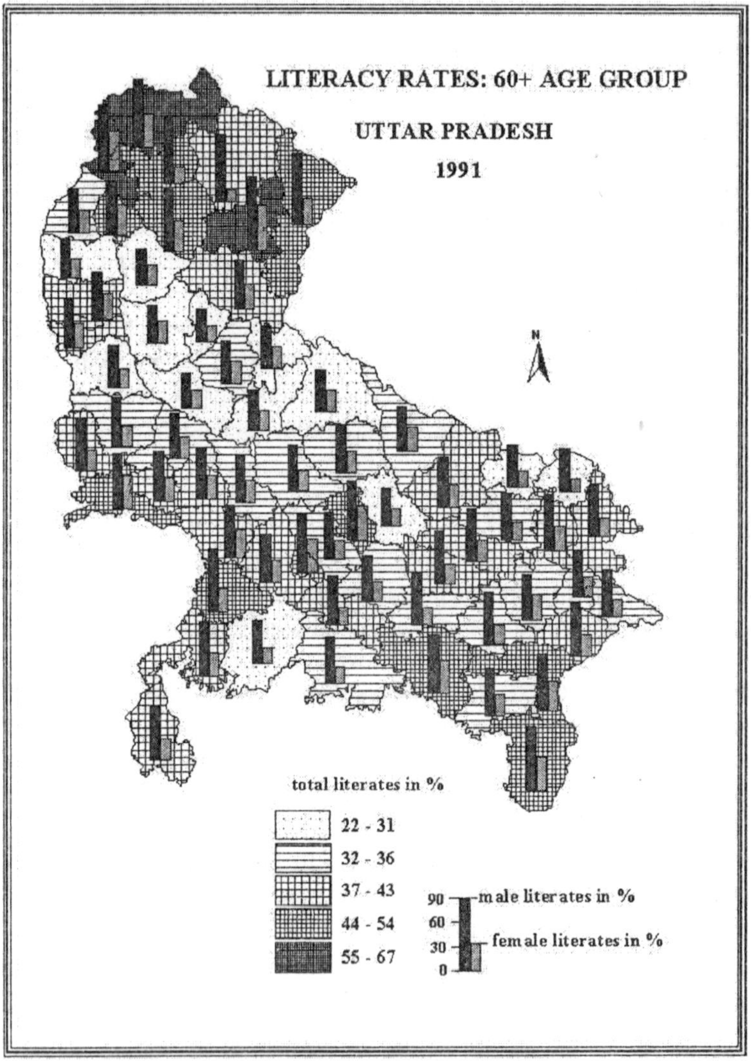
LITERACY RATES: 60+ AGE GROUP
UTTAR PRADESH
1991
N
total literates in %
22 - 31
32 - 36
37 - 43
44 - 54
55 - 67
90
60
30
0
male literates in %
female literates in %

Fig. 21

within 46-25 per cent of female literates in 60+ age group. The districts of Dehradun and Almora have a number of academic institutions and government organization which points the post-retirement stay of educated females in these areas. There might have been also after marriage or job based migration of females in that age group at any point of time in the past. Another concentration around 60 per cent of female literates in 60+ age group occurs in Kanpur Nagar, Lucknow, Agra, Varanasi, Allahabad, Sonbhadra and Etawah. All these areas stand high on female work participation scenario as per 1991 census as well. However, the dominance of literate females in 60+ age group represent both the working group as well as non-working females in this age group as these districts have an old history of urbanization and basically represent an affluent population with an urban culture.

It is, however, insignificant for most of the parts of Ganga Plain since it represents basically an agricultural community in which the culture of female education was not encouraged. There are few exceptions as in Ghaziabad, Meerut, Moradabad, Bareilly and along the foothill as Nanital, Bahraich, Gonda and south eastern margins in Jhansi, Jalaun, Firozabad, Mainpuri. In general, the degree of effective urbanization and female in migration rates seems to correspond with this variable.

EDUCATIONAL LEVELS

The attainment of educational levels is a sign of growing awareness of the demands of modern times. It also reflects the behavioral changes in urban society in response to changing life styles. As such the centers for learning, research and professional trainings are generally located in large towns or cities of higher order population size.

The intricate link between attainment of educational levels and increased labour productivity for over all economic development is well established. To optimize the available human resource powers, the formally organized sector of elementary, primary, secondary and higher-level education is pre-requisite. For international comparison of economic efficiency and potential use of human resource, two important parameters are: firstly the level of educational attainments in respective levels, secondly the percentage of higher education degree holders engaged in selected occupational groups. For the present study, only educational attainment levels are considered.

In India education is still not given its due recognition in respective plan periods. During eighth five-year plan only 4.9 per cent of the public sector outlay was allocated to education. Although, the National Policy on Education in 1985 envisaged universalization of primary education and adult literacy by 1990, the higher education area still waits to be prioritized.

Males: Matric but below Graduate

Educational attainment below graduation is a sign of either incomplete degree course or taking up a technical course just after metric. This is a character of generally families with either economic constraints or low educational background. Considering job markets, urban areas not always demand highly trained professionals rather job specific training with some basic education also helps in for self started business for which loans are available. Thus the potential market for jobs in the city influences the trends in educational attainment of the males. Even migrants from rural areas with some level of education can get them absorbed in diversified base of urban economy.

Spatial Process

In Uttar Pradesh in 1991, this variable does not show any specific association with percentage of urban population suggesting of it a feature of even less urbanized areas. However, male workers less than graduate (+0.81) are strongly correlated with the males within 15-59 age group (+0.67). A corresponding high correlation (+0.64) for male in-migrants is also an indicative of migratory character of such males.

Spatial Patterns

The percentage distribution of low educational of males shows certain regularity over geographical surface (Fig.22).

Between 32-35 per cent lie very high category in which 6 districts cover mostly the northern hilly region along with Kanpur

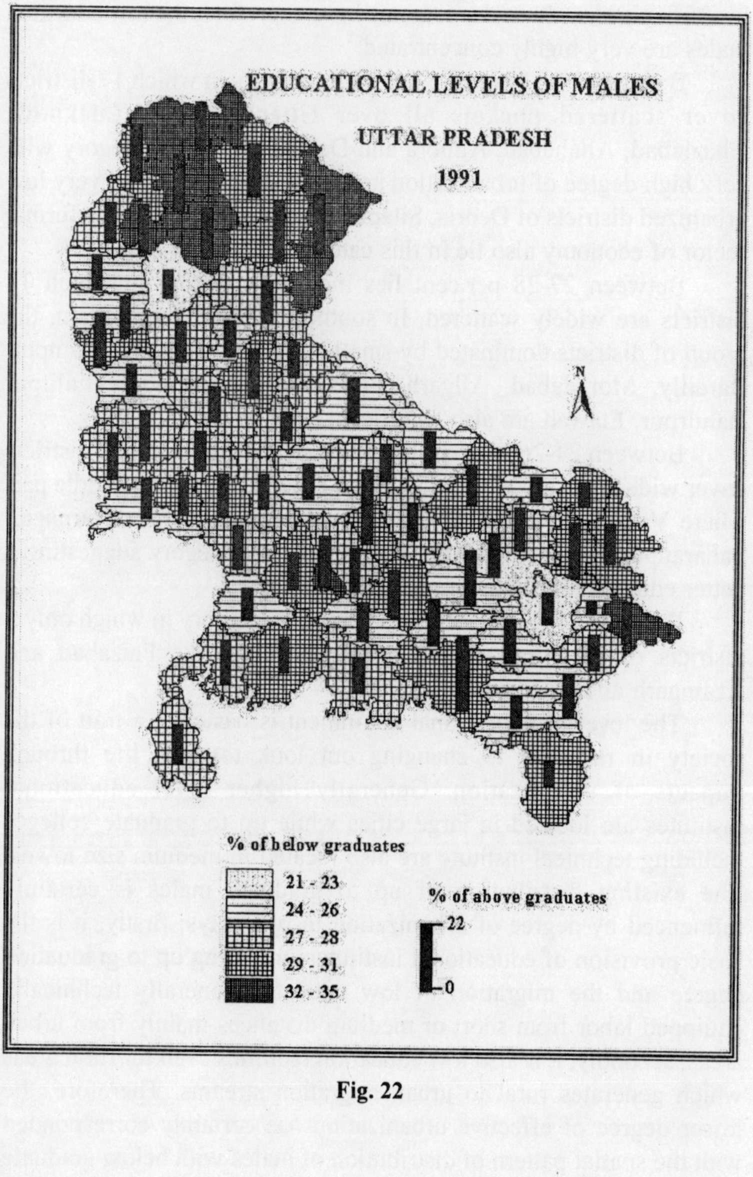
EDUCATIONAL LEVELS OF MALES
UTTAR PRADESH
1991
N
% of below graduates
21 - 23
24 - 26
27 - 28
29 - 31
32 - 35
% of above graduates
22
0

Fig. 22

Nagar and Ballia in the Ganga Plain. The service sector of economy is well developed in case of hill districts like Pithoragah. Kanpur Nagar has diversified economic base of cities while Ballia is very low urbanized with weak economic base, therefore, the low educated males are very highly concentrated.

Between 29-31 per cent lies high category in which 17 districts cover scattered pockets all over Uttar Pradesh. Lucknow, Ghaziabad, Allahabad, Almora and Dehradun in this category with very high degree of urbanization are significant. While the very low urbanized districts of Deoria, Sitapur, Banda on account of informal sector of economy also lie in this category.

Between 27-28 per cent lies medium category in which 19 districts are widely scattered. In southern Upper Ganga Plain, the group of districts dominated by small-scale industries like Rampur, Bareilly, Moradabad, Aligarh, Firozabad are included. Lalitpur Hamirpur, Etawah are also significant.

Between 24-26 per cent lies low category in which 17 districts cover wide areas all over Ganga Plain especially eastern middle part where Varanasi, Mau and Mirzapur are important. Muzaffarnagar, Saharanpur, Meerut and Agra also lie in this category suggesting a better educational status of population.

Between 21-23 per cent lies very low category in which only 3 districts of very low degree of urbanization like Faizabad and Azamgarh and Bijnor are included.

The level of educational attainment is basically a trait of the society in response to changing out look towards life through impacts of urbanization. Generally higher level educational institutes are located in large cities while up to graduate colleges including technical institute are also located in medium size towns. The existing distribution of up to graduate males is certainly influenced by degree of urbanization in two ways: firstly, it is the basic provision of educational institutes imparting up to graduation degree and the migration of low educated generally technically equipped labor from short or medium distances mainly from urban areas, secondly, it is also low education facilities even for rural areas which generates rural to urban migration streams. Therefore, the lesser degree of effective urbanization has certainly corresponded with the spatial pattern of distribution of males with below graduate degree.

Males: Graduate and Above

The formal and higher level education depict either the favourable socio-economic conditions of the family or impact of urbanism upon the society. The initial avenues for getting higher education are available in large cities. Various mechanisms operate in the functioning, employment avenues and income generation capacities of the industry determining the over all level of development of any urban area. It is the assurance of continued job availability in a particular sector of urban economy as a result of its sustained development, which opens up avenues for specialized education and job skills.

Education is positively related to in-migration. Various studies have confirmed that differential education accounts for differential rates and patterns of migration streams. Higher education is essential for eradication of poverty, for promotion of economic development, social upliftment and political maturity. Education also has a significant role in defining the demographic structure of age at marriage and number of children. Thus, it is an over all indicator of the pace at which the socio-economic transformation of a society is taking place.

Spatial Process

In 1991, Uttar Pradesh records 14.6 per cent of total males in above graduate degree category which correlates strongly with male workers above graduate (+0.90), with the active age group of total male (+0.62) and total tertiary workers (+0.60). It certainly defines a process in which active age group working males are being absorbed in mainly tertiary sector. It also correlates with household size of 3-5 persons (+0.59) suggesting it to be phenomena of medium household size.

Spatial Patterns

There seems to be a spatial regularity in the distribution pattern of males with higher education (Fig.22).

On a generalized level, the concentration of males with above graduate education is highly localized in space. Only 13 or 20.5 per cent of the districts record high values within 16-22 per cent, in which Lucknow and Allahabad are significant due to the administrative cum service nature of the economy that demands high educated and technically trained professionals.

While 11 districts cover most part of hilly region in which Dehrdun is significant along with Almora, Tehri Garhwal, Gahwal and others. Gorakhpur, Aligarh and Faizabad are all areas with higher educational facilities and renowned universities.

The majority of the northern Upper Ganga Plain including districts of Meerut, Mathura, Agra, Jhansi and the Middle Ganga Plain except the eastern most districts show a moderate value around 15 per cent of males with higher educational levels. Varanasi also records moderate values on this variable.

However, the easrern Middle Ganga plain and the southern plateau region along with Bijnor, Barielly, Firozabad, Shahjahanpur, and Budaun show low to very low percentage, within 6-11 per cent of highly educated males.

The over all patt rn of distribution revels that highly urbanized areas especially with development of tertiary sector are employing highly educated males. While industry based urbanized areas recording slightly lower values as there is a mix of labor of all educational levels. In general low urbanized areas around large cities especially in the eastern part of Uttar Pradesh are recording an improvement in the educational status of males which in due course of time might lead to the socio economic upliftment of the areas like Fatehpur, Jaunpur, Pratapgarh, Faizabad, Gonda and Basti.

Females: Matric but below Graduate

Female educational attainment is a sign of a modernizing society. However, in urban areas female education up to graduation level is not exceptional as institutions to provide education up to graduation are not uncommon even in small urban centers. The discontinuity in education might be due to the early marriage system in urban areas, reflecting a tradition bound society which is a common feature of Indian cities. However, the attainment of some short-term technical courses certainly signifies a will to be economically active.

Spatial Process

In Uttar Pradesh, the percentage of secondary workers corresponds strongly (+0.66) with the education of females below graduate. It also relates mildly with metric but less than graduate males (+0.46). A high correlation with density of households (+0.56) and juvenile dependency (+0.47) suggest the socio-economic status of such less educated females.

Spatial Patterns

The females with matric but below graduate degree are widely distributed all over Uttar Pradesh showing specific spatial patterns (Fig.23).

Between 25-27 per cent lies very high category in which 14 districts cover most part of Upper Ganga Plain and few districts in the hill region and eastern Middle Ganga Plain. Notable among them are Kanpur Nagar, Lucknow, Dehradun, Hardwar, Aligarh, Mathura and Allahabad, All these areas have good educational facilities. Incidentally these are also areas of female in migration from other urban areas of the state. Kanpur Dehat, Badaun, Rampur, Barielly are other areas where female education is high compared to their infrastructural development.

Between 23-24 per cent lies high category in which 22 districts cover mostly the foot hill region of Himalayas and extend in the form of a belt encompassing the districts around Lucknow and Kanpur Nagar. Saharanpur, Muzaffarnagar, Ghaziabad, Moradabad, Rampur and Nainital which are sound in urbanization scenario along with very low urbanized districts in this category like Almora, Tehri Garhwal Bahraich, Unnao, Maharajganj. This group of districts seems to have been benefited by the educational sphere of influence of high-urbanized centers of Lucknow, Kanpur and Aligarh.

Between 21-22 per cent lies medium category in which 13 districts cover scattered pockets of very low urbanized areas of southern Plateau Region, northern hill region along with Ghaziabad, Agra are significant in this category showing a mix of females from various educational back ground.

Between 17-20 per cent lies low category in which 10 districts cover mostly very low urbanized part except Varanasi and

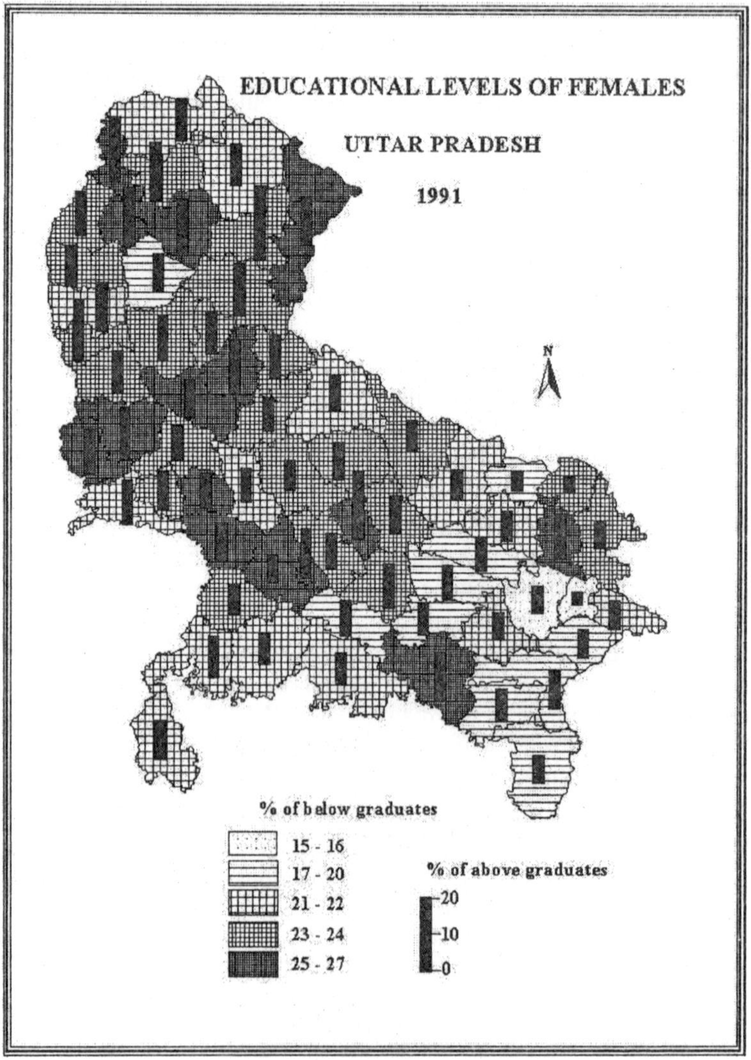
EDUCATIONAL LEVELS OF FEMALES
UTTAR PRADESH
1991
N
% of below graduates
15 - 16
17 - 20
21 - 22
23 - 24
25 - 27
% of above graduates
20
10
0

Fig. 23

Sonbhadra where it is rather more educated females that are prominent.

Between 15-16 per cent lies very low category in which only 2 districts of Mau and Azamgarh are included. Since both are occupied by traditional communities, the culture of education of females is less.

In Uttar Pradesh, the general lower educational attainments of females are highly influenced by the age at marriage. In addition, the socio-cultural background of families also restricts avenues for higher education of females. Therefore, it is not just degree of urbanization which is affecting attitudes towards getting females educated, it is also the socio-economic set up which counts. Though this indicator reflects the low educational levels of females as could be expected in a socio-economically backward state, the spread of even undergraduate level of education in very low urbanized areas is a welcoming signs of social equity.

Females: Graduate and Above

Female education is a definite sign of the impact of urbanization. The role of female as an economic producer necessitates females' education at higher levels. The desirability of female workers especially at higher wage services is rising due to their efficiency and managerial skills. Awareness about the status of females, their active role in economy and society is being acknowledged. Therefore, female education in specialized skills and higher educational programmes in all spheres of knowledge are being promoted. This definitely reflects a change in the outlook of the Indian society as a whole. Therefore, this variable though a simple measure of educational level, translates into several important dimensions of urbanization and modernization.

Spatial Process

In Uttar Pradesh in 1991, the rising educational level of females is strongly correlated with higher mean age at marriage (+0.83) especially within the age group of 15-59 (+0.60) in which migration from abroad is also significant (+0.58). There is also a corresponding rise in percentage of urban population (+0.52) with good standard of living like electricity connections (+0.57), cooking gas supply (+0.82), Pucca houses (+0.51). However, striking feature is the family size, which are reflected in household size of 3-5 persons (+0.77).

Spatial Patterns

The highly educated females are only 12 per cent of the total females. However, there is a spatial regularity regarding the distribution pattern (Fig.23).

The highly educated females have a disproportionately high concentration in the Hill districts and northern Upper Ganga Plain. Dehradun, Tehri Garhwal, Almora, Ghaziabad, Lucknow record a value within 16-20 per cent. While Nainital, Pithoragarh, Hardwar, Saharanpur, Agra, Mathura, Aligarh, Muzaffarnagar, Bareilly, Kanpur Nagar and Allahabad have 12-15 per cent of females with graduate and above degree. The service sectors of all the above districts have a potential to absorb such females who are generally long distance migrants from other urban areas outside the state. However, districts like Barabanki, Gorakhpur are signifying a forthcoming change in the economy of eastern Uttar Pradesh as these are at present backward areas.

The moderately urbanized districts like Muzaffarnagar, Bulandshahr, Budaun, Etawah; the low urbanized part like Firozabad, Pilibhit and very low urbanized districts of Chamoli, Lalitpur, Barabanki and Sitapur lie at par with Varanasi with a moderate degree of female education, around 10 per cent.

The whole of Middle Ganga Plain and southern Upper Ganga Plain with few exceptions have low values, around 8 per cent. This is the most prevalent category consisting of 30 or 47.6 per cent districts of low to very low degree of urbanization.

In general the degree of urbanization seems to commensurate with the distribution of highly educated females. Areas with effective urbanization are also significant like Moradabad, Firozabad, Jalaun, Gorakhpur with hill districts of Almora and Dehradun. It seems that the traditional society under the modernization impacts precipitated basically from the highly urbanized areas, is being transformed educationally, which is a welcoming signs of further socio-economic implications in Uttar Pradesh.

5

LIVING ENVIRONMENT AND URBANIZATION

The urban living environment is a multi-dimensional phenomenon, the concept of which is defined by the welfare levels of living of its own inhabitants. The livability of urban areas in terms of the carrying capacity of its urban environment is continually under strain and being challenged by the rapid rise in its population both through the rate of natural increase and in-migration. Cities serve both as a physical and social space in which population live, interact and survive. Thus, cities become a spatial manifestation of on-going socio-economic process, recording changes in its ambient environment and affecting the surrounding environment in return on regional and global scale.

In India, the lop sided development of urban economy has favoured an unusually high concentration of urban population into large cities, around 65 per cent of total urban population lives in class I cities. Due to urbanization economies, the industrial and manufacturing activities in large cities have attracted migrants from both rural and urban areas. The rate of natural increase of population becomes rather more decisive in urban growth than the rate of in-migration in case of large cities as a result of concentration of active age group. Thus, the role of economy in selecting, encouraging and accommodating migrants of specific ages, sex, various educational and economic background defines the demographic profile of urban population.

The city population is, thus, always on rise with corresponding increase in demand for infrastructural facilities and social services like housing, transport network, basic sanitation including safe drinking water supply, electricity. The large investment to be incurred by the government in the provision of basic services is discouraged by the gap that exist between the per head marginal cost of provision of such services and the average cost. The net effect of cost in provision of urban amenities is further influenced by the socio-economic status of population including migrants since rural migrants are generally not gainfully employed. Thus, there is an evident deterioration in the physical environment and quality of life in urban areas, caused by a widening gap between demand and supply of essential services and their level of affordability by different sections of urban society itself.

The dimensions attached to urban living environment are difficult to discern due to the subjectivity of perception and analysis. However, the livability of given urban environment in Indian context, can best be measured in terms of relative assessment of the degree of provision of basic services as reflected in the quality of indoor living environment.

HOUSING QUALITY

Housing quality is the most visible dimension of livability of urban environment in physical terms. It is an important indicator of the socio-economic status of urbanites as well as prevailing government policies especially in case of India. The World Bank Report (1975) rightly observes the role of housing through shelter provision to sanitation facilities in ensuring a welfare effect for both physical and intellectual grooming of an individual.

The norms of quality of housing in terms of the construction material are set up by National Building Organization and Building Material and Technology Provision Council (1990). This important aspect in India was overlooked till in 7th Plan period measures were taken to promote production of building material with cost effective technology.

In 1991, the index of housing shortage of urban areas calculated as the number of residential/partly residential census houses for 1000 households is recorded as 980/1000. The quality of housing in terms of its physical planning and quality of construction material used are far below the prescribed norms on internationally accepted criteria. Despite of its far-reaching effects in ensuring a healthy society, housing quality is still an underdeveloped sector of urban planning and financing. The formulation of National Housing Policy and setting up of National Housing Bank with an initial investment of Rs. 1000 millions is the most sought after step in this regard.

Pucca Houses

Pucca houses as defined by Census of India, are those that have both wall and roof made of Pucca material. The walls are made of burnt bricks, metalled sheets, stone and cement concrete. The roof is made of tiles, slate, shingle, corrugated iron, zinc or other metal along with asbestos and cement sheets, brick stone, concrete and RBC and RCC. These houses ensure a healthy life style with security from drudgeries of nature as well as and safety from vectors of diseases, pathogens and rodents. However, the financial aspect involved in initial planning and instituting the plan necessitates the desirability of the area in its socio-economic terms. Generally short duration stay or short distance migrants do not invest in this sector of housing. They generally prefer remittance to be paid at their place of origin. Age is also a deciding factor as in India, as near retirement age generally defines the final phase of stay after which the investments in housing sector becomes considerable. So this indicator is both a socio-economic as well as behavioral measure of livability of urban environment.

Spatial Process

The percentage of urban household with Pucca houses in 1991 is 75.95 per cent, which relates strongly with the literacy level of total household of 60+age group (+0.63) as well as the male literacy in 60+ age group (+0.66). Total literates in age group of 15-59 (+0.60), and male literates in 15-59 age group (+0.55) especially females (0.61) show a definite correlation with percentage of urban households with Pucca houses. More importantly, the educational attainment of male workers above graduate (+0.61) and also below graduate (+0.57), with percentage of tertiary workers (+0.53), all reflect the role of education, absorption in service sector of economy and age specificity in determining the percentage of such households.

Spatial Patterns

The combination of factors in bringing about the existing percentage of 75.93 per cent at an aggregate level might not be operative on the same level of intensity at district level, however certain spatial regularities exist in percentage distribution of urban household with Pucca houses (Fig.24).

The households between 87-95 per cent form the very high category under which 9 districts cover the whole of northern hilly region. Except Dehradun all other districts stand low to very low on the scene of urbanization. However, these districts are urbanizing rapidly with high rates of in-migration especially well educated males and female in active age group. Therefore, the investments in this sector of housings are high. In Ganga Plain, industrial centers of Mathura, Agra, Varanasi due to variable sectoral development of economy, have high density of urban population. Effective urbanization is also marked in these areas necessitating multi-storied buildings to cope with space congestion in residential-cum-industrial areas.

The high category includes 80-86 per cent in which 10 districts lie mostly in Middle Ganga Plain. In case of industrial centers of Kanpur Nagar and Ghaziabad the secondary workers especially in other than household industry, the females work participation in non-agricultural sector with general high education scenario creates an atmosphere of affluence which permits expenditure in housing sector. Allahabad and Lucknow have administrative-cum-service character with considerable development of tertiary sector of economy. Although the active age group of workers is low, it is perhaps the remittance paid in these areas by out-migrants in active age group, which has raised investment in Pucca housings. Similar phenomena may be operative in Jaunpur and Gorakhpur. Gonda, Siddharthnagar, Maharajganj that are upcoming centers of economic opportunities inviting expenditure in this particular sector of housing.

The category of 73-79 per cent forms medium group, which covers 17 districts. A belt consisting of Aligarh, Etah, Mainpuri and

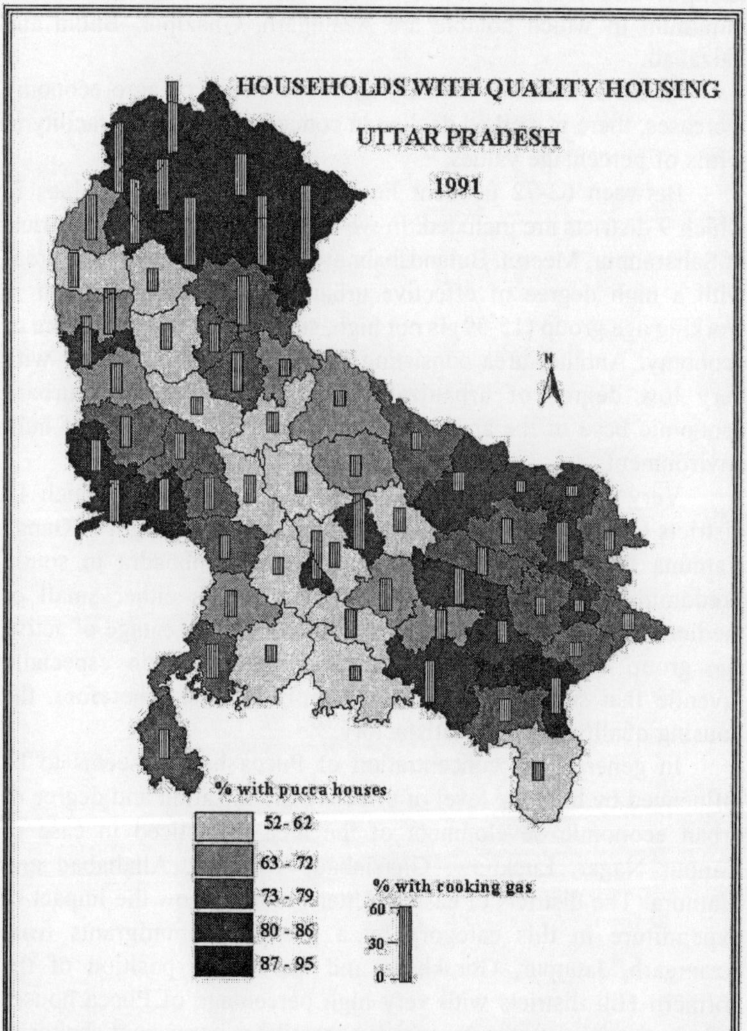
HOUSEHOLDS WITH QUALITY HOUSING
UTTAR PRADESH
1991
N
% with pucca houses
52 - 62
63 - 72
73 - 79
80 - 86
87 - 95
% with cooking gas
60
30
0

Fig. 24

Etawah surround the Agra-Mathura industrial belt. Another cluster of districts lies in the northern Ganga Plain consisting of Nainital, Rampur and Bareilly. Towards the east, the concentration is minimum in which notable are Azamgarh, Ghazipur, Ballia and Faizabad.

As the small-scale industry and dependence on agro-economy increases, there is marked decline in concentration of this facility in terms of percentage values.

Between 63-72 per cent lies the category of low values in which 9 districts are included. In western Uttar Pradesh the districts of Saharanpur, Meerut, Bulandshahr are medium urban density areas with a high degree of effective urbanization. Still population in working age group (15-59) is not high, suggesting stagnant nature of economy. Another area consisting of Pilibhit, Kheri, Sitapur with very low degree of urbanization suggest the unstable urban-economic base of the area, it remains backward on scene of built environment.

Very low category lies between 52-62 per cent in which 15 districts form a prominent belt running all along the length of Ganga Yamuna Doab till Allahabad and includes Sonbhadra in south. Predominantly agricultural, the whole area has either small or medium sized towns with a high sex-ratio, low percentage of active age group of population and high dependency ratio especially juvenile that suggest strains upon family income. Therefore, the housing quality is below satisfactory.

In general, the concentration of Pucca houses seems to be influenced by both the level of effective urbanization and degree of urban economic development of the area as noticed in case of Kanpur Nagar, Lucknow, Ghaziabad, Varanasi, Allahabad and Mathura. The districts of eastern Uttar Pradesh show the impact of expenditure in this category by a group of emmigrants from Azamgarh, Jaunpur, Gorakhpur and Basti. The position of the northern Hill districts with very high percentage of Pucca houses reflects the role of climate, which necessitates permanent shelter in face of natural hazards.

Cooking Gas

The environmental implication of the contemporary urbanization is highly significant. It is the indoor air quality assessed through the type of fuel used for cooking which has a wider environmental implication for rising pollution levels inside the house. In Indian case, still the most frequently used fuels are kerosene, wood and electricity. It reflects in general the levels of affordability of the inhabitant for cooking gas on one hand and the efficiency of public distribution system on the other, both of which are suffering at one level or the other in India.

Spatial Process

In Uttar Pradesh the process underlying the provision of cooking gas supply to urban households seems to be reflecting education, earning capacity and affluency of households. Only 25.58 per cent of households in Uttar Pradesh posses this facility which seems to be the most strongly related with all literacy and educational levels (+0.65 to +0.80) especially in migrants from urban areas (+0.66) and also international migrants (+0.60). Active age population (+0.77) also strongly correlates. The safe drinking water supply, electricity and serviceable toilets show strong correlation (+0.81) with gas supply connections. Overall this indicator emerges as a measure of socio-economic development and level of modernization in case of Uttar Pradesh.

Spatial Patterns

In general, there is a spatial regularity in percentage distribution and its concentration of cooking gas supply over the geographical space (Fig.24).

The very high category is defined by 28-56 per cent in which 16 districts cover Pithoragarh, Almora, Gahrwal, and Uttar Kashi. Except Dehradun, rest of the area though less urbanized with few economic activities, population is gainfully employed. Dehradun due to its high air of affluency of the economic status of population lies in this category. The areas with a high degree of urbanization like Kanpur Nagar, Lucknow, Agra, Ghaziabad, Meerut along with Allahabad and Nainital with medium degree of urbanization are showing the efficacy of the public distribution system and degree of affordability of the population.

Medium category is defined by 20-27 per cent in which 13 districts cover mostly either northern Upper Ganga Plain or scattered pocket in the eastern Middle Ganga Plain in which notable district are Varanasi, Jhansi, Mathura, Aligarh, and Bareilly. The crowding and congestion along with large household size reflects economic strains in this category.

Within low category 35 districts record a value between 4-19 per cent of the urban house holds with this facility. Approximately the whole southern part of Upper Ganga Plain extending in the form of a belt encompassing the eastern parts of Middle Ganga Plain is low to very low urbanized except Moradabad, Rampur, Etah and Etawah. In this category both the effect of high population pressure on this facility as in Moradabad and low demand in economically backward districts like Unnao and Fatehpur are well marked.

All along the Tarai belt and southern plateau region except Sonbhadra, there is an underdeveloped base of economy and very low level of urbanization is supportive only of a series of medium or small towns therefore, affordability of population is certainly less.

In general, this indicator corresponds to the degree of urbanization in a positive manner. In addition, the basic purchasing power of the population seems to have determined the regional variations. The public distribution system of cooking gas supply seems to have favored for large cities irrespective of the degree of urbanization of the district.

URBAN BASIC AMENITIES

The sustainability of urban living environment primarily is dependent on the degree of pressure of population upon its given infrstructural facilities and urban amenities. India is experiencing a substantial growth of its urban population of about 2 to percent, in case of large cities while the slum and squatters settlement are recording even 5 to 7 per cent of growth rate. A rough estimate suggests that 10 to 50 per cent of the population of medium and small size cities lives either in slums or slum like conditions. The proliferation of slums is largely associated with the expanding size of urban informal sector of economy, and slum like conditions exist even in the areas managed by Municipal Corporation and other Urban Local Bodies.

The paucity of various urban services in face of rising urban growth is one of the main features of Indian urbanization. However, the dynamics underlying the lack of amenities in the extremes of urban size hierarchy are different. In large cities the average cost of providing basic amenities to the entire set of population including rural migrants who are generally engaged in unproductive sector of economy, is excessive. It cuts down the facility margins of the original claimer of such facilities. In case of medium and small size towns it is rather the lack of the facility payer in economic terms due to which government expenditure on urban development tends to become low.

For analyzing the level of provision of basic amenities to urban households in Uttar Prdesh, few amenities are selected which form the basic criteria for minimum need programme for the welfare of population. Four variables combinedly cover this indicator of urban amenities in which the households with safe drinking water supply, serviceable toilet facilities, electricity supply and number of connection of cooking gas are thought to be significant considering the socio-economic scenario of urban Uttar Pradesh.

These indicators are divided into two parts for the purpose of effective analysis. The first consist of a single indicator of cooking gas supply, which is analyzed along with Pucca houses as a part of quality housing. The second consist of electricity, safe drinking water supply and serviceable toilet facility combined under the category of all three amenities.

Drinking Water-Electricity-Serviceable Toilets

Urban households with electricity, safe drinking water supply and serviceable toilet facilities collectively cover a more effective aspect of quality of living environment. Regional economic disparities result in uneven levels of urbanization. The question of availability of minimum basic services is critical at present and going to be grave in future. The urban development policies though properly planned, are ineffectively implemented, therefore, the increasing pressure upon these amenities is creating a fast deteriorating living environment of urban areas of all size categories.

Spatial Process

In Uttar Pradesh, the basic urban amenities of electricity, safe drinking water supply and toilet exist at varying levels of provision as electricity is provided to 67.76 per cent of urban households, in case of safe drinking water supply the percentage of household is 85.78 per cent while serviceable toilet facilities are available to 66.54 per cent of the urban households. It is the provision of all these three facilities together which becomes a more effective indicator. Thus, in Uttar Prdesh, only 53.72 per cent of the urban households have all three amenities in 1991. The active age of population within 15 to 59 (+0.57), both males and females above graduate (+0.51 and +0.71) along with educational levels of both males and females workers above graduate (+0.480 and +0.73) and total secondary other than household workers (+0.49) also correspond to provision to all three amenities. The medium family size (+0.55) and Pucca houses also mildly correlate (+0.47) with all three amenities. Thus, the provision of basic amenities associates itself with the socio-economic status of urban population in Uttar Pradesh.

Spatial Patterns

The emerging spatial pattern of the distribution of households with all three facilities shows great variation over various districts of Uttar Pradesh (Fig.25).

Between 65-73 per cent, is the very high category in which 7 districts lie in the hill and foothill regions of Uttar Pradesh, which include Tehri Garhwal, Uttar Kashi, Garhwal, Pithoragarh and Dehradun with less density of population except Saharanpur. High rate of in-migration have been recorded with a corresponding rise in service sector of economy therefore, the population due to sound economic conditions is able to afford quality housing in areas where these facilities are available.

Between 54-64 per cent, is the high category in which 14 districts lie with maximum concentration in the northern Upper Ganga Plain, from Bulandshahr to Muzaffarnagar in the form of a belt. Though this area has high percentage of urban population, the workers are engaged in other than household industry. Almora,

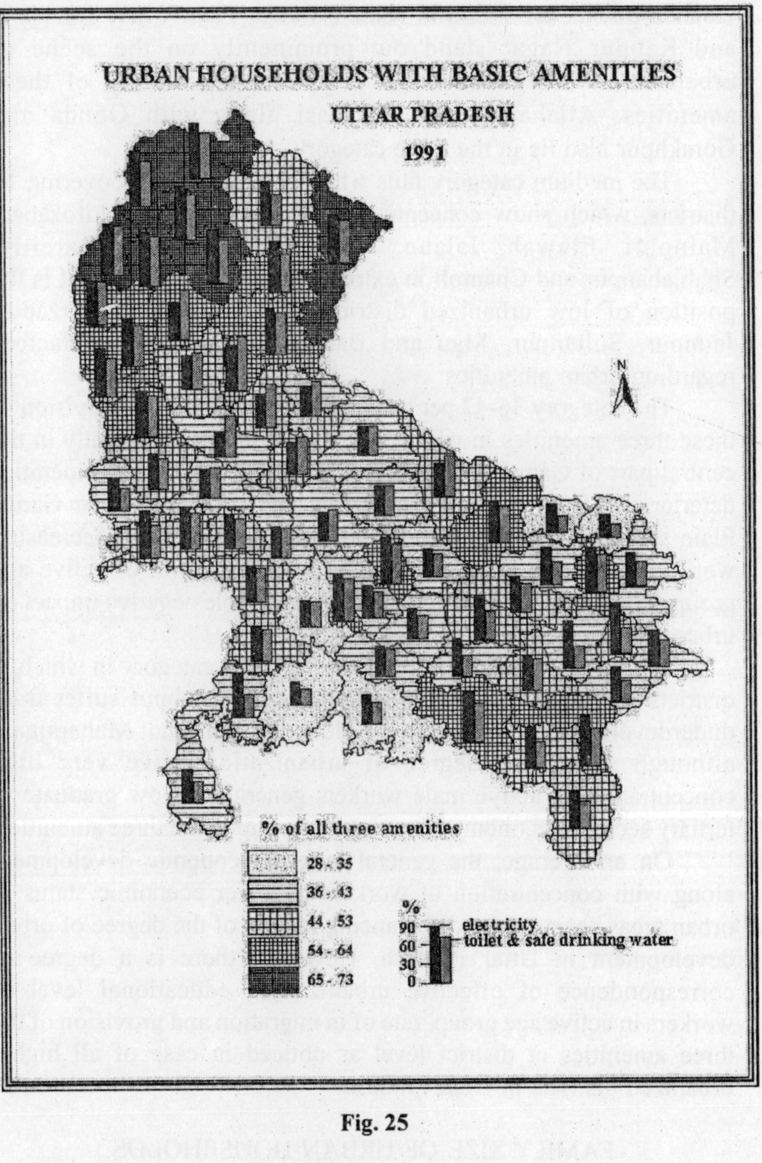
URBAN HOUSEHOLDS WITH BASIC AMENITIES
UTTAR PRADESH
1991
N
% of all three amenities
28 - 35
36 - 43
44 - 53
54 - 64
65 - 73
%
90
60
30
0
electricity
toilet & safe drinking water

Fig. 25

Hardwar, Nainital and Rampur also lie in the same category with varied but expanding tourism based economy and educated workers. Isolated pocket are found in Middle Ganga Plain where Lucknow and Kanpur Nagar stand out prominently on the scene of urbanization along with high degree of availability of these amenities. Allahabad and Varanasi along with Gonda and Gorakhpur also lie in the same category.

The medium category falls within 44-53 per cent covering 17 districts, which show concentration in a belt in Agra, Firozabad, Mainpuri, Etawah, Jalaun, Aligarh, Moradabad, Bareilly, Shahjahanpur and Chamoli in extreme north. Towards east it is the position of low urbanized districts like Sonbhadra, Mirzapur, Jaunpur, Sultanpur, Mau and Bahraich, which is satisfactory regarding urban amenities.

The category 36-43 per cent defines low degree of provision of these three amenities in which 20 districts lie. It is generally in the central part of Ganga Plains where the provision of basic amenities deteriorates. Both the western Middle and southern Upper Ganga Plain are suffering from lack of industrial development, decreasing work participation rates of males and out-migration of active age group male population, which had a considerable negative impact on urban development.

Within 28-35 per cent forms the very low category in which, 5 districts are included. Hamirpur, Banda and Fatehpur suffer from underdevelopment in general. Siddharthnagar and Maharajganj although show low degree of urbanization, have very high concentration of active male workers generally below graduate in tertiary sector of economy, showing strains upon the three amenities.

On an average, the general lack of economic development along with concentration of workers of lower economic status in urban areas seems to be disbalancing factors of the degree of urban development in Uttar Pradesh. However, there is a degree of correspondence of effective urbanization, educational level of workers in active age group, rate of in migration and provision of the three amenities at district level as noticed in case of all highly urbanized districts in Uttar Pradesh.

FAMILY SIZE OF URBAN HOUSEHOLDS

Urbanization reflects a revolutionary change in the whole pattern of social life of an urbanite, brought about by economic and technological developments which affect every aspect of urban society (Davis, K.: 1962). It also leads to perceptible changes in the life style of the city dweller which is distinct from their counterpart in rural areas, a phenomena identified as urbanism (Wirth, L.: 1938).

India is basically an agricultural country. The rural lifestyle favor the large family size with joint or extended family systems with a patriarchal hold. The indicator of family size of urban households becomes highly significant in face of the facts that in Indian set up of society, blood relations and family ties are very strong in a state like Uttar Pradesh where urbanization is not systematically evolving.

The census defines household as a group of persons, who commonly live together to share their meal from a common kitchen, it coincides with the basic concept of a family, which is sociological. Therefore, for the present study, size of the family is identified through number of persons per household. Three indicators are selected. To identify nucleated or small family size it is an urban household with up to 3 persons, for joint or medium family size it is an urban households with 3-5 persons and extended or large size family is on the basis of more than 5 persons per urban household. Each of these indicators is distinct in terms of its processual characteristics showing a combination of underlying dynamics of social transformation occurring rapidly in the society through urbanization. However, the distribution of above categories over space is complimentary, as one indicator's concentration value becomes less, it gives way to the dominance of the concentration value of the next indicator. This is more so common in case of small family size and large family size.

Extended Family: More than 5 Persons per Household

Urban migration proceeds in a cyclic manner in which all members of the family do not migrate all at once. Definite phases of migrants flow are recorded in which active age group migrate first particularly males, remaining members of the family also migrate if economic opportunities permit them.The information flow through migrants also encourages even the friends and relatives to join and even accommodated with them. The economic hardship and struggle for respectable ways of life is joined both by males and females in urban areas. Thus, an expanding base of urban economy is able to absorb growing streams of migrants leading to medium and then large family size.

In addition, large family size norms are still found in economically backward areas. The financial and emotional dependency of senile age group on working age group is a well-accepted norm of Indian society. Thus, both senile and juvenile dependency ratio is high in the large households. The process indicates a condition of economic struggle and missing links of desired channels of spread of urbanization effects. Therefore, this variable measures important urban aspects.

Spatial Process

In 1991 Uttar Pradesh has 52.76 per cent of households with more than 5 persons. The larger family size indicates an extended family system that seems to be an outcome of high sex ratio (+0.85) of population with dependency ratio for both old (+0.79) and young (+0.85) along with high density of population in urban areas (+0.53) and high degree of crowding (+0.57).

This is suggestive of either lack of mobility within the males themselves for economic motives or may also be an indication of the late stage of migration cycle where family has also joined. However, the short distance migration is significant (+0.61) for such households with large family size.

Spatial Patterns

Although, the distribution confirms the process operative on Uttar Pradesh as a whole, the emerging spatial patterns highlights the role of regional socio-economic set up (Fig.26).

Between 62-70 per cent, of the households with large family size form the very high category under which 6 districts lie in eastern Middle Ganga Plain. The agriculture in this region is under strain with one or two large cities dominating the urban scene in which the concentration of population is very high. Deoria, Ballia, Mau and Jaunpur are significant. The urban sex ratio is very high along with high dependency ratio of especially juvenile population resulting in large family size. Except Mau, the percentage of main workers is

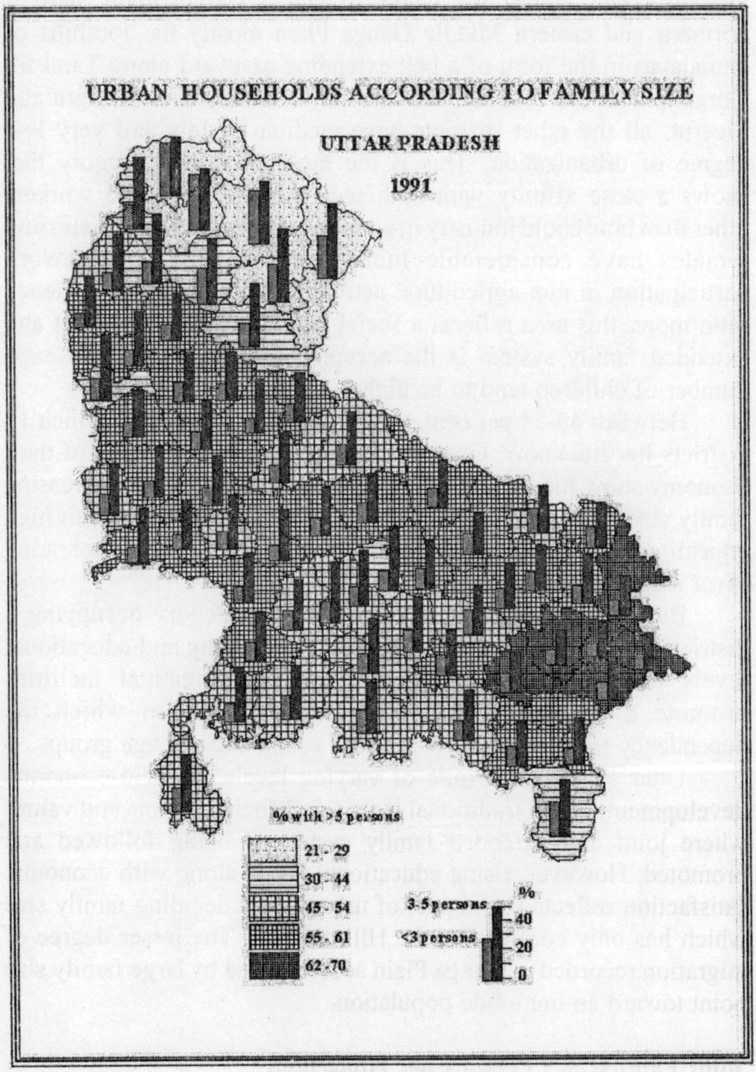
URBAN HOUSEHOLDS ACCORDING TO FAMILY SIZE
UTTAR PRADESH
1991
% with >5 persons
21 - 29
30 - 44
45 - 54
55 - 61
62 - 70
3-5 persons
<3 persons
%
40
20
0

Fig. 26

very low in the whole area suggesting the prevalence of economic stagnation in this region.

Between 55-61 per cent lies the high category in which 30 districts cover almost the whole of Upper Ganga Plain, part of northern and eastern Middle Ganga Plain mostly the foothills of Himalayas in the form of a belt extending eastward along Tarai till Gorakhpur in the east and Varanasi in the south. Except Agra and Meerut, all the other districts have medium to low and very low degree of urbanization. This is the most prevalent category that shows a close affinity with both secondary workers and workers other than household industry in active age group and both males and females have considerable literacy levels with female work participation in non-agricultural activities. With senile dependency ratio more, this area reflects a social set up in which the joint and extended family system is the accepted form of living and even number of children tend to be high.

Between 45-54 per cent, lies the medium category in which 17 districts lie. Lucknow, Ghaziabad and Dehradun by virtue of their economy show the impact of urbanization in the form of decreasing family size. However, the percentage of tertiary workers with high educational levels especially in case of Lucknow and Dehradun favor smaller family size.

Between 29-21 per cent lies very low category occupying 6 districts of Uttar Pradesh Himalayas. The economy and educational levels with lesser strains upon given environmental facilities promote a culture of nucleated family system in which the dependency ratio is very low for both young and old age groups.

Uttar Pradesh, in spite of varying levels of socio-economic development, is still traditional in its set of society norms and values where joint and extended family system is being followed and promoted. However, rising educational levels along with economic satisfaction reflects the impact of urbanism in deciding family size which has only confined to the Hill districts. The lesser degree of migration recorded in Ganga Plain accompanied by large family size point toward an immobile population.

Joint Family: 3-5 Persons per Household

The close emotional bonds within the families in case of India results in generally joint family system. In Uttar Pradesh basically an agricultural based middle class society dominates, in which even after settling down in urban areas, the behavioral changes are occurring slowly but gradually. The process of migration along with the family has also promoted increase in family size. The medium family size and percentage of household cannot necessarily be correlated with lower economic or educational status it is rather a behavioral attitude determined by inherent and prevalent socio-cultural ethos of the society itself.

Spatial Process

In 1991, 35.93 per cent of households with medium family size are recorded in Uttar Pradesh. The spatial process underlying the outcome of present proportion of such households seems to be determined by the interaction of variables in which educational level of females above graduate (+0.77), especially female workers above graduate (+0.75) with mean age of females high at marriage (+0.73) are significant. Males within active age group (+0.74), male migrants (+0.62) along with male main workers (+0.61) are all important aspects. This process is particularly operative in high urban density areas (+0.78). A negative weak correlation (–0.37) with number of children per female suggests it to be a phenomenon of adjustment of old persons or relatives. Thus, it is rather a character of migrant families with high education levels of both males and females, having medium size families reflecting the impact of traditional societies, which they originally belong to.

Spatial Patterns

The spatial distribution of joint family system with medium household size has a variable degree of concentration that results in definite spatial patterns (Fig.26).

Between 40-50 per cent, lies the very high category in which 10 districts including Dehradun, Pithoragarh, Almora with Nainital cover the northern hill region, suggesting a household structure in which the medium family size might results from more number of children or relatives in a house. Since the hill region receives tourists and pilgrims it may also be a residential-cum-commercial place like a tourist resort. The districts of Kanpur Nagar,

Lucknow and Ghaziabad with a very high urbanization degree, record a high concentration of such households due to both within the family increase of members by natural increase itself as these districts record a high concentration of population in active age group.

The whole of southern plateau region and parts of southern Upper Ganga Plains with Agra, Mathura, Jhansi, Allahabad and Sonbhadra record around 35 per cent of households in this category. Except the districts dominated by large cities where density itself is high, rest of the area has low concentration of urban population resulting in variable household size.

While the northern Upper Ganga Plain, the Tarai belt and parts of eastern Middle Ganga Plain including Varanasi, Aligarh, Gorakhpur, Mirzapur record low values. In Varanasi, it is rather the extended family, which is recording more compared to this indicator. The rest of the districts in face of lesser density of urban population and lesser economic pulls are not encouraging medium family size showing only around 25 per cent of such house holds.

Thus, medium size of households is a reflective of the on going socio-economic changes in the area. The districts of Ganga Plain are lying in either medium category around the two highly urbanized districts of Kanpur Nagar and Lucknow or merge to low westward and low to and very low eastward to be replaced by households with large family size.

Nucleated Family: Up to 3 Persons per Household

The emergence of nucleated families in urban societies might be a common phenomenon to developed countries, where rapid developments in technological innovations and information diffusion necessitate increased mobility of workers in various specialized economic sectors. In India, family bonds, the traditions and culture are very strong influencing the decision to move for economic or other reasons. However, with increasing functional segregation through urbanization, nucleated family system is on rise more specifically in large urban areas, which sustains the potential movers. The rising cost of living in urban areas is another limiting factor for family size. Since the culture of working women is cn rise in urban India, economic satisfaction level is manifesting itself rapidly in households with nucleated and small family size.

In Uttar Pradesh, the phenomenon reflects two important processes. In the first process, it is a single-family migration generally for large urban areas. Secondly, it might also be the old members left behind once the active age group members have out-migrated for economic or other reasons as in case of small or medium towns. It further reflects the preference of small family itself, which is generally associated with the impact of urbanization or 'urbanism'.

Spatial Process

In Uttar Pradesh only 11.31 per cent of the household have nucleated family with household size up to 3 that reflects the lack of general impact of urbanism. Though, the present figure of small family size is low, however, it shows a very strong influence of education and economic status of population as suggested by correlation matrix. It is both the male and female workers above graduate (+0.76 and +0.77) along with educational levels of both the male and female with above graduate (+0.58 and +0.63) highlighting the role of education and income in limiting the family size. The cost of living in urban areas also discourages the large family system as reflected by households with nucleated family with active age of migrants of males (+0.83), male main workers (+0.87) with high standards of living as shown by the provision of all three urban amenities (+0.81).

Spatial Patterns

The type of economy, culture, tradition and educational levels all seem to have affected this phenomenon at local scale (Fig.26).

Between 17-37 per cent of households form the very high category under which only 8 or 12.7 per cent of the districts cover mainly the Kumaon Himalaya. Although negligent on the scene of urbanization, these districts especially Chamoli and Tehri Garhwal, with few industries and limited employment opportunities are encouraging migrants only in specialized services. Therefore, nucleated family in migration of both males and females with high educational levels is on rise. Sonbhadra has low population concentration and family size tends to be small, as it is an area experiencing rapid in-migration of workers of all educational levels.

The most dominant category identified all throughout Ganga Plain is the low to very low concentration of nucleated families recording a value within 7-13 per cent in which 47 or 75 per cent of the districts lie. The northern Upper Ganga Plain including highly urbanized districts of Mathura, Ghaziabad, Agra, Meerut, Aligarh along with Lucknow and Kanpur Nagar, the Tarai region including all low urbanized districts and in the western Middle Ganga Plain till Varanasi, the family size remains large irrespective of the degree of urbanization. This category shows a rather negative relation with urbanization except in Dehra Dun while, Nainital, Banda, Hamirpur, Rae Bareili, Sultanpur and Mau are basically under-developed recording low mobility of population and moderate concentration of nucleated families.

CROWDING

In India, urbanization represents a uniqueness of the process of population distribution over the geographical surface. The rapid locational mobility of population towards urban cities does not necessarily mean a corresponding sectoral shift of economy. The hierarchy of towns and cities clearly reflect the outcome of this process in which 65% of the total urban population is concentrated in class I cities. In Uttar Pradesh, the number of such cities is just 8% of the total numbers of urban places enumerated in 1991. The metropolitan growth continues unabated in terms of population. It is the residential quarters of the cities that bear the brunt of rising population. Even the residential location decisions at intra-urban or even inter-urban levels are taken within the constraints of economic and socio-cultural set up (Reginold and Stimson: 1987).

Thus, the degree of crowding though a negative aspect while deciding upon quality of living environment reflects the individual location decisions made in response to changing needs and aspirations. Crowding expressed as number of persons per room reflects broadly the shortage of housing demands.

The concept of territoriality as suggested by crowding theory (Adrey: 1966) elaborates upon the relation between crowding in terms of living and moving space inside the house, and resultant strains and stresses in both physical and psychological terms. The physical space thus, emerges as the prime requirement for a feeling of privacy, building up of personality and rationale behavior of an individual in the society (Knox, P.: 1987).

The number of rooms considered in calculating crowding or density of household is a matter of concern. The possession of at least two rooms per household reflects a monetary status of a middle class family, the concept of which is most relevant in Indian society and more so, for the study area. Therefore, for the present study, the criterion of two rooms possession remains fixed against which number of members per household are considered, to work out an index of crowding in terms of density per household.

Density of Large Households

Urbanization encourages functional segregation of population. It is positively related with the size of urban population where growing large number of migrants can be absorbed into a multi-functional economy through multiplier effect. However, the workforce structure does not always reflect the economic viability of urban environment as the economy of surrounding areas has a major role to play especially setting in motion streams of rural to urban migrants.

In Uttar Pradesh the agricultural background of the economy promotes and sustains large families with more than 5 persons per household as anywhere else in the developing world. The urban density in general is high in Uttar Pradesh with a tendency for the metropolitan growth and development. Thus, the housing density invariably becomes high more so in case of migrants who are generally absorbed in low paid jobs.

The cost of living itself is high in urban areas. Along with large families the cost of accommodation near the place of work compels for adjustments between the quality housing and easy commuting and to opt for small living space. Therefore, the highly urbanized places have higher crowding status for joint and extended families. In less urbanized areas it is rather the lack of resources that results in again higher crowding status of households with large family size.

Spatial Process

In 1991, Uttar Prdesh recorded 31.67 per cent of households with more than 5 persons with 2 rooms facility. The urban density correlates strongly (+0.66), the in migration of males (+0.60) and sex-ratio (+0.55) along with dependency ratio of young (+0.51) clearly reflects the male based family migration resulting in high crowding status of households. The mild positive relation of places of more than 20,000 (+0.41) and inter-sate migration from urban areas (+0.42) clearly reflect that higher crowding is also a feature of places of higher population size.

Spatial patterns

The dynamics underlying this measure of stress in territoriality has manifested itself in the correlation values as noticed. But the association of factor has variability over space, which expresses itself in definite spatial patterns (Fig.27).

Between 39-47 per cent lies the very high category in which 7 districts covering an area of medium urbanized regions of Bareilly, Badaun, Pilibhit, Etah and Shahjahanpur are inhabited by traditional societies. These areas are neither much industrialized nor much urbanized resulting in higher space congestion and resultant crowding through in-migration generally of low educated persons who are generally self-absorbed or marginally employed.

Between 31-38 per cent lies high category in which 15 districts cover mainly the Upper Ganga Plain. Kanpur Nagar, Mathura, Agra, Meerut and Aligarh are worth mentioning. In general the degree of crowding is decreasing towards eastward, almost in correspondence with the degree of urbanization. However, places like Farrukhabad, Hardoi and Kheri also lie at par with highly urbanized districts irrespective of size of urban population.

Between 26-30 per cent lies medium category with 17 districts cover the highly crowded parts of central and western Uttar Pradesh including Lucknow, Allahabad, Varanasi, Ghaziabad and Jhansi with very high degree of urbanization along with places like Unnao, Sitapur and Gonda with very low level of urbanization. A belt of Himalayan foothill districts along with Dehradun is also included.

Between 16-25 per cent lies low category in which 19 districts cover either the southern Plateau Region or eastern Middle Ganga Plain except areas around Varanasi. Dehradun in northern hill region is a well-advanced region supportive of a thriving economy along with Nainital, do not suffer from this phenomenon. Banda,

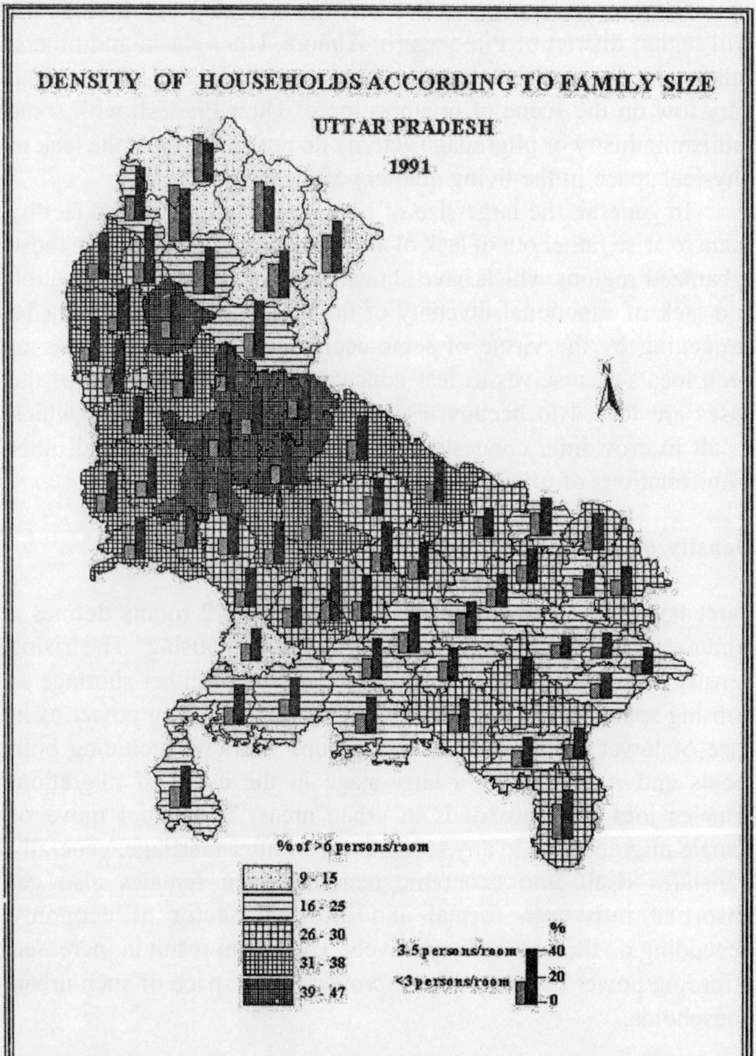
DENSITY OF HOUSEHOLDS ACCORDING TO FAMILY SIZE
UTTAR PRADESH
1991
N
% of >6 persons/room
9 - 15
16 - 25
26 - 30
31 - 38
39 - 47
%
3-5 persons/room
<3 persons/room
40
20
0

Fig. 27

Hamirpur, Hardoi, Faizabad are areas where due to low degree of urbanization, congestion status is low.

Between 9-15 per cent lies very low category that include the Hill region district of Pithoragarh, Almora, Uttar Kashi and others. Jalaun also lies in this category. These districts except Jalaun, stand very low on the scene of urbanization of Uttar Pradesh with some tourism industry or pilgrimage activity do not suffer from the lack of physical space in the living quarters of the houses.

In general, the large size of households with 2 rooms facility seem to arise rather out of lack of affording power especially in those urbanized regions which have shown signs of economic stagnation and lack of functional diversity of urban economy. This might be happening by the virtue of socio-economic nature of migrants or even locals themselves as less educated persons in majority of the cases are forced to occupy less desirable location in cities which result in crowding, congestion, lack of urban amenities and other manifestations of urban environmental degradation.

Density of Medium Households

Percentage of households with 3-5 persons per 2 rooms defines a parameter for decreasing crowding status in housing. The rising density of population per room is a suggestive of either shortage of housing space as in case of large city or less affording power as in case of lower or medium income groups in a city including both locals and migrants. At a later stage in the cycle of migration, females join their husbands in urban areas. The initial move of female migrants due to any social cause or after marriage, generally translates itself into economic benefits when females also get absorbed into both formal and informal sector of economy depending on their educational levels. This might result in increased affording power consequently improved living space of such urban households.

Spatial Process

In Uttar Pradesh, during 1981-1991, the density of households with 3-5 persons per 2 rooms is strongly correlated with female workers more than graduate (+0.72), and also with female mean age at marriage (+0.68). The male main workers also correlate strongly (+0.69) especially in other than household industry (+0.50). The age structure within 15-59 years also corresponds well (+0.54) especially of males in active age group (+0.52). There is a movement of population from long distance, though mild (0.44) from other urban areas. There is an unsatisfactory provision of basic amenities (+0.40) associated with rising density.

Spatial Patterns

In 1991, 26.21% of total households are having medium family size with 3-5 persons with 2 rooms facility. The process bringing about the above percentage in Uttar Prdesh is not equal; rather it shows regional variations in its intensity of concentration under the influence of some local factors (Fig.27).

Approximately 21 or 33.3 per cent of the districts record a value within 27-35 per cent covering either the Uttar Pradesh Himalayas in Pithoragarh, Nainital, Tehri Garhwal, Hardwar or the highly urbanized areas of Dehradun, Lucknow, Kanpur Nagar, Ghaziabad and Sonbhadra. Another concentration comprising of of the industrial areas of Rampur, Bareilly, Meerut lies at par with areas of limited economic opportunities like Budaun, Shahjahanpur, Pilibhit, Unnao, Garhwal and Chamoli. The heavy concentration of population in few cities or degree of effective urbanization results in an increasing urban density per household.

Surrounding the high concentration region towards the west and south of it, lies a zone of medium degree of concentration of around 25 per cent of such households covering 22 or 34.9 per cent of the districts in areas of varying degree of urbanization. Agra, Mathura, Aligarh, Etawah lie at par with Kanpur Dehat, Mainpuri, Farrukhabad, Sitapur and others with low degree of urbanization.

Nearly 21 or 33.3 per cent of the districts record a low value within 12-22 per cent in which mainly the Middle Ganga Plain lies. Apart from Varanasi and Allahabad, the rest of the area has a very low degree of urbanization, which signifies not necessarily a decrease in space congestion, but simply a lesser percentage of medium size households with 2 room facility due to availability of space. The districts occupying the eastern part of Middle Ganga

Plain like Ballia, Deoria, Mau, and Azamgarh, which are already experiencing low pace of urbanization as well record lesser crowding status.

In general the decreasing family size along with 2 room facilities seems to be a characteristics of two distinct types of socio-economic set up. It is either industrialized and highly urbanized areas with higher concentration of migrant population and greater degree of effective urbanization which show strains upon the living space like Kanpur Nagar, Lucknow and Ghaziabad, on the other, the mono or bi-functional towns with obvious high degree of concentration population into few cities resulting in increasing territorial stress. Less urbanized areas, due to small size of towns and limited economic base of urban places do not suffer from space congestion.

Density of Small Households

A criterion of 3 persons with 2 rooms facility is considered respectable enough to depict the comfortable living condition of a middle class family. It constitutes a section of urban society where either small family norm are practicable or nucleated family is in existence, not necessarily consisting of active age group. It can also represent senile group of population consisting of old people who are left behind once the working age group from the family migrates for economic reasons. However, this criterion certainly reflects some changing norms of the urban society apart from economic independency, which encourages this type of households.

Spatial Process

As per 1991 figures, 9.32 per cent of households with a family size of up to 3 persons with 2 rooms facility are the outcome of a number of factors. The housing density is generally a function of small family size (+0.98) with male migrants (+0.85), which are generally main workers (+0.88) in active age group (+0.83). A correlation also exists with total literacy of males in +60 age group (+0.65) suggesting the level of living in independent dwelling mainly by working males in active age group and post retirement group of males as well.

Spatial Patterns

The percentage of small size household with 2 rooms facility itself is very low in Uttar Pradesh in 1991. Still, the spatial pattern certainly corresponds to the regional urban economic set up (Fig.27).

Only 6 or 9.5 per cent of the districts record a value within 15-35 per cent of households lying in this category. Chamoli, Uttar Kashi, Pithoragarh, Almora and Garhwal though very low urbanized, have the highest percentage of nucleated families due to more male in migrants. Sonbhadra is also included in this category. Nearly all the hill districts show a rising proportion of active age group workers that signify economic self-sufficiency resulting in very high to high percentage of nucleated families with 2 room facility.

It is only a part of the foothills of Himalayas in Hardwar, Nainital and Kanpur Nagar, Ghaziabad, Dehradun which due to high degree of urbanization and rising density of population show just sufficient picture. Lalitpur, Pratapgarh, Sultanpur due to low density and low degree of urbanization shows a comfortable position regarding crowding status of small families.

However, a great contrast exists in Ganga Plain where 47 or 75 per cent of the districts record low to very low percentage within 5 to 10 per cent of small size family with 2 room facility. The districts important on scene of urbanization like Kanpur Nagar, Lucknow, Allahabad, Varanasi, Agra, Meerut, Jhansi and Mathura stand at par with very low urbanized districts like Hamirpur, Pilibnhit, Kheri, Fatehpur Ballia, Deoria and others. Medium urbanized districts like Saharanpur, Muzaffarnagar, Aligarh, Firozabad are also included in this category.

This phenomenon is highly localized in space. Apart from the Hill districts, the rest of Uttar Pradesh has a low, rather very low percentage of small household size with 2 room facility. The whole of Ganga plain irrespective of the degree of urbanization is highly populated. Due to deep-rooted socio-cultural norms, more number of children with joint family system is generally the way of life, as could be visualized even in cases of large cities. This partly explains the near absence of small household size with 2-room facility in Uttar Pradesh.

6

DIMENSIONS OF LEVELS OF URBANIZATION

The spatial analysis of a number of indicators pertaining to various aspects of urbanization have successfully identified the role of individual variables in context with the on-going process of urbanization in Uttar Pradesh as a whole through correlation matrix with all other variables. However, the exploration of intrinsic patterns of urbanization underlying the multitude of variables is lacking. Each variable since an indicator of urbanization is supposed to contribute equally in determining the degree of urbanization. There is a need to compress the results into few easily identifiable and interpretable sets of deterministic variables for causing variations in levels of urbanization in Uttar Pradesh. Therefore, the multivariate analysis technique of Principal Component Analysis is being applied to ascertain the underlying dimensions affecting levels of urbanization and to address these dimensions into spatial context.

Principal Component Analysis: Component Structure

A set of fifty-seven variables related to four broad aspects of urbanization was taken up for sixty-three districts of Uttar Pradesh, which has yielded 10 principal components. Together these factors account for 86.56 per cent of the total variance in the date set. However, for concise description and meaningful analysis of the data set, only 4 major principal components were selected which together accounted for 69.20 per cent of the total variance in the data set. The principal component, later on referred as PC, has shown that PCI accounted for 39.38 per cent of total variance in the data set, PC II for 15.41 per cent, PC III for 8.73 per cent, and PC IV for 5.86. The rest of the principal components were not considered, as these were mainly one or two variable dominated components.

Principal Component	*Eigen Values*	*% Variance explained*	*Cumulative percentage*
PC I	22.4480	39.38	39.38
PC II	8.78243	15.41	54.79
PC III	4.97582	8.73	63.52
PC IV	3.33903	5.86	69.38

The grouping of the variables under summary dimensions brings out clearly the contradictory nature of urbanization in Uttar Pradesh. It has all been brought about by the large number of principal components into which the variables are grouped. Further more, the intensity of loadings both on negative and positive side is almost the same suggesting a complementarity of the process of urbanization in negative and positive aspects. This has further been aggravated by the fact that three out of four principal components have loaded more negative loadings than positive under the dimensions concerned.

Principal Component I: Dysfunctional Urbanization and Lack of Urban Development

The first principal component, as expected grouped together most of the variables into a vast summary dimension, which has more negative loadings than positive over the given set of variables. This further suggests the vulnerability of the process of urbanization in Uttar Pradesh.The variables recording very high positive loadings are juvenile dependency ratio (+0.93), senile dependency ratio (+0.79) and higher number of females (+0.85) suggesting the urban scenario to be characterized by high dependency ratio and a shortage of working population. The high positive loading on household size more than 5 persons (+0.91) further confirms the severity of the problem associated with specifically large family size. The centralized economics pull of the urban areas is identified through district-to-district migration stream originating from urban areas (+0.59).

The variables that record high negative loadings are active age group population (-0.93), the literacy rates for the active age group (-0.85), males at under-graduate level (-0.79) and post-graduate level (-0.81). The medium household size between 3-5 persons records very high loading (-0.83) with a corresponding high loading on availability of urban amenities (-0.88). The mean age of marriage (-0.74), female workers more than graduates (-0.79), the male workers more than graduate (-0.81) and male workers less than graduate (-0.79), are all significant. The variables on nearly all the aspects of urban amenities record strong negative loadings.

These loadings and their corresponding signs are consistent and complementary to each other suggesting a general level of degradation in the urbanization scenario of Uttar Pradesh. The conditions brought about by the Principal Component-I point out to a situation where the economy is not any more supportive of the level of urbanization. It rather emphasizes a situation where most of the dynamics of urbanization have ceased to be operative any more. Thus the lack of well defined occupational structure of working population with the low educational levels of workers even in active age group, presence of non working population reflected in the lessening economic pull of the area, high juvenile and senile dependency ratio with medium household size and a high density of households along with a corresponding low quality of housing in terms of basic amenities, suggest the lack of urban economic development in Uttar Pradesh. On the basis of above findings, the first dimension is labeled as 'Dysfunctional Urbanization and Lack of Urban Development'.

However, the above process is manifesting itself in various degree of combination of the forces of urbanization. The determination of factor scores, thus, permits a more accurate weighing of these variables by districts. On the basis of the range of variation in the component scores, five categories are identified on the basis of natural breaks, as argued earlier, which differentiate areas from very high to very low status of the dimension under study. The districts scoring more on this component are characterized by more intensity of the problems as identified through the dimension, while the districts scoring very low are better in terms of the functional aspects of urbanization.

The range of component scores from 11 to 17 identifies the very high category. The districts within this range represent the most vulnerable areas on urbanization scenario of Uttar Pradesh. There are 9 district out of which Moradabad, Bijnor and Bulandshahr in northern Upper Ganga Plain have medium degree of urbanization while Ghazipur, Jaunpur, Azamgarh, Mau and Ballia have very low degree of urbanization except Varanasi, lying in the eastern Middle Ganga Plain (Fig.28).

The percentage of males in active age group all throughout these districts is very low. The urban sex ratio varies from high in western Uttar Pradesh to very high in eastern Uttar Pradesh. The nature of industrial employment as shown by workers in registered factories per lakh of population records a value of 159 for eastern part of Uttar Pradesh and 526 for western part compared to a state average of 420. Apart from Varanasi, Moradabad and Bijnor all other districts are dotted by small-scale industries.

The district of Bijnor and Moradabad along with Bulandshahr form a zone in the Ganga Plain. Bijnor and Moradabad are part of the historical Rohilkhand Plain that has a rich history of urbanization but suffers from the lack of enough mineral and power resources. Due to less diversified industrial base of economy, these districts along with Bulandshahr, seem to have reached at a saturation point as reflected by the rate of in-migration which is lowest in this area suggesting a lesser economic pull for potential workers. Further more, due to large family size with very low literacy levels, a high dependency ratio results.

The next group of districts covering the central part of the eastern Middle Ganga Plain includes Ghazipur, Jaunpur, Azamgarh, Mau and Ballia. All these districts incidentally lie in the mineral resource and power deficit region. These districts mainly survive on the basis of agriculture related occupations and could not get enough economic stimulus to promote a well knitted hierarchy of towns, therefore, only one or two cities on the urban economic scenario have attracted disproportionately large percentage of urban population with resultant pressure upon existing urban job market and deteriorating urban facilities.

On the scene of urban amenities like safe drinking water supply, serviceable toilet and electricity, the western group of districts is comparatively better off than eastern except Varanasi. It seems that the remittance paid by out migrated active age group of males from eastern Uttar Pradesh have made the quality of housing comparatively better while public distribution system has been in

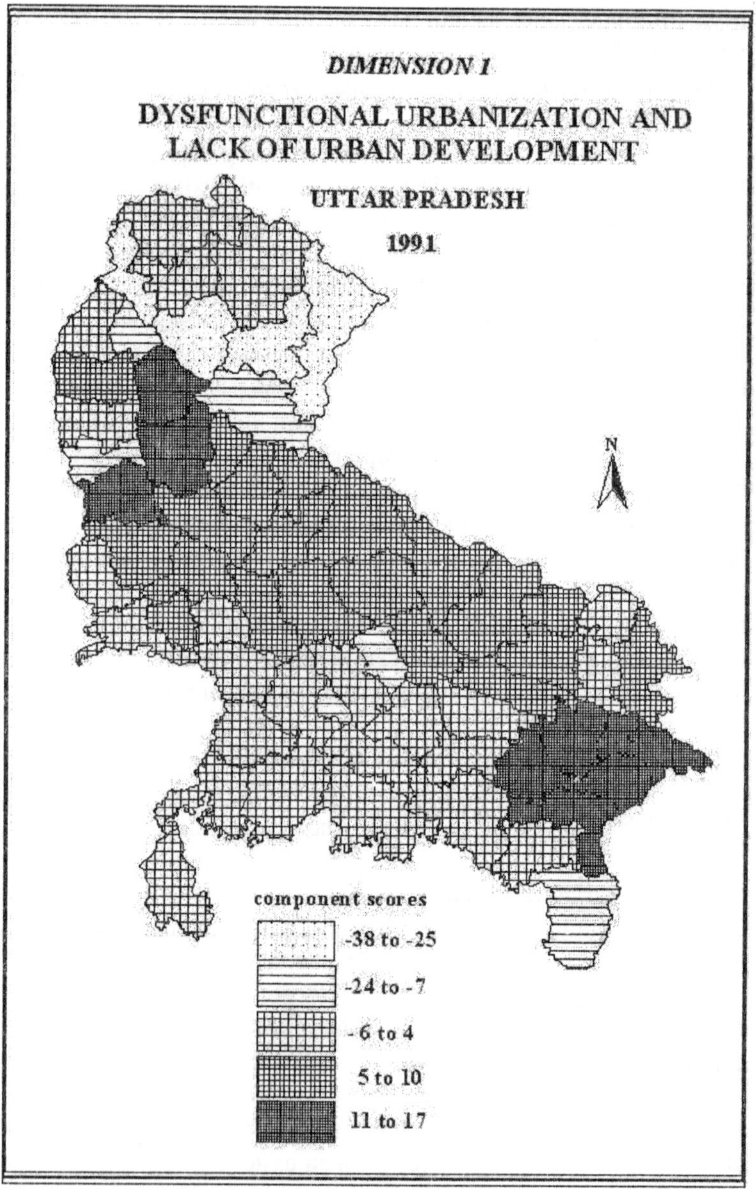
DIMENSION 1
DYSFUNCTIONAL URBANIZATION AND LACK OF URBAN DEVELOPMENT
UTTAR PRADESH
1991
N
component scores
-38 to -25
-24 to -7
-6 to 4
5 to 10
11 to 17

Fig. 28

favor of large cities irrespective of level of urbanization as is the case with western group of districts.

On the educational scene, the total literacy levels of western group of districts is very low compared to the eastern group of districts. This is a significant aspect as it indicates the economic value of the set of population of eastern Uttar Pradesh for future human resource base planning.

The component scores between 5 to 10 form the high category. It encompasses 20 districts in the form of a belt from west to east through the entire length of Upper and Middle Ganga Plain along Tarai region showing a decrease in the percentage of urban population from west to east with few exceptions. In the southern Upper Ganga Plain, the group of districts is formed by Aligarh, Etah, Firozabad, Mainpuri, Farrukhabad, Kheri, Shahjahanur, Pilibhit, Bareilly, Rampur, Budaun and Etah. The other group occupies Middle Ganga Plain, mostly the western part where Bahraich, Sitapur, Hardoi, Bara Banki, Faizabad, Gonda along with Sidharthnagar, and Basti form a continuous belt. Deoria in the extreme east also lies in this category. In general, to the north of River Ganga all along Tarai, there is an area of under development in face of lack of economic resources due to which small and medium urban centers are stagnating. The workers in registered factories also record a value of roughly 150 for the whole set of districts, highest recorded by Rampur 532, lowest by Firozabad with zero and second lowest by Etah with 40. There seems to be little incentive for further industrial development in the districts of Rampur, Bareilly, Moradabad and Aligarh, which already have very high degree of effective urbanization and have recorded a general decrease in the percentage of in-migrants. Muzaffarnagar lying in the northern Upper Ganga Plain records a medium degree of urbanization and medium rate of in-migration. A general character for this whole belt is that it receives more seasonal rural migrants from short distances.

This whole belt forms an area where percentage of migrants is low to very low suggesting an economy unsupportive of further developmental activities. Even in 1991, the total main workers are very low especially in active age group and resultant high sex ratio with large generally more than 5 persons family size is experienced with high status of crowding. However, the urban amenity provision seems to be correlated with general degree of urbanization, in particular effective urbanization and is insufficient all throughout this region.

In general, the agrarian base of the society dominates the life style with norms of large family. Therefore, dependency in general is very high for both juvenile and senile group of population resulting in economic burdens and sub standard urban living environment.

Along the Southern Plateau region, a belt of 24 districts records loadings between -6 to -4 that can be treated as medium category considering the nature of distribution of the component scores. Mathura, Agra, Jhansi and Allahabad with a sound degree of urbanization are able to absorb migrant workers from various educational categories with a heavy concentration in tertiary sector resulting in moderate strain upon all developmental aspects of urbanization. Etawah and Firozabad though dominated by small scale industries, record medium scores as the female work participation rates in this area are also high especially in an around Aligrh, Mathura and Agra. Towards the southeast, it is again a preponderance of educated workers that defines its degree of comparative relaxation from economic deprival and urban development as in case of Mirzapur, Jaunpur, Faizabad. While Lalitpur, Jalaun, Hamirpur, Banda, Fatehpur are dotted by a number of small scale and household industries that support the streams of across the state migrants. In Uttar Pradesh Himalayas, Uttarkashi, Chamoli and Tehri Garhwal have shown a moderate degree of strains as the area is comparatively under developed compared to the rest of the Hill districts.

Since this dimension was related with the basic problems of urbanization, understandably, only few districts could come above it. Therefore, the low category lying between -24 tc -7 component scores has covered only 6 districts that are widely distributed all throughout. The most urbanized districts of Kanpur Nagar followed by Lucknow and Ghaziabad on urbanization scale, have recorded low values. Kanpur Nagar being the industrial nerve of the economy of Uttar Pradesh along with Ghaziabad has shown a sound degree of deviation from the phenomena of dysfunctional urbanization and lack of urban development. Hardwar, Nainital and Sonbhadra have a vibrant economy and experiencing active age in migrants, and lesser dependency ratio and resultant better provision of urban amenities.

The very low component scores ranging between -38 to -25 were loaded by 4 districts of Uttar Pradesh Himalayan region in which Dehradun, Almora, Garhwal and Pithoragarh are included. This category signifies a functional urban economy in which percentage of main workers are more especially in higher education as in case of Dehradun. The size of household in all these districts including Dehradun is less, density is also less, with rising income levels as suggested by provision of urban amenities, there is an acceptable quality of life attached to these districts. However, apart from Dehradun, due to a small population base the component scores have recorded strongly negative on this dimension.

Thus the PC I has successfully brought into focus the hidden dimension of the urbanization dynamics of Uttar Pradesh. The foremost impression of the urbanization scenario of Uttar Pradesh, as per 1991 data set, is that the imprints of economic saturation and urban degradation are marked all throughout Ganga Plain especially in districts towards the east and along Tarai belt. Two important aspects out of the above dimension further emerge: first, is the inability of existing centers of agro-economic base and small scale industrial centers to absorb any more main workers except seasonal, and secondly, the relative immobility of active age group both sectoral or economy wise and location or space-wise all throughout Ganga Plain. This hints at an agrarian based and traditional bound society on the verge of transformation of its values in selected parts as suggested by increase in literacy rates and increased female work participation rates in backward region of eastern Uttar Pradesh.

The simple bi-variable analysis in the preliminary exercises has shown the vulnerability of Lucknow and Kanpur Nagar on many developmental aspects of on urbanization scenario. However, in the present analysis both these districts along with Ghaziabad have managed to come above the average picture of dismay and economic stagnation. The results of Sonbhadra, an upcoming area on economic scenario with hydel power projects Hardwar with a service and tourism based economy, Almora with forest resources and tourism are all pointing to better future stimulants of economic growth in Uttar Pradesh. The active urbanization seems to be occurring in Dehradun where the educational facilities, small family size and higher economic opportunities along with educated male and female work participation rates have made this district as a future generator of urban economic growth.

Principal Component II: Dynamic Urbanization and Urban Development

The broader concept of functional stagnation of urbanization process through the interpretation of PC I has already highlighted areas of comparative prosperity and economic development. This dimension is revealed by the PC II, which has fully focused upon the areas of active urbanization and socio economic progress, accounting for 15.41 per cent of the variance explained in the data set.

The dimension associates itself with percentage of urban population (+0.62), urban density (+0.46) and effective urbanization (+0.44). The work participation rates are defined by both secondary workers in other than household industry (+0.52) and tertiary workers (+0.61). The educational level of workers is also highlighted in which male workers of less than graduate (+0.51) and above graduate (+0.46) show a moderate degree of occurrence. However, the educational levels of female workers with less than graduate (+0.41) and above graduate (+0.69) show increasing work participation rates in non-agricultural activities (+0.55) especially jobs requiring higher skills. The very high loadings on female mean age at marriage (+0.78) defines the common phenomena of delayed marriage due to either achievement of higher education or economic causes. This is further indicated by the family size of households of 3-5 persons (+0.46) along with density of households with medium family size of 3-5 persons with 2 rooms facility (+0.56). The rates of in-migrant from urban areas within the state (+0.41) and urban areas outside the state (+0.36) suggest the economic opportunities attracting migrants are moderate in intensity. There is a corresponding negative loading of district to district migration from rural areas (-0.49). A decrease in juvenile dependency ratio (-0.39) suggests the role of females in sharing the economic burden of the households. Regarding urban amenities, there seems to be a satisfactory level of provision of basic urban facilities like service able toilets (+0.92), electricity (+0.62), cooking gas (+0.61) and safe drinking water supply (+0.47). The variables are closely related with the signs of a healthy urbanization in which the degree of effective urbanization, work force structure of population, educational status of workers especially females, resultant migration streams from urban areas of other states and over all a satisfactory level of urban development are found. Therefore, this component is identified as 'Dynamic Urbanization and Urban Development'.

The variable structure of the component identifies higher scores with higher quality of urbanization and low scores with degradation in the dimension concerned. The component scores were recorded on varying degree of intensity over the districts. However, on the basis of the range of variation, five categories were identified to analyze the phenomena in spatial perspective (Fig.29) .

Very high component scores between 16-27 are recorded in 6 districts covering two areas. The first group of districts lies in the Uttar Pradesh Himalaya with Dehradun, Garhwal, Almora and Haridwar. Two districts of Kanpur Nagar and Lucknow lying in the western Middle Ganga Plain form the second group. All these districts have a marked degree of effective urbanization.

In case of northern hill districts, the dynamics underlying the urbanization process are different. Except Dehradun with a very high degree of urbanization, all other districts are very low on levels of urbanization. The whole area is rich in forest resources and shows a potential for hydel power generation. The development of tourism industry and location of a number of religious places like Haridwar, Rishikesh have been the prime force behind the pilgrimage related urban activities. In case of Dehradun, a number of prestigious government offices and institutions have promoted the dominance of tertiary sector of economy. There is noticed a multiplier effect in the urban economy as a result of which the migrated educated males and females in active age group are absorbed. Although the absolute volume of migration is meager, it is the proportional share in the urban population that ranks these districts very high. The size of the family remains medium but a general level of affluency is a suggestive of the contribution in income made by earning females.

Lying in this category, Kanpur Nagar is the most highly urbanized district of Uttar Pradesh. It forms an isolated pocket of urbanization along with Lucknow in the whole Middle Ganga Plain.

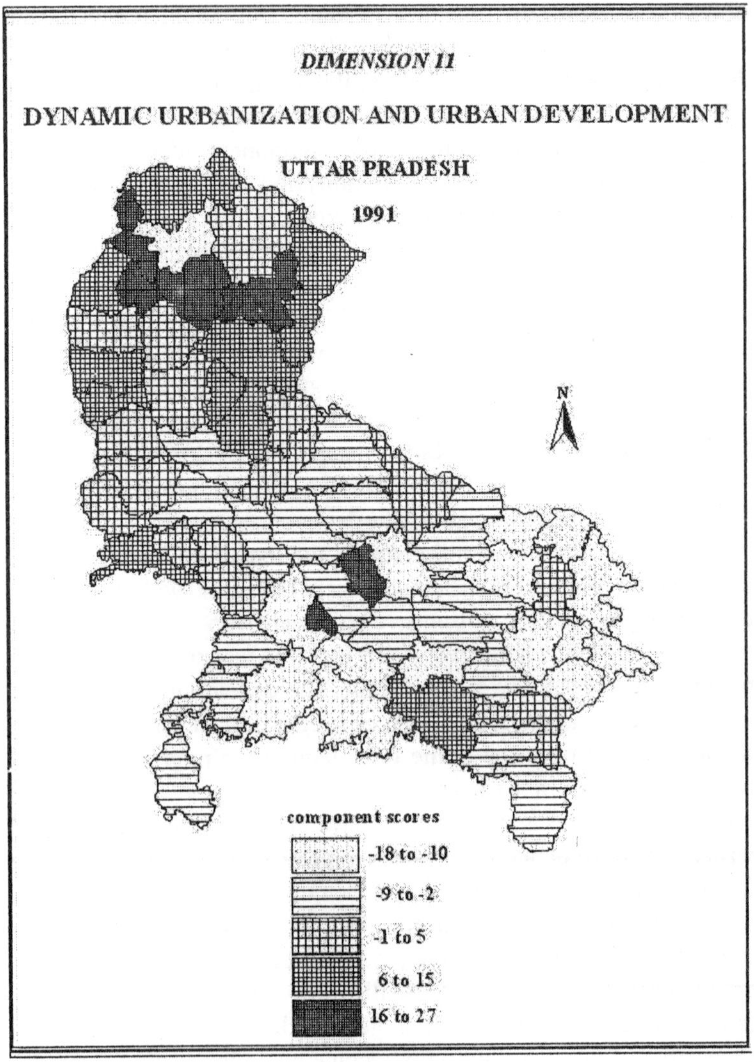
DIMENSION 11
DYNAMIC URBANIZATION AND URBAN DEVELOPMENT
UTTAR PRADESH
1991
N
component scores
-18 to -10
-9 to -2
-1 to 5
6 to 15
16 to 27

Fig. 29

The urbanization dynamics are suggestive of an increasing concentration of population into large cities as degree of effective urbanization is highest with a trend towards metropolitan growth. Kanpur U.A. alone has accommodates 12.7 per cent out of 55.2 per cent of total urban population in class I cities of Uttar Pradesh. The concentration of industrial establishments of medium and large scale has already attracted high concentration of active age group population of males. A corresponding decrease in urban sex ratio is also noticed. Male workers, however, are more with below graduate educational levels in other than household industries. Lucknow basically an administrative center has shown a concentration of educated workers in tertiary sector. The workers are active age group remain high. The family size for both these districts is almost same. Lucknow in comparison to Kanpur Nagar shows lesser concentration of large household size of more than 6 persons per family. This can be attributed to its higher educational levels or the impact of urbanism on its population. On the scale of provision of urban amenities both districts are almost the same. However, Kanpur, due to more density of urban population and larger size of the family have a shortage the three amenities of electricity, safe drinking water supply and serviceable toilets in comparison to Lucknow. Further more, the decadal variation of population in Kanpur Nagar is far below than Lucknow, thereby suggesting that the multiplier effect of urban economy of Kanpur Nagar is on decline and Lucknow might take up lead in urbanization scenario of Uttar Pradesh.

The component scores define the high category within 6-15 in which 10 districts lie. Except Allahabad, all other districts extend from Uttar Pradesh Himalaya to the foothill region encompassing Shaharanpur, Meerut, Ghaziabad and Agra in the western Uttar Pradesh. The hill districts of Pithoragarh, Almora, Uttarkashi, are all areas where tourism industry and hydel power stations have promoted in migration of workers into productive sector of economy. All these areas are sparsely populated with only one or two cities dominating the urban scenario. In face of the small base of urban population of hill districts, the parameters of quality urbanization have recorded high.

The link between prosperous agriculture and resultant urbanization is well established for nearly all the districts of Upper

Ganga Plains which have received benefits of Green Revolution and established a network of agro industry based towns of various sizes. The district of Saharanpur, known for its sugar mills, Ghaziabad for multi functional industrial establishments, Meerut for metal based small scale industries along with textiles, Agra with burgeoning tourism industry due to Taj Mahal, apart from leather industry are few of the basic functions attached to these districts. The functional linkages established with National Capital Region of Delhi have certainly streamlined the course of urban development of these districts. However, excluding these externalities, the internal factors are of more decisive in nature. The degree of effective urbanization is high and consistent in spatial distribution within this part of the region. The industrial sector at present is showing a consistently high concentration of educated workers in other than households industry and also in tertiary sector of economy. The more important is the female work participation rates in non-agricultural sector of economy by mostly highly educated females. However, all these districts are experiencing short distance in migration rates from urban areas within the state and long distance in migration rates by rural workers outside the state. This result is an increase in active age group population. Excluding Agra and Ghaziabad, other districts are recording considerable decadal variation of population suggesting a potential for further urban growth. Urban amenities are sufficient on provision scale. The family size is also medium with lesser dependency ratio.

Allahabad lying at the confluence of Ganga Yamuna is basically an administrative center where the degree of effective urbanization is very high though the present level of urbanization is just medium. The tertiary sector of economy is heavy with workers belonging to both sexes from various educational levels. The secondary sector of economy especially other than household industries is deficient resulting in the low percentage of total main workers with a corresponding low rate of in migration, suggesting a low potential for this district for future development. Although with present income levels and provision of amenities, the living urban environment seems respectable on every criteria of quality of life.

Bareilly and Rampur are the two old industrially established areas with a history of urbanization dating back to colonial period.

However, at present the urban scenario unfolds itself in the form of a well-established agro base of industries and numerous small-scale industries mainly metal based which thrive on local articraft. With a high concentration of male workers belonging to mainly lower educational group in secondary sector and female workers with more sound educational levels in tertiary sector, these two districts are experiencing high density and high sex ratio. The quality of housing in terms of Pucca might not be satisfactory but the basic amenities of safe drinking water supply and serviceable toilets are available, attaching a credential to Rampur and Bareilly.

The medium category is defined by component scores within -1 to -5 in which 15 districts lie, concentrated mainly in the Upper Ganga Plain. The coverage of this category closely confines itself to the areas with varying degree of urban economic development. The western belt of districts covering Muzaffarnagar, Moradabad, Bulandshahr, Aligarh, Mathura, Firozabad is almost homogenous with medium degree of urbanization. Mathura with the oil refineries, Aligarh and Moradabad with small and medium size industrial units of metal works are supplementing their economy apart from agro based small-scale industrial units lying in high urbanized category.

The existing capabilities of the economic units seem to have been reaching at a threshold points in case of Bijnor, Morabadad, Bulandshahr, Aligarh where the rate of in-migration of active males have considerably been declined. The nature of industries in all these districts is either household industry using local articraft or small-scale industries that does not submit their income returns. The seasonal or cyclic nature of the availability of work corresponds to lesser percentage of main workers. Consequently, it also reflects a decreasing trend in the long distance migration streams especially from rural areas. However, along the bordering districts of agriculturally backward states of Rajasthan and Madhya Pradesh or even from Bihar, rural workers are coming from outside the states. However, inter district migration seems to be a more preferred stream of mobility of population especially rural workers from within the districts.

In Middle Ganga Plain the position of Varanasi is very striking as the district serves the whole of eastern Middle Ganga Plain in terms of basic goods and services. Though it is known for its textiles, the industrial structure is mainly dominated by small-scale industries running on power or even handloom to produce fabric to cater export needs. The workers, consequently, include both males and females of having either just a literacy or even low educational background. Only the organizational sector demands qualified personnel who are generally migrants from outside the state. The religious significance of Varanasi is of utmost importance that attracts heavy crowd during religious festivities and rituals. The density of population is very high and decadal variation is showing a slowing down of urbanization process with a pronounced degree of effective urbanization.

Gorakhpur known for its terracotta industry, though low on degree of urbanization is recording very high decadal growth rates with a rise in educated secondary workers in other than household industries. Bahraich, lying in very low category of urbanization levels has loaded medium component sectors. The on going urbanization process suggests a medium level of concentration of workers in other than household industries, with a high degree of low educated total male workers in active age group.

In the entire region lying in medium category, the dependency ratio is variable ranging from high in the western and eastern parts to low in the central part of the state. The provision of urban amenities is generally medium except Varanasi. The family size, which is a more significant indictor to records growing strains on the urban living environment is invariably large, generally more than 6 persons per household with high crowding status all throughout.

On a generalized level, the results of this dimension seem to be commiserating with the degree of urbanization. As the degree of urbanization is decreasing from west to east, the loadings on this component are also lessening in almost the same fashion.

The low category is defined by the component scores between -9 to -2 in which 17 districts are lying in an irregular belt running from the southern Upper Ganga Plain through western to eastern Middle Ganga Plain particularly to the north, continuing into the southern plateau region barring the districts of Hamirpur and Banda. The Middle Ganga Plain though agriculturally fertile is not developed properly and the eastern part of it is suffering from the uncertainty of rainfall, frequent floods and droughts. The net effective is the lack of development in these areas, which calls for proper agricultural planning. However, this region has shown a dominance of literates especially males with post graduate degree like in Faizabad, Sultanpur, Pratapgarh while in the southern part of Upper Ganga Plain, it is the excess of males with below graduate level like in Etah, Budaun, Kheri. The female work participation rates in this whole region varies in accordance with the degree of effective urbanization which is turn has had an impact on the avenues of better educational attainment and better job opportunities of female workers as noticed in Etah, Mainpuri, Gonda and Kheri. The quality of urban living environment in this category is variable. While lesser degree of effective urbanization results in lesser congestion and crowding, the amenities provision is however, negatively related the small size towns as in case of Unnao and Sultanpur.

There are potential areas where at present the degree of urbanization might be very less but the loadings have given certain credibility to Barabanki, Sultanpur, Jaunpur and Gonda. It is probably the rise in agro based textile industry especially handicraft and cottage which is capturing a wider market even outside India. The rise of tertiary workers in the above district especially females with varying educational levels are a suggestive of this phenomenon. On the contrary, Mau, Banda and Hamirpur seem to have lost some of its economic attraction as have recorded very low component scores on this dimension.

The very low category includes 15 districts within -18 to -11 component scores. The whole of northern part of eastern Middle Ganga Plain along with remaining district of Western Middle Ganga Plain are included in it. As discussed earlier, this whole belt seems to be devoid of any economic stimuli for further development and the tertiary sector is dominant in the bordering districts of east where outside state migration is taking place from Bihar, Madhya Pradesh and even West Bengal. There are two prominent groups of districts. The first encompasses eastern Uttar Pradesh where Jaunpur, Mau, Ghazaipur, Ballia, Deoria, Siddharthnagar, Maharajganj,Basti and Pratapgarh form a core of urban economic under-development along with a second group to the south of Kanpur Nagar, including Banda, Hamirpur, Fatehpur and Kanpur Dehat.

This dimension was able to differentiate and identify the dynamics of urbanization as a concomitant of economic growth and the resultant urban development. Since the dimension has shown a close affinity with the degree of urbanization along with effective urbanization to certain extent, it may rightly be the representative of the process of healthy urbanization in Uttar Pradesh as the key variables, all suggestive of a degree of urban economic development have loaded very high. Still the high loadings on the family size make this dimension a proxy of demographic and socio-economic status of urban society of Uttar Pradesh which is reflected in the absolute growth of urban population and very low very low level of urbanization. The increase in urban population is being curtailed by equally fast growth rate in rural population in Uttar Pradesh. Therefore, the real problems related with urbanization, is not the level of it. It is rather the absolute volume of urban growth, which is more significant.

Thus, the dimension is capable to distinguish and discover the dynamics of urbanization at present at work and the potential areas where further urban growth and expansion could take place.

Principal Component III: Traditional Urbanization and Urban Decay

The discussion on the preceding dimension of dynamic urbanization and urban development has broadly identified areas of lesser urban dynamism regarding economic sustainability of growing population base. The third principal component which explain 8.73% of the total variance in data set has successfully brought out the above phenomena through a set of variables which identify themselves positively with over concentration of economically active population with lesser mobility and work participation rates resulting in congestion, crowding, large family size and high dependency ratio. This principal component also identifies itself negatively with all the developmental aspect of healthy urban attribute like educational levels in general and especially of workers, female work participation rate, workers in other than household industry, quality housing with basic urban amenities and so on. Therefore, this principal component is being labeled as 'Traditional Urbanization and Urban Decay'.

In Indian set up of urban society, the history and tradition of urbanization dynamics are significant. Earlier cities in case of Uttar Pradesh were mainly originated due to their strategic location with a stable agro based economy. In the entire Ganga Plain especially in Upper Ganga Plain, the towns evolved as a result of functional linkages provided by an agricultural economy. The prime condition, of the initiation of the urbanization process as well established, is the release of sizeable agricultural workers from the occupations of land. This had set in the process of urbanization in the historical past, the tradition of which is still continued. The agriculture related small scale and cottage industries dot the number of small size towns, which after attaining a certain level of self-sufficiency show no sign of further growth and expansion. No fresh economic incentives for attracting migrants seem to be at work. The population seems to be rooted in the place of origin mainly engrossed in the traditional work inherited from their forefathers

The above phenomenon is reflected in a very high positive loading on main workers within active age group (+0.78) especially males (+0.76). The corresponding negative loadings on the educational level of workers particularly males above graduate (-0.86) also commensurate with a negative loading (-0.77) on tertiary workers. Even other than household workers record a weak positive loading (+0.24). However, a mild negative loading (-0.40) on female workers in active age group and negative loading (-0.39) with female literacy within 15-59 age group bespeak of the status of women in the society. With more number of children within the child bearing age group of 15-49 (+0.51) and less age at marriage for females (+0.24), it seems a tradition bound society with a joint family system in which dependency ratio both for juvenile (+0.36) and senile (+0.30) are significant. The household size is large, more than 5 persons (+0.52) with a high crowding status of more than 6 persons with 2-room facility (+0.71). Other developmental parameters are all either highly insignificant or inversely related.

However, the above process has manifested itself in spatial perspective in varying degree of intensity resulting in definition spatial patterns. The districts recording higher component scores signify a degenerative urban environment and vice versa (Fig.30).

Within the component scores of 13-25 lies very high category under which 11 districts of Ganga Plain cover Pilibhit, Budaun,

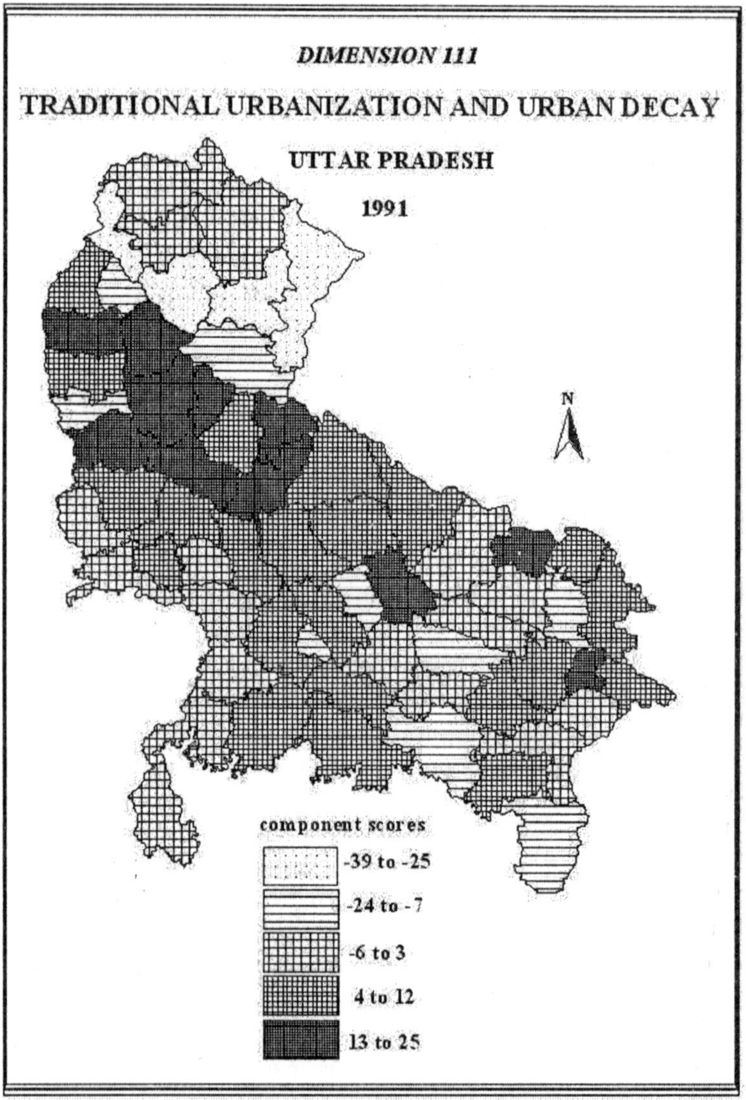
DIMENSION 111
TRADITIONAL URBANIZATION AND URBAN DECAY
UTTAR PRADESH
1991
N
component scores
-39 to -25
-24 to -7
-6 to 3
4 to 12
13 to 25

Fig. 30

Moradabad, Bijnor, Bulandshahr Muzaffarnagar, and Hardwar, forming mainly a part of the traditional Rohilkhand Division of Upper Ganga Plain. As noticed earlier in PC II, this region has lost its former glory and regressing into economic backwardness due to lack of resources other than agriculture accompanied by a generally less educated less mobile population. Small-scale private enterprises even on household basis is a common mode of earnings. Due to prevalence of early marriage system, females are generally below graduate, with a resultant large family size and economic strains. Female literacy is not promoted as such. Another concentration occurs in Barabanki which suffer from very low level of urbanization and economic stagnation. Mau and Siddharthnagar are economically upcoming areas, though at present showing signs of degenerative quality of urban life.

The component loadings between 4 to 12 forms the high category recording 22 districts which cover considerable parts in southern Upper Ganga Plain and part of western Middle Ganga Plain extending south through Unnao and Kanpur Dehat to Fetahpur, Banda and Hamirpur. The eastern Ganga Plain includes Ballia, Azamgarh, Jaunpur, Deoria and Maharajganj along with Mirzapur in south. In western Uttar Pradesh, the districts of Saharanpur, Meerut, Rampur, Bulandshahr, Shahjahanpur, Aligarh and Mainpuri with a number of household industries have medium degree of urbanization. These districts are centers of small-scale industries as well as medium sized industries submitting returns. Apart from the economic variations, a culture of family value and system seems to be running through all these districts. On a broader scale of generalization a rather rural oriented, upper middle class family with its own sets values and culture, seems to be currently engaged mainly in tertiary occupations. Thus, this dimension is more oriented towards socio-cultural differentiation than economic segregation of urban population of Uttar Pradesh.

The medium category is defined by -6 to 3 component scores which are loaded by 17 districts covering the south western plateau region in Lalitpur, Jhansi, Etawah, Agra to Mathura. The next belt is defined by a group of district in eastern Uttar Pradesh in which Ghazipur, Varanasi, Pratapgarh, Rai Bareily, Faizabad, Basti and Gonda are included. In the hill districts, Chamoli, Garhwal and Uttar

Kashi also lie in the same category. It is the highly urbanized districts of Agra, Jhansi along with Varanasi in this group that reflect the streak of traditionalism as practiced even in highly urbanized areas. In Uttar Pradesh, as only where else in any agricultural society, it is the local tradition bond population that has to interact with culturally different and educated migrants from outside the state. As a result, a dualistic nature of urban society results with a broad traditional and a narrow modern base of population, as is being experienced in the above regions. In contrast, the industrial cities of Mathura, Agra, Etawah, are experiencing in migrants of rural back ground with a norm of large family size. The hill districts of extreme north like Uttar Kashi, Chamoli, Tehri-Garhwal since have a narrow economic base; a limit is naturally imposed by the physical environment and lack of infrastructure. All the above district are experiencing problems of urban infrastructural development, lack of basic urban amenities and decreasing quality of life due to local as well regional urban economic influences.

The low category records component scores within the range of -7 to -24 within which 9 districts cover isolated pockets all over the Ganga Plain. Understandably this category includes places where due to modernization a change in the outlook towards society is being recorded. These include the highly urbanized districts of Kanpur Nagar, Lucknow and Ghaziabad. However, the inclusion of Hardwar, Faizabad and Gorakhpur along with Sonbhadra forms an area of socio-cultural change. Nainital rich in educational institutes, though low urbanized holds bright future prospects as its fast emerging as a service centre.

The very low category defined by the component scores between -25 to -39 in which 4 districts of hill region lie, signifying higher scale of development. With a culture of its own, this area has come up as either for tourism, pilgrimage, forestry or establishment institutions of higher prestige like Survey of India, Regional Remote Sensing Center, Forest Research Institute in Dehradun. Thus Dehradun, Tehri Garhwal and Pithoragarh to a certain extent justify the category which they occupy otherwise it is basically the small base of urban population which yields higher percentage values in face of very small absolute values on nearly all developmental parameter of urbanization.

Thus, the present dimension has been able to delineate areas in Uttar Pradesh that had a history of indigenous pattern of urbanization and isolated areas where urbanization developed due to excess of rural workers in relation to rural occupations. The high rate of growth of population in general, both for urban and rural areas characterize it. The increasing man land ratio has promoted out migration of agricultural population to cities. In face of lack of mineral resources, cities evolved through the mechanism operated by agricultural economy. The hierarchy of the towns was defined by mainly medium and small sized towns. Few mono or bi functional cities dominated urban landscape but could not serve for surrounding region consistently due to rapid changes occurring in the behavior of consumer society itself. A degenerative effect is thus on sight in which the population uphold by the past history of galore, continues to reside and adjust itself in spite of all environmental problems arising out of an stagnant rather regressing urban economy. The over all efficiency of this dimension can however, is best explain by its role in highlighting the socio cultural aspect of urbanization in Uttar Pradesh.

Principal Component IV: Female Education and Tertiary Urbanization

As opposed to the preceding dimension in which the role of traditional societies in determining the direction of urbanization was identified, the present dimension associates the effects of modern urbanization explaining 4.33 per cent of the total variance in the data set. The impact of urbanization on any urbanizing society can be assessed through urbanism (Wirth, L: 1965) in which female literacy, education and work participation rates emerge as a strong index of modernization. In western world, female education and urbanization are synonyms but in case of Uttar Pradesh, a typical traditional bound society with its deep roots in agricultural economy, the emerging dimension assumes greater significance.

The indicators that load significantly on this dimension are educational levels of female in general along with urbanization. The females with less than graduate but above metric load very high (+0.83) followed by female workers less than graduate (+0.63) with strong positive loadings. The females with above graduate load moderate (+0.49) and female workers with more than graduate (+0.39) record a weak positive loading. The tertiary workers load moderately (+0.53) with a corresponding moderate positive loadings on intra district migration (+0.55) from rural areas and intra state migration (+0.45) from urban areas. The negative loadings commensurate and the strong negative loadings on secondary workers (-0.78) and migration outside the state from rural areas (-0.59) suggest that female mobility from rural areas in case of long distance migration is discouraged. The female work participation is also not in favor of secondary sector of economy. A corresponding higher loading (+0.61) on large household size with more than 6 persons suggest this phenomena is generally common in middle class status families, possibly more for economic compulsion for majority of undergraduate females who generally take up jobs through intra district migration from rural areas. However, for postgraduate females it seems to be a long migration stream mainly from urban areas and further indicates a desire to be economically independent, a sign of fast modernizing urban society. The phenomena conceptualized in a set up of a traditional society reflects the on going socio cultural changes that a convention bound society like Uttar Pradesh is experiencing. Thus the dimension is labeled as 'Female Education and Tertiary Urbanization'.

The districts loading high on this dimension are better representative of female literacy and tertiary urbanization and vice versa. The manifestation of this process in spatial perspective highlights certain areas, in terms of distribution of component score (Fig.31).

In the very high category between 5-8 component loadings, 7 districts are included. In Hill region, Dehradun a highly urbanized area has already a quality status on urbanization scenario. It has very less density of urban population and in general an air of affluency with medium household size. The nature of the service sector needs two types of female workers, either in highly specialized jobs, the institutions demand especially trained females or the tourism industry which is capable of absorbing female workers belonging to both educated and less educated background. Pithoragarh, Almora, Garhwal, Tehri Garhwal and Hardwar are manifesting very high

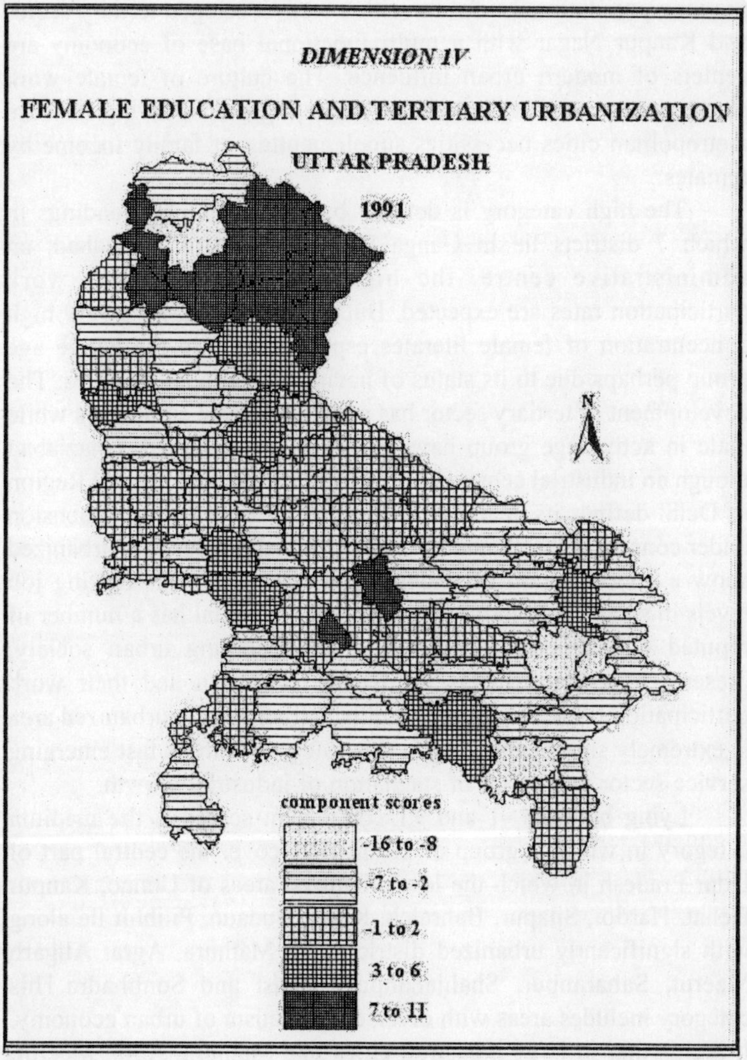
DIMENSION IV
FEMALE EDUCATION AND TERTIARY URBANIZATION
UTTAR PRADESH
1991
N
component scores
-16 to -8
-7 to -2
-1 to 2
3 to 6
7 to 11

Fig. 31

concentration of population in active age group. The economy though mono functional, is opening up new economic vistas for growing population. Lucknow with a well-developed tertiary sector and Kanpur Nagar with a multi functional base of economy are centers of modern urban influence. The culture of female work participitation is prevalent as the escalating cost of living in these metropolitan cities necessities supplementing of family income by females.

The high category is defined by 2-4 component loadings in which 7 districts lie in Ganga Plain. In case of Allahabad, an administrative centre, the higher educated females work participation rates are expected. But Gorakhpur shows a very high concentration of female literates especially within the active age group perhaps due to its status of having educational facilities. The development of tertiary sector has attracted female employees while male in active age group have generally out migrated. Ghaziabad though an industrial center, its proximity to National Capital Region of Delhi defines its degree of modernity in terms of the dimension under concern. Etawah and Firozabad, though moderately urbanized show a concentration of undergraduate females with varying job levels in small-scale industries especially. Nainital has a number of reputed educational institutes and an upcoming urban society, presents a good prospects for female education and their work participation rates. However, Bareilly, a traditionally urbanized area is extremely significant lying in this category with its fast emerging service sector as a result of stagnation of industrial growth.

Lying between -1 and +1 component scores is the medium category in which a group of 20 districts cover the central part of Uttar Pradesh in which the low urbanized areas of Unnao, Kanpur Dehat, Hardoi, Sitapur, Bahraich, Kheri, Budaun, Pilibhit lie along with significantly urbanized districts like Mathura, Agra, Aligarh Meerut, Saharanpur, Shahjahanpur, Jhansi and Sonbhadra.This category includes areas with diverse mechanism of urban economy. It seems that in large industrial cities like Mathura, Agra, Meerut, there is a rather more absorption of females in educated categories only perhaps on basis of job related requirements, while areas manifesting lower industrial concentration and higher service sector are absorbing females from various educational background in various jobs of related economic importance.

The low category lying between -11 to -6 component scores consists of 24 districts covering most part of Middle Ganga Plain especially in the east. This region roughly coincides with the area having very low level of urbanization. Bulandshahr, Bijnor, Moradabad, Rampur; along Tarai in Kheri, Pilibhit, Bahraich; in the eastern margins of the state and southern plateau region in Ballia, Deoria, Azamgarh, Gonda including Varanasi. In general, the districts identified under PC III as areas inhibited by traditional urban societies, are recording low on this dimension irrespective of their degree of urbanization. The reason may be the more number of females in the active age group who are non-working or simple housewives in spite of up to graduation level of education in most of the urban areas as female work participation is discouraged under such socio economic set up of the society.

The very low category loads component scores between -5 to -2 in which 4 districts cover eastern Uttar Pradesh in Azamgarh, Mau, Mirzapur and Tehri Garhwal in the northern hill region. In case of eastern Uttar Pradesh it is again a case of either traditionally urbanized area like Azamgarh not favoring working females or secondary workers dominating areas like Tehri Garhwal where limited economic opportunities are not conducive for development of service sector of economy for the absorption of female work force.

Over all, this dimension clearly isolated areas of female work participation in service sector of economy from mainly two strata of society.The first is the region where effective urbanization has promoted development of tertiary sector through multiplier effects of economy in which educated females either by choice or under economic compulsion are getting jobs like Kanpur Nagar, Lucknow and Allahabad. This category also shows female long distance migration from mainly urban areas. The second group comprises of districts, which are newly emerging on scene of urbanization catering to the services offered by females in higher, educational and socio economic strata like Dehradun, Nainital and Etawah. However, places dominated by traditional urban societies show slackness towards formal education of females and their resultant scope for absorption to service sector of economy. This dimension has further emphasized the attitude of females towards adoption of career. It seems that females prefer tertiary or service sector as the more suitable work environment.

The remaining dimension from V to X though significant as employed by the percentage trace through PCA does not help in any summary analysis of the results. A closer examination of the variables loading high under remaining respective PCA fail to unfold any underlying mechanism of urbanization in Uttar Pradesh. By closely scrutinizing the loadings on such principal components, a spurious correlation was found under which the high loadings does not reveal the process that has generated them

Thus, the principal component analysis produced a number of descriptive dimensions of levels of urbanization by sifting through a set of indicators conceived of as measuring a similar phenomena and identifying those with maximum variance within and least variation between themselves. It is noticeable that the indicators thus emerged a deterministic in defining direction and status to the levels of urbanization were not picked up so clearly by simply using bi-variate analysis as explained with every indictor for summarizing the process at state level in the preceding discussion.

CONCLUSION AND SUGGESTIONS

The study is focused on the spatial differentiation of urbanization status than its process, which could be more effectively displayed by spatio-temporal data. Despite of the limitations and constraints imposed by the selection of indicators and data set, the study has been successful in even finding out some on going dynamics of urbanization along with its present status in terms of levels of urbanization.

The foremost conclusion of the present study is that the levels of urbanization in Uttar Pradesh though very low, is showing extremely high regional variations exposing the underlying dynamics of urbanization which have ceased to be operative in most of the area irrespective of their present levels of urbanization. As could be expected it is not unfolding a mechanism conducive for further urban-economic development, rather is leading to a situation where saturations in degree of urbanization is resulting. The concept of inter-dependent development (Bannister: 1975, Sheppard: 1977) emphasizes the role of regional economy, as an interdependent part of the national economy and the regional growth and development which seem to be lacking here. Though the nature of uneven development over space highlights the role of relative dominance of concentration and dispersion forces over time, in the present study area it seems that the role of concentration forces have subsided and the resultant spatial differentiation is related more to the forces of dispersion acting at various levels of intensity. This is more so noticeable in case of areas where regional economy has ceased to be dominated by any city or economic activity of prime importance. This phenomenon of urban deconcentrtion or spatial decentralization has been identified as 'polarization reversal' (Richardson:1977) which was also equated with the idea of counter urbanization and regional dispersal (Berry and Gillard: 1977, Hall and Hay: 1980). However, in case of less developed countries,

LDCs, the concept was analyzed with the fast growth rates of urban population reaching a transitional stage in their patterns of economic development (Townroe and Keen: 1984) in case of São Paulo, Brazil. In the present study no temporal data was available to trace the point of time at which reversal of urbanization has started. However, while analyzing the patterns arising out of process of urbanization in Uttar Pradesh, the same phenomena was noticed broadly on the basis of the existing levels of urbanization and the cessation of the developmental dynamics as reflected by the key variables which are discussed briefly below.

The striking feature of the urbanization pattern and underlying process is hinting at the areas in Ganga Plain where initial economic feasibility has declined. A stagnant rather dysfunctional economy has resulted in which the parameters point at a situation where out-migration of active age group males has already reached a point where higher urban sex ratio has resulted. It further leads to an increase in proportion of females with more dependency ratio both juvenile and senile. A corresponding increase in household size with lack of basic amenities points towards the standards of living that suggest middle-income group scenario of congested parts of cities, possibly the old residential areas. The whole of Ganga Plain extending from western Uttar Pradesh, with sound agricultural economy and high to medium levels of urbanization mainly agro-based, to the eastern Uttar Pradesh where agriculture is suffering and percentage of urban population is also low in absence of any supportive industries, under the third dimension identifies itself with traditional urbanization and urban decay. The few districts of western Uttar Pradesh in which Bijnor, Moradabad and Rampur are part of traditional urban society of Rohilkhand division along with Budaun, Shahjahanpur, Pilibhit, Muzaffarnagar, Bulandshahr with Barabanki, Mau and Maharajganj are analyzed as areas in which population is less mobile, more tradition bound and less exposed to modernization effect par se of urbanization. Therefore, early marriage of females and resultant break in their education acquisition process in general deprives them to be an economically productive member of the family. Since the community is engaged mainly in business and commerce related activities with textiles, sugar mills, wood craft, brassware and other handicraft, the share of female workers is highly selective either to low paid jobs or very highly paid service sector of economy. The household industries widespread all over the above region employ less educated workers at minimal wages. Large family size with medium income levels is bringing down living standards in most of the area especially medium urbanized areas with effective urbanization.

Rohilkhand division consisting of Bijnor, Moradabad, Budaun, Bareilly, Shahjahanpur, Pilibhit and Rampur is the worst sufferer. Culturally a very rich region, the lack of industrial resources has kept this region into backwardness on educational levels in general. However, the metropolitan influence of National Capital Region of Delhi has benefited these areas in establishing small-scale industries.

The eastern part of Middle Ganga Plain consisting mainly of core group of districts of Ballia, Mau, Azamgarh, Jaunpur, Deoria, Maharajgang and Sidharthnagar is suffering from natural calamities, decreasing land productivity, lack of natural resources and consequently a low level of urbanization. Regional economic disparities are very sharp here resulting in highly uneven development of towns of generally medium and small population size. In case of Jaunpur, Ballia, Azamgarh there has been out-migration of active population of males. Remittances paid to the places of origin by migrants have tried to maintain a minimum level of living standard but general atmosphere of traditional culture of conservatism has reflected in all aspect of life including female literacy and their working status. Large family size, high dependency ratio and lesser mobility of females clearly reflect the aspects of modernism as associated with degree of urbanization are lacking in this area. Thus, economic causes seem to have aggravated non-economic causes. However, Planning Commission of India has also identified eastern part of Uttar Pradesh as economically backward region.

The northern Upper Ganga Plain, since agriculturally prosperous has also promoted a more stabilized scenario of urbanization in terms of space hierarchy of towns. Meerut, Ghaziabad, Aligarh, Mathura, Agra, have availed the locational benefits of proximity to National Capital Region (NCR) of Delhi. The functional diversity of these districts has considerably reflected itself in increasing job opportunities through multiplier effect. However, the small-scale industries of Meerut, the industrial base of Mathura and Agra seem to have lost their former hold on the economy. The weakening functional linkage is suggested by lesser percentage of in-migrant as a result of decreasing economic pull of these districts. The family status shows large family size with an increasing work participation ratio by low educated females especially in non-agricultural category. This was further confirmed by the medium value recorded by the fourth dimension of female education and tertiary urbanization. Ghaziabad is emerging very strong on the industrialization scenario of Uttar Pradesh being a part of National Capital Region of Delhi. The districts of modern urbanization are relatively few. Kanpur Nagar tops the urbanization scene of Uttar Pradesh with 84.24 per cent of its population as urban it has a density of 6622 persons per square kilometer, the decadal variation of population was only 23.89 per cent compared with a state average of 38.73 per cent showing signs of saturation during 1981-91. Even the sex ratio there is declining suggesting the presence of more males in active age group. This might result in slowing down the natural growth rate of its urban population in future. So the present status of Kanpur Nagar in the urban scenario of Uttar Pradesh seeks further enlightenment. The urban living condition are going to be appalling. The active age group population concentration might result in over-population if the families of the migrant workers join in. Medium sized families are common with high room density and shortage of electricity and drinking water. Lucknow is an administrative centre, has limited industrial base. However, the growing tertiary sector is attracting migrants especially highly educated females. Allahabad another administrative centre, has maintained its position on level of urbanization due to expanding tertiary sector in which again female work participation is appreciable. The region in and around the bipolar region of urban growth of Lucknow and Kanpur Nagar, seem to have generated pulses for economic growth as is shown under the second dimension of dynamic urbanization and urban development. Districts like Faizabad. Barabanki, Bahraich, Gonda, Sultanpur, Jaunpur, connecting Varanasi, Mirzapur till Sonbhadra form almost a continuous region with economic potential for development.

However, Jhansi, though very high on urbanization level with its military base, seems to have lost its former attraction for migrants. The Ganga Plain, in general, is showing tendency towards economic saturation as suggested by the lesser percentage of in migrants.

The hill region by virtue of their physiography imposes a limit upon physical expansion of agricultural activities and development of infrastructure. However, at present the tourism, pilgrimage, hydel-power projects and location of government institutions have certainly given a direction to the present level of urbanization. Although the hill districts are declared backward region of Uttar Pradesh, the position of Dehradun and Tehri Garhwal is different.

Dehradun has already emerged as a strong centre for urbanization with its multifunctional urban economic base. Apart from its strategic significance, it is a centre for establishment of prestigious government offices and institutions like Forest Research Institute, Indian Institute for Remote Sensing, Survey of India and many others. Dehradun is also providing a beautiful site for the resettlement colonies of retired service personnel from Indian Army and other prestigious government organizations due to its environmental sustainability as against the congested and polluted urban places of Ganga Plain. The growing farmhouse culture is also inviting migration of affluent members of the Indian society. It is widely selected for its tourist. Tehri Garhwal with its water resources has enormous potential for hydro-electricity generation. Almora and Nainital by virtue of their significance on service sector especially education and tourism are fast developing. The rest of the hill region districts are areas of under development being further depressed by the natural calamities and harsh climate. However, the recent insurgence of tourism and religious activities are attracting large volume of migrants to there areas.

The southern Plateau Region of Uttar Pradesh presents a contrast in the respective eastern and western plateau of Jhansi and Mirzapur divisions. The states of Rajasthan, Madhaya Pradesh and Bihar, all of which are agriculturally under developed surround the east, south and south-western margins of Uttar Pradesh. There are mostly short distance migrants both rural and urban who prefer the border districts due to the availability of economic opportunities especially in Sonbhadra with its mega projects while the rest of the southern plateau records medium rate of in migrants. Lalitpur in the west also has a hydel-power project with limited job opportunities

The dimensions underlying the process of urbanization are not defining any particular mechanism of urbanization in southern plateau region. Basically areas with either traditional urbanization as in Jhansi, Hamirpur or nearly stagnated economy as in Lalitpur, Banda, Jalaun and Mirzapur are suffering. The economic viability of the areas is not very promising except Sonbhadra. A noticeable feature of the area is percentage of total female workers, which is medium to high base with higher education background in Sonbhadra and Jhansi and with lower educational background in rest of southern plateau are basically engaged in tertiary services. The dependency ratio in all these districts excluding Lalitpur and Sonbhadra is high suggesting an economic pressure upon the family income as shown by decreasing quality of houses with depleting basic urban amenities and corresponding rise in household size. Since the area is not densely populated, the density of household records low.

From the preceding discussion few significant dynamics further emerge regarding levels of urbanization in Uttar Pradesh.

The first, is the significantly low to very low percentage of males in active age group in the whole Ganga Plain barring Kanpur Nagar and Lucknow. This seemingly low active population results in persistently high urban sex ratio compared to the state average, all over Ganga Plain. It further reflects the phenomena of out-migration of active population since the in-migration rates of males are also low to very low suggesting the underlying dynamics of urbanization. The whole area is surviving on agriculture and its related occupations in the absence of any other competitive economic resource. It seems that the initial pull of the area in the form of either agro based industries or allied service sector has lessened therefore, there is a de-polarization of urbanization process rather decentralization of concentrated agricultural economy. This is also brought about by the decadal variation of urban population for 1981 to 1991 where the whole Ganga plain is recording medium to low rates of urban growth excluding few districts like Ghaziabad, and Lucknow with very high degree of urbanization along with district like Faizabad, Gorakhpur, Mahrajganj with low levels of urbanization. This phenomena can better be termed as 'subsistence urbanization', in which non-basic service sector has taken over the basic sector of urban economy.

The second point of concern is the evidence of the phenomena of polarization reversal as was noticed in western cities in face of highly urbanized centers with developed economies (Richardson: 1977). In case of less developed countries, there was fast growth rates of population, which are reaching a transitional stage in their pattern of economic development (Townroe and Keen: 1984). However, the phenomenon of reversal is generally traced in spatio-temporal perspective, which is outside the purview of the present study. Therefore, the study makes use of the indicators recording the present status of urbanization, which was able to delineate areas of spatial contiguity but functional continuity in the form of spatial patterns of urbanization.

At any given point of time the emerging level of urbanization is an outcome of the underlying dynamics of urban growth. The process variable like decadal variation of population easily evaluates the cumulative outcome of urbanization process. But the spatial differentiation of any phenomena in terms of emerging patterns also explains the trend of spatial concentration of population, industry, income or other socio-political forces. In this context, the position of Kanpur Nagar and Agra, need special mention. Urbanization necessitates in-migration of specialized skilled workers for the functioning of various sectors of urban economy. Both Kanpur Nagar and Agra are very highly urbanized with a dominant industrial sector of large and medium industries per lakh of population of 19.20 and 15.20 respectively compared to a state average of 5.4 in 1991. Though on the dimension of dynamic urbanization and urban development these two districts recorded very high and high respectively, still lesser male and female in-migration, very low in-migration from short distance both from rural and urban areas are recorded. Considering the districts are surrounded by an underdeveloped hinterland with very low to low percentage of total workers in active age group, one of the lowest decadal variation rate during 18-91 is recorded which is a reflective of decreasing economic pull of the area. It is further suggestive of a stage when the economies of scale are rather giving way to urbanization diseconomies. A stagnation level in the present economy is indicated which might be an early sign of the onset of polarization reversal especially in case of Kanpur Nagar.

For Agra, the tourism industry requires tertiary sector development. However, the concentration of semi-skilled in-migrants mainly from rural areas across the state is forming a major share of urban growth, consequently urbanization. However, stagnation in economy is again pointed out which can be taken as a sign of polarization reversal. Although in the present study, the phenomena is being generalized on district level, it is the location of cities in relation to their interaction field within and across district boundaries that define their mechanism.

Thus, a fragile balance in the urbanization economies of Uttar Pradesh can be noticed. The whole of Ganga Plain is studded with towns with generally medium and small size whose economic base is highly tilted towards agriculture related occupations. The economy is already showing signs of saturation in an urban society which was itself only surviving at a subsistence level regarding dissemination of urban functions. The absence of any core region of urban economic development or growth even in case of Kanpur Nagar, is a suggestive of a saturation level where the existing urban economy is not any more supportive of the level of urbanization.

Districts with higher percentage of urbanization are showing trends towards metropolitan growth under the impact of which lop-sided development of the urban hierarchy is taking place like in case of Ghaziabad. The multiplier effect of large cities in Ganga Plain is on decrease due to the absence of a balanced industrial development. As a result, the marginally urbanized areas like the northern hill region and southern plateau region are showing signs of further concentration of population on the basis of power resources and its related employment potentials. However, the region lying between Lucknow, Kanpur Nagar, and Varanasi, Mirzapur form aregion for potential economic growth. This belt is composed of districts of Rae Bareli, Sultanpur, Faizabad, Jaunpur and includes Bahraich, Gonda in Tarai region. Along with the forest based industries, handicraft industries especially handloom and handiwork, there is a scope for future employment generation potentials as these items have a ready market for foreign countries.

Thus, it can be concluded that Uttar Pradesh though a low urbanized and economically backward state is showing pronounced variations in the level of urbanization under the impact of a dual set of urbanization forces. A narrow modern urbanization economy exists side by side with a broad based agriculturally oriented urban economy.

Suggestions

The impact of National capital Region is very well marked on the urbanization pattern of Uttar Pradesh. Apart from the inclusion of Meerut, Ghaziabad and Bulandshahr in NCR, other 7 priority urban centers have also been identified. The direct beneficiary of this project is going to be the western Uttar Pradesh which is though highly urbanized, will be experiencing more rate of urban growth and urbanization in near future. Already the urbanization influence of NCR is perpetuating from the west encompassing the area around Ghaziabad, Saharanpur, Meerut, Aligarh, Mathura, Firozabad and Etawah, with full development of Rapid Mass Transit System, a burden on already congested urbanized parts like Mathura, Agra and Meerut is in purview.

The Integrated Development of Small and Medium Towns (IDSMT) initiated in 1979-80 has helped to control flow of out-migration from small and medium size towns, subsequently reducing flow to large cities leading to a balanced and integrated development of rural and urban areas. However, IDMST had a localized effect on the urbanization scenario of Uttar Pradesh under which 24 towns have been identified giving preference to districts towns, sub-divisional towns, and mandi towns. It is being implemented in towns having 5 lakh (earlier it was 3 lakhs) as per 1991 estimates. The scheme provides for development of a related number of potential growth centers by adopting a whole 'town-development' approach rather than diluting the funds among a large number of towns.

At the grass root level, the role of Peri-Urban Growth Satellite Towns can prove effective under the Cooperative Sector, it focuses upon to develop new township in areas adjoining large or metro-cities to promote spatially balanced system of urban settlements.

This strategy can be significant for districts having effective urbanization on one hand and on the other suffering from decreasing decadal growth rates like Kanpur Nagar, Agra, Varanasi, Mathura, Allahabad and Mirzapur.

Age and sex specificity of literacy levels have shown a higher occurrence in the hill districts of Uttar Pradesh Himalayas. In Ganga Plain, it is surprisingly the districts of Etawah, Rai Bareli and Bahraich, which are emerging on the aspect. The female work participation in tertiary services with higher education is a phenomenon of Dehradun, which is an administrative cum service centre. However, the position of Etawah and Bulandshahr is instigating and encouraging, as these two districts are experiencing problems of under-development due to small household industries. If these areas are provided with the Urban Self Employment Programme (USEP) a part of SJRSY, to help poor women group for setting up micro-enterprises, it will help with coping of the existing urban employment problem.

The pockets of very high dependency ratio and weak economic base have been identified in the eastern most part of eastern Middle Ganga Plain in which Deoria, Ballia, Gorakhpur including Varanasi spread in the form a belt. Employment generation programmes especially home based economic activities for handloom workers and such economic groups by Urban Basic Services for the Poor (UBSP), Nehru Rojgar Yojna (NRY) and Integrated Rural Development Programme (IRDP) for micro-enterprises can prove beneficial. Swarna Jayanti Shahri Rozgar Yojna (SJRSY) launched in 1997 was aimed for community empowerment through self-employment generation programmes, should be implemented more rigorously.

The whole of Ganga Plain is suffering from lack of quality housing irrespective of degree of urbanization. The eastern part of Uttar Pradesh represents a picture of dismay in face of economic deprivations. Therefore, a need to promote adequate and affordable housing as promoted by NHHP of 1998, through activating housing cooperatives. In case of large urban centers, a private sector partnership in housing as developed in Lucknow through Lucknow Development Authority Model can be practiced for congested areas having effective urbanization along with high degree of urbanization.

For urban areas without effective urbanization, there is a need for economically affordable housing along with basic amenities through a social mandate on private sector, to provide a specific percentage reservation for the poor in the form of MIG and LIG housings as directed by NHHP in 1998.The basic difference between shortage and requirement has to be taken care of as it is the 'will to spend' and 'will to live' as independent family system that assumes greater significance in case of tradition bound societies of Uttar Pradesh. The Building Material and Technology Promotion Council (BMTPC) and the Housing Urban Development Corporation (HUDCO) have promoted cost effective building material and technology in this regard for providing shelter to urban poor. There is need for reassessing housing need in the socio-economic background of Uttar Pradesh as single-family dwelling might not work in face of the culture of joint family system or even extended as is noticed in especially eastern part of Uttar Pradesh.

Thus, shelter delivery, access to basic services and a sustained livelihood with a view to sustained urban economic development should be targeted with a time frame. The slums and low income informal settlements house nearly 25 per cent of the population of the urban population of Uttar Pradesh living in semi-permanent or even temporary structures. Only 53 per cent of the total urban population is supplied with the basic minimum needs of drinking water, electricity and serviceable toilets. Access to basic services programme was instituted by National Housing and Habitat Policy 1998, through policy initiatives and programme ascertained to supply water, sanitations facilities, waste management system to both urban areas and slums, has to be more effectively implemented.

Though a land locked state with the urban economic influence perpetuating from National Capital Region of Delhi, there is going to be an increasing pressure of urban population within the sphere of influence defined by 24 priority regions of NCR, which encompasses areas around Ghaziabad. The regional distribution of the proposed investment of Rs 51,02,00 million, out of which the western districts especially Ghaziabad and its neighboring region has claimed for nearly half of the proposed investment due to localization of urbanization economies. The regional urban economy is going to be more skewed with its implementation.

The Centre for Monitoring Indian Economy (CMIE) has

identified the low level of total investment in Central Government undertaking which is only 8.6 per cent in 1992-93 (India's average of 16.6%). Though the Uttar Pradesh Urban Planning and Development Act, 1973, have covered KAVAL towns (Kanpur, Agra, Varanasi, Allahabad and Lucknow), as a part of comprehensive planning, still the unified hierarchy of urban settlements could not be expected. A fast increase of urban population in western Uttar Pradesh after the completion of Mass Transit System is under preview, which can further accentuate the disparities in the regional pattern of urbanization.

With pronounced regional disparities in the forces of urbanization, its environmental implication has to be given due attention. The model plans working in this direction should be reviewed like the Environmental Management Plan (EMP) of Kanpur which is aimed for sustainable management of Urban environment of Kanpur city. The plan preparative includes assessment of the environment quality, identification of the environmental 'hot' spots through extensive services, environmental modeling and G I S mapping to propose an Environmental Management Plan. Such studies in other industrial cities like, Mathura, Agra and Ghaziabad are required

However, the basic problem is how to modulate the future course of urbanization in Uttar Pradesh? Kanpur Nagar, Agra and the whole of Rohilkhand Divsion have started showing signs of regressing urban economy. A phenomena of saturated urbanization rather reversal is being noticed especially in Agra and in Kanpur Nagar. The economy of these areas is showing signs of saturation as multiplier effect of the economy is on decline with resultant urban decay. The Government plans like Generator of Economic Momentum (GEMS), National Capital Region (NCR) and Integrated Development of Small and Medium Towns (IDSMT) are definitely going to be beneficial for the area under immediate focus. However, the NCR can further accentuate the regional disparities between the western Uttar Pradesh and eastern Uttar Pradesh. IDSMT will benefit Uttar Pradesh as the limit for these towns has been raised from 3 to 5 lakhs. The central and eastern part of Uttar Pradesh have been showing very poor growth rate of urban population, there is a need to enhance the urban economic base as the region has a hinterland susceptible to send out-migrants like Bihar, West Bengal,

Orissa and Madhya Pradesh. The area is well served with communication lines and has rich human resource base as reflected upon by increased literacy levels. There is a need for re-assessing the resources, both economic and non-economic, from the point of view of a comprehensive regional planning perspective, which should be based on carrying capacity planning concept (NIUA: 1996) for sustainable urban development and urbanization in the area. Since it is generally a slowly developing area with tradition bound families with very less mobility, the community participation power has to be realized in every field of urban economic policy plans as also proposed through the emerging concept of 'Urban Governance' so to attain a balanced and integrated urbanization levels in Uttar Pradesh.

BIBLIOGRAPHY

Books and Journals

Abler, R. Adams, J. and Gould, P. 1971. *Spatial Organization: The Geographer's View of the World,* Prentice Hall, N.J.

Adhikari, S. 1978. Origin and Evolution of Capital Cities in Ancient India: A Politico-geographical Analysis, *Geographical Bulletin of India*, vol. III: 31-37.

Adrey, R.1966. *The Territorial Imperative*, Dell, New York.

Aggarwal, A.N. 1976. *Indian Economy*, Vikas Publishing House, New Delhi.

Aggarwal, P.C. and Khan, Z.T. 1982. Functional Characteristics of the Outgrowth of Class I and II Towns of Madhya Pradesh, *The Geographer*, Vol XXIX, No.1: 41-55.

Ahmad A. and Anjani K. S. 1981. Public Distribution Systems in Indian Cites, *Geojournal*, Supplement Issue, Vol. IV, pp. 27-35.

Alam, S.M. 1976. Indian Cities and Western Theories of Urban Growth. In *Urbanization in Developing Countries*, Alam and Pokshishevsky (eds.), Osmania University, Hyderabad, pp. 455-474.

Alam, S.M., Rao, R.M. and Gopi, K.N. 1974. Trends and Patterns of Metropolitan Development in India, *Occasional Paper, No. 3,* Centre for Urban Research, Osmania University, Hyderabad.

Alonso, W. 1968. Urban and Regional Imbalances in Economic Development, *Economic Development and Cultural Change*, No. 3, pp. 1-14.

Alonso, W. 1971. A Theory of the Urban Land Market. In *Internal Structure of theCity: Readings and Space and Environment,* L. Bourne (ed.), Oxford University Press, pp. 154-59.

Amis, P. 1992. *Urban Management in Uganda: Survival Under Stress*, The Institutional Framework of Urban Government: Case Study no. 5, Development Administration Group, INLOGOV, University of Birmingham, Birmingham.

Amos, F.J.C. 1984. Madras Metamorphosis : Spatial Planning for Growth, *Nagarlok*, Vol. XVI, No 4, pp. 11-19.

Ara, R. 1980. Distortions in the Isotropism of Urban Influence in Lucknow District, *The Geographer*, Vol.XXVII, No.1, pp.51-55.

Aziz, A. 1981a. Dimension of Urbanization and Quality of Urban Life in Uttar Prdesh, *The Geographer*; Vol. XXVIII, No.1, pp. 17-22.

Aziz, A. 1981b. System of Cities in India, *The Geographer*,Vol. XXIII, No. 2, pp. 47-60.

Aziz, A. 1982. Growth Status of Towns of Uttar Pradesh, *The Geographer*, Vol. XXIX, No.1, pp. 25-30.

Aziz, A. 1983. Man land Ratio in the Towns of Uttar Pradesh, *The Geographer*, Vol. XXX, No. 2, pp. 37-48.

Baer, W. 1964. Regional Inequality and Economic Growth in Brazil, *Economic Development and Cultural Change,* No. 12, pp. 258-65.

Bagchi, K.G. 1980. Urban Renewal-Some Thoughts, *Geographical Review of India*, Vol. XIII, No. 3, pp. 201-205.

Bala, R. 1980. Some Hypothesis on Urban Growth in India, *Population Geography*, Vol. 2, pp. 59-77.

Bannister,G. 1975.Population Change in Southern Ontario, *Annals of Association of American Geographers* 65,177-88.

Bansal, S.C. 1974. Adequacy of Services in the Saharanpur City Region, *The Geographical Observer*, Vol. X, pp. 1-8.

Bartone, C. 1990. Sustainable Responses to Growing Urban Environmental Crisis, Urban Development Division, *(mimeo),* World Bank, Washington D.C.

Batty, M. 1978. Urban Models in Planning Process. In *Geography and the Urban Environment,* D. Herbert and R. Johnston (eds.), John Wiley, New York.

Beaver, S.1975. *Demographic Transition Theory Re-interpreted,* Lexington Books, Lexington.

Berry, B. 1988. Counterurbanization, *International Regional Science Review*, No. 11, pp. 221-6.

Berry, B., Conkling, E. and Ray, D. 1976. The *Geography of Economic System,* Prentice Hall, Englewood Cliffs, N.J.

Berry, B.J. 1963. Commercial Structure and Commercial Blight. *Research Paper No:85,* Department of Geography, University of Chicago.

Berry, B.J. 1973. *The Human Consequences of Urbanization: Divergent Paths in the Urban Experience of Twentieth Century*, St. Martin's Press, New York.

Berry, B.J.L and Gillard,Q. 1977. *The Changing Shape of Metropolitan America : Commuting Patterns, Urban Fields and Decentralization Processes 1960-70*, Ballinger, Cambridge.

Berry, B.J.L. 1968. A Synthesis of Formal and Functional Regions Using a General Field Theory of Spatial Behaviour. In *Spatial Analysis : A Reader,* B.J.L. Berry and D.F. Marble (eds.), Prentice Hall, Engle Wood Cliff, New Jersey, pp. 419-28.

Berry, B.J.L. 1976. *Urbanization and Counter Urbanization,* Sage Publications, Beverly Hills, Calif.

Berzina, M. Ya and Pokshishevsky, V.V. 1976. Non-Indigenous Population in Indian Cities", In *Urbanization in Developing Countries*, Alam and Pokshishevsky (eds.), Osmania University, Hyderabad, pp. 307-320.

Betroglia, C., Leonardi, G. and Wilson, A. (eds.),1990: *Urban Dynamics: Designing an Integrated Model*, Routledge, New York.

Bhalla, G.S. 1983. Small and Intermediate Towns in India's Regional Development, *Indian Architect*, Vol. XXV, pp. 79-80.

Bhalla, G.S. and Kundu, A. 1982. Small and Intermediate Cities in India – Regional Development. In *Small Cities and National Development*, O.P. Mathur, (ed.), United Nation Center for Regional Development, Nagoya.

Bhattacharya, B. 1979. *Urban Development in India*, Shree Publishing House. New Delhi.

Bisht, H.S., Tiwari, M.M.and Wihard V.K. 1980. A Short History of Urbanization of Almora, *Geographical Review of India*, Vol. XLII, No.3, pp. 245-253.

Biswas, K. 1983. Evolution and Implementation of the IUDP Scheme: A Policy Review, *Nagarlok*, Vol.XV, No.2, pp. 34-59.

Bondi, L. 1990. Feminism, Postmodernism and Geography: Space for Women, *Antipode*, Vol. 22, pp. 156-67.

Booth, A. 1976. *Urban Crowding and its Consequences*, Praeger Publishers, New York.

Bogue, J.B. and Zacharia, K.C. 1962. Urbanization and Migration in India. In *India's Urban Future*, Roy Turner (ed.), University of California, Berkley.

Bose, A. 1965. Six Decades of Urbanization in India, *Indian Economic and Social History Review*, Vol. II, No.1, January, pp. 23-41.

Bose, A. 1973. *Studies in India's Urbanization, 1901-71*, Tata McGraw Hill Publishing Company Ltd, New Delhi,

Bose, A. 1978. *India's Urbanization 1901-2001*, Tata McGraw Hill Publishing Company Ltd., New Delhi.

Bourne, L. 1981 *The Geography of Housing,* Wiley, New York.

Bourne, L.S. 1975. Conceptual Issues in Designing and Evaluating Strategies for National Urban Settlement Systems. In *National Settlement Strategies, East and West*, Harry Swain(Ed.), IIASA-CP, Luxembourg.

Bradley, David, Stephens, Carolyn, Cairncross, Sandy and Harpham, T. 1991. *A Review of Environmental Health Impacts in Developing Country Cities,* Urban Management Programme Discussion Paper No. 6, World Bank, UNDP and UNCHS (Habitat), Washington DC.

Brush, J. E. 1977. Growth and Spatial Structure of Indian Cities. In, *Indian Urbanization and Planning,* Allan G. Noble and A.K. Dutta (Eds.) Tata McGraw Hill Publishing Co., New Delhi.

Brush, J.E. 1972. The Spatial Structure of Cities in India: Pre-industrial or Post-colonial. In *International Geography*, W.P. Adams and Frederick M. Helleiner (Eds.), University of Toronto Press, Toronto, pp. 1303-1305.

Buch, M. N. 1979. The Fundamentals of a National Housing Policy, *Nagarlok* ;Vol. XI, No. 4, pp. 52-59.

Buch, M.N., 1981. Towards a Human Settlement Policy : Alternatives and Options, *Urban India*, Vol.I, pp.17-21.

Buch, M.N. 1982. Cities, *Urban India*, Vol. II, No. 3, pp. 3-6.

Bulsara, J. F. 1964. *Problems of Rapid Urbanization in India*, Popular Book Prakashan, Bombay.

Burnel, J. and Galster, G. 1992. Quality of Life: Measurement and Urban Size: An Empirical Note, *Urban Studies,* 29 pp. 727-35.

Burns, I. 1982. Metropolitan Growth in Transition. *Journal of Urban Economics* 11:112-29.

Cadman D. and Payne, G. (eds.) 1990. *The Living City: Towards a Sustainable Future*, Routledge, London.

Cadwallader, M. 1988. Urban Geography and Social Theory, *Urban Geography,* 9:227-51.

Cadwallader, M.1978. Urban Information and Preference Surfaces: Their Patterns, Structures and Interrelationship, *Geografiska Annaler*, 608, pp. 97-106.

Cadwallader, M.1986. Migration and Intra-urban Mobility. In *Population Geography: Progress and Prospect,* M. Pacione, (eds.),Croon and Helm, London. 257-83.

Cairncross, S, Hardoy, J. E. and Satterthwaite, D. 1990. TheUrban Context. In *The Poor Die Young: Housing and Health in Third World Cities*, Jorge E. Hardoy *et al.* (eds.), Earthscan Publications, London.

Cairncross, S. 1990. Water Supply and the Urban Poor. In *The Poor Die Young: Housing and Health in Third World Cities*, Jorge E Hardoy *et al* (eds.), Earthscan Publications, London. pp. 257-83.

Carter, H. 1981. *The Study of Urban Geography*, Edward Arnold, London.

Chakravarty, B. 1983. Dominance Pattern of Size Classes of Cities and Its Implications, *Nagarlok*, Vol. XV, No. 4, pp. 66-76.

Champion, T. 1983. A New Definition of Cities, *Town and Country Planning*, Vol. LII, pp. 305-307.

Chapman, G. and Wanmali, S. 1981. Urban Rural Relationship in India: A Macro-scale Approach Using Population Potentials, *Geoforum,* Vol. XII, pp. 19-44.

Chatterji, L. 1983. Migration, Housing and Equity in Developing Countries: A Comparative Systems Approach, *Regional Development Dialogue*, Vol. IV, No. 1, pp. 105-23.

Chatterji, M.N. 1978. System Approach to Urban and Regional Planning, *Urban and Rural Planning Thought*, Vol. XXI, Nos. 1-2, pp. 1-17.

Childe, V.G. 1950. The Urban evolution, *Town Planning Review*, 21.3

Chitranjan, K.V. 1983. Functional Specialization of Cities and Urban Growth in Gujarat, *Indian Journal of Regional Science*, Vol. XV, No.2, pp. 27-35.

Chitranjan, K.V. 1984. Urban and Regional Growth Patterns in Gujarat: A Cross Section Analysis, *Urban India*, Vol. IV, No. 4, pp. 32-58.

Clark, G. 1982. Urban Population Densities, *Journal of the Royal Statistical Society,* Series A, 114:490-96

Clark, W. 1986. *Human Migration*, Sage, Beverly Hills, Calif.

Clarke, M. and Wilson, A. 1985. The Dynamics of Urban Spatial Structure: The Progress of a Research Program, *Transactions of The Institute of British Geographers*, n.s.10, pp 427-51.

Coffey, W.G. 1981. *Geography : Towards General Spatial Systems Approach*, Methuen, London.

Cohen, M. A. 1987. Macroeconomic adjustment and the city, *Cities*, Vol. 7, No. 1, pp 49-59.

Connell, John *et al.* 1976. *Migration from Rural Areas*, Oxford University Press, New Delhi.

Converse, P.E. 1972. Country Differences in the Use of Time. In *The Use of Time* A. Szalai(ed.), Mouton, Hague, pp.145-78.

Conway, D. and Shrestha, N.R. 1981. Causes and Consequences of rural-to-rural Migration in Nepal, *Ford Foundation Research Report*, Department of Geography, Indiana University Press.

Crook N. 1993. *India's Industrial Cities*, Oxford University Press, Oxford.

Daniel, P. and Hopkinson, M., 1987. *The Geography of Settlement*, Oliver and Boyed, Hong Kong.

Darigo, G. and Tobler, W. 1983. Push-Pull Migration Laws .*Annals Association of American Geographer* 73 (1):1-17.

Datta, A. 1983. Planning of Urban Development: The Basic Policy Issues, *Nagarlok*, Vol. XV, No. 4, pp 8-23.

Davies, W. and Herbert, D. 1993. *Communities Within Cities, An Urban Social Geography*, Belhaven Press, London.

Davis, K. 1962. Urbanization in India: Past and Future. *Economic Development and Cultural Change* 3, pp. 6-26.

Davis, K. and Hilda, H. 1957. Urbanization and the Development of Pre-Industrial Areas. In *Cities and Society*, P. K. Hatt and A .J. Reiss (eds),New York, 1957, pp.120-131.

Dawra, S., 2001. *Environmental Economics*, Mohit Publications, New Delhi.

De Jong, G. F. and Fawcett, J. 1981. Multi disciplinary Framework: A Model of Migration in Decision Making. In *Migration, Decision Making: Multi-disciplinary Approach to Micro-level Studies in Developed and Developing Countries*, De Jong, G. F. and R. W. Gardner (eds), Pergamon Press, New York.

De, Jong, G.F. and Robert, W. G. 1981. *Migration, Decision Making*, Pergamon Press, New York.

Deolalikar, S.G. 2001. Futuristic Planning of Human Settlements Infrastructure Issues, *Shelter*, Vol. 4, No.1, pp. 16-18.

Desai, A. 1980a. The Environmental Perception of an Urban Landscape: The Case of Ahmedabad, *Ekistics*, Vol. CCXXIII, pp. 279-285.

Deshpande, C.D. 1975-76. Spatial Dynamics in the Indian Suburban Zone, *Indian Journal of Social Work*, Vol. XXXVI, Nos. 3-4, pp 305-309.

Deshpande, C.D. 1976. Trends in Cities and Towns of Western India, 1961-71. In *Urbanization in Developing Countries*, S. Manzoor Alam and V.V. Pokshevshivsky (eds.), Osmania University Press, Hyderabad.

Deshpande, C.D., Arunachalam, B. and Bhat, L.S. 1980. *Impact of a Metropolitan City on the Surrounding Region*, Concept Publishing Company, New Delhi.

Dhurandhar, K.P. 1978. Urbanization As a Function of Structure, Process and Stage: A Conceptural Frame, *Uttar Bharat Bhoogol Patrika,* Vol. XIV, No. 1, pp. 66-70.

Dixit, R.S. 1981. The Transport Accessibility of Market of Kanpur Metropolis, *Deccan Geographer*, Vol.XIX, No.45-52.

Donald, A. K. and Arthur, S. 1976. *Urban Planning Analysis: Methods and Models,* John Wiley and Sons. New York.

Douglas, I. 1983. *The Urban Environment*, Edward Arnold, London.

Douglass, M. 1992. The Political Economy of Urban Poverty and

Environmental Management in Asia: Access, Empowerment and Community based Alternatives, *Environment and Urbanization*, Vol. 4, No. 2

Doxiadis, C.A. and Papaionnou, J.G. 1974. *Ecumenopolis, the Inevitable City of the Future*, Athens Publishing House, Athens.

Dutta, A. and Agarwal, M.M.1992. *The Quality of Life*, Indian Institute of Advanced Study, New Delhi.

Dutta, S.S. 1985. Information System for Urban Development: Some Conceptual Issues; *Nagarlok*, Vol XVII, No. 4, pp. 1-8.

Elhance, A. 1983. Location of Social Facilities: An Analytical Approach, *Indian Journal of Regional Science*, Vol. XV, No. 1, pp. 53-58.

Friedmann, J. (ed.), 1974. New Concepts and Technologies in *Third World Urbanization*, SAUP, University of California, Los Angeles, pp. 101-127.

Friedmann, J. 1966. *Regional Development Policy: A Case Study of Venezuela*, M.I.T. Press, Cambridge.

Gatrell, A.C. 1977. Complexity and Redundancy in Binary Maps, *Geographical Analysis*, 9, pp. 29-41.

Geyer, H.S. 1990. Implications of Differential Urbanization on Deconcentration in the Pretoria–Witwatersrland–Vaal Triangle Metropolitan Area, *Geoforum* 21, pp. 385-96.

Geyer, H.S. and Kontuly, T. 1993. A Theoretical Foundation for the Concept of Differential Urbanization, *International Regional Science Review*, Vol.17, No.2, pp. 157-77.

Gilbert, A. and Gugler, J. 1981. *Cities, Poverty and Development – Urbanization in the Third World*, Oxford University Press.

Gober, M. P. 1878. Employment Motivated Migration and Economic Growth in Post-industrial Market Economies, *Progress in Human Geography*,2, pp. 207-29

Gohman, V.M. Lapoo, I., Maegoiz, M. and Mashbits Y.G. 1976. The Economic-geographical Aspects of World Urbanization and its Specific Features in the Developing Countires. In *op.cit.*, Alam and Pokshishevsky (eds.), pp. 25-46.

Goldstein, G. 1990. Acess to Life Saving Services in Urban Aras. In *The Poor Die Young: Housing and Health in Third World Cities*, Jorge, E. Hardoy, *et al.* (ed.), Earthscan Publications, London.

Gopi, K.N. 1980. *Urban Growth and Industrial Locations*, Indian Book House, New Delhi.

Goryacheva, A.M. 1977. Factor Analysis of the Growth of India's Largest Cities and Differentiation of Economic Functions, *Soviet Geography*, Vol XVIII, pp. 384-306.

Goryacheva, A.M. and Lipyets, Y.G. 1976. Inter-relation of Factors of Growth in the System of Indian Cities, in *op.cit.*, Alam and Pokshishevsky (eds.), pp. 283-306.

Gould, P. 1975. Acquiring Spatial Information, *Economic Geography*, 51, 87-99.

Gras, N.S.B. 1965. An Introduction to Economic History. In *The Study of Urbanization,* Hauser, P.M. and Leo, F. Schnore (eds.), John Wiley and Sons, New York.

Groenon, W.W.V. 1977. Crowding: A Report on India, *The Indian Journal of Social Work*, Vol. XXXVIII, No. 1, pp. 27-36.

Habeeb, A. 1982. Economic Structure of Colonial Cities in India: A Review of Sectoral Trends (1872-1982). In *Studies in urban History*, J.S. Grewal and Indu Banga (eds.). Guru Nanak Dev University, Amritsar.

Habib, A. and Moonis, R. 1983. Urbanization in a Fragmented World: Some Aspects of International Inequalities, *Urban India*, Vol. III, No. 2.

Hagerstrand, T. 1966. Aspects of the Spatial Structure of Social Communications and the Diffusion of Innovations, *Papers and Proceedings of the Regional Science Association*, 16, pp. 27-42.

Haggett, P. 1965. *Geography—A Modern Synthesis*. Harper and Row, London.

Halder, D.K. 1976. Integration of Spatially Separated Towns and Regional Development, *Indian Journal of Regional Science*, Vol. VIII, pp. 66-70.

Hall, P.G. and Hay, D. 1980. *Growth Centres in The European Urban System*, Heinmann, London.

Hardoy, J. E. 1975. Two Thousand Years of Latin American Urbanization. In *Urbanization in Latin America: Approaches and Issues,* J.E. Hardoy (ed.), Anchor Books, New York.

Harris, N. 1990. Environmental Issues in the Cities of the Developing World, *DPU Working Paper No. 20*, University College, London.

Hartshorn, T. 1992. *Interpreting the City,* John Wiley, New York.

Harvey, D. 1969. *Explanations in Geography*, Edward Arnold, London.

Harvey, D. 1969. *Social Justice and the City*. Edward Arnold, London.

Henderson, J. V. 1982. The Impact of Government Policies on Urban Concentration, *Journal of Urban Economics,* Vol. 12, No. 3, pp. 280-303.

Herbert, D. and Thomas, C. 1990. *Cities in Space: City as Place,* David Fulton Publishers, London.

Hirchman, A.O. 1958. *The Strategy of Economic Development*, Yale University Press, New Haven, Connecticut.

Hussain, M. I. and Siddiqui N.A. 1977. Urban Encroachment on Rural Lands, A Case Study of Ghaziabad City, *The Geographer*, Vol. XXIX, No. 2, pp. 44-57.

Jagmohan, A. 1982. The Hierarchical Organization of Structural Pattern of Urban Centres: A Multivariate Analysis, *Transactions of the Institute of Indian Geographers*, Vol. IV, No. 1, pp. 25-38.

Jain, M.K. 1977. Interstate Variations in the Trends of Urbanization in India 1951-71, *International Institute of Population Studies,* Bombay.

Jaypal, P. 2001. Urban Management: Strategies for sustainable Development of Cities, *Shelter,* Vol. 4, No. 2, pp. 39-43.

Jenks, G.F. and Colson, R.C. 1963. Class Intervals for Statistical Maps, *International Year Book of Cartography*, 3, pp. 119-133.

Jocobson, L.V. and Prakash, V. 1977. Urbanization in India: The Need for Normative Regional Development Strategies. In *op, cit.,* A.G. Noble and A.K. Dutt (eds.), pp.159-169.

Johnston, R.J. 1983. *Philosophy and Human Geography,* Edward Arnold, London.

Jones, G.W. 1983. Structural Change and Prospects for Urbanization in Asian Countries, *Papers of the East West Population Institute*, No. 88, East West Centre, Honolulu.

Karnnevar, M.F. 1976. A Quantitative Analysis of the Pattern of Urban Settlements in Karnataka State, *Geographical Review of India*, Vol. XXXVIII, pp. 78-84.

Kayastha, S.L. and Singh, S.N. 1977. A Study of Preferences and Behaviour Pattern of Tourists in Varanasi: A Geographical

Analysis, *National Geographical Journal of India*, Vol. XXIII, pp. 3-4.

Kelley, A., Jeffrey, W. and Russell C. 1972. *Dualistic Economic Development,* Chicago University Press, Chicago.

Knox, P. 1987. *Urban Social Geography : An Introduction*, Longman, New York.

Kulaba, S. 1989. Local Government and the Management of Urban Services in Tanzania. In *African Cities in Crisis*, Richard E. Stren and Rodney R. White (eds.), Westview Press, USA, pp. 203-245.

Kulkarni, S. 1984. *Geography of Crowding and Human Response*, Concept Publishing Company, New Delhi.

Kundu, A. 1992. *Urban Development and Urban Research in India*, Khanna, New Delhi.

Kundu, A., 2000. Poverty and Employment in Urban India : A Perspective for Formulating a Development Strategy, *Shelter,* Vol. III, pp. 14-18.

Lahiri, K. and Numrich, R.P. 1983. An Econometric Study on the Dynamics of Urban Spatial Structure, *Journal of Urban Economic*, Vol. XIV, pp. 55-79.

Lahiri, M. 1981. Trends in Urban Growth in India, 1901-1971, *Geographical Review of India*, Vol. XLIII, No. 4, pp. 385-389.

Lampard, E.E. 1967. Historical Aspects of Urbanization. In *The Study of Urbanization*, Schnore, L.F. and Hauser, P.M. (ed.), John Wiley and Sons, New York.

Lee, E. 1969. A theory of migration. In *Migration*, Jakson, J.A. (ed.), University Press Cambridge.

Lee, T. 1970. Perceived Distance as a Function of Direction in the City, *Environment and Behaviour* 2, pp. 40-51.

Lewis, M. 1954. *In the Name of Sanity*. Harcourt Brace & Co. New York.

Lowry, I.S. 1966. *Migration and Metropolitan Growth: Two Analytical Models*, Chandler, San Francisco.

Mahmood, A. and Raza, M. 1982. Urban Redistribution of Population in Regional Space: A Case Study of India, *Working paper No. 82-85 UNCERD,* Nagaya.

Mahmood, A. 1994. Role of Small and Medium Towns in Regional Context Specially Linkages and Their Effect on Growth and Such Towns, *The Geographer*, Vol. XLI, No. 2, pp. 32-39.

Mallick, U.C. 1981. A Profile in India's Urbanization: Problems and Policy Issues. In *Urban Problems and Policy Perspectives,* Gopal Bhargava (ed.), Abhinav Publishers, New Delhi.

Mandal, R.B. (ed.) 1982. *Urbanization and Regional Development*, Concept Publishing Company, New Delhi.

Mathur, A. 1983. Regional Migration in India: A Sectoral Analysis, *Economic Development and Cultural Change, Vol.* 31, No. 3, pp 475-505.

Mc Gee, T.G. 1971. *The Urbanization Process in the Third World*, G. Bell and Sons, London.

Mehra, A.K., 1991. *The Politics of Urban Re-development – A study of Old Delhi*, Sage Publications, New Delhi.

Mera, K, 1973. On the Urban Agglomeration and Economic Efficiency, *Economic Development and Cultural Change,* No. 21, pp 309-24.

Mills, E.S. 1972. *Urban Economics*, Scott, Foreman and Company, London.

Mills, E.S. 1983. The Concept of Over-Urbanization; *Nagarlok*; Vol. XV, No.2, pp 1-8.

Mills, E.S. and Becker, C.M.1986. *Studies in Indian Urban Development,* World Bank Research Publications, Oxford University Press.

Misra, H.N. and Bhagat, B. 1980. Spatial System of Intermediate Towns of Uttar Pradesh, India, *The Geographer*; Vol. XXVII. No. 2, pp 14-30.

Misra, H.N. 1982. Role of Small and Intermediate Towns in Regional Development Process: *A Project Report*, HED, London.

Misra, R.P. 1978. *Million Cities of India*, Vikas Publishers, New Delhi.

Mitra, A. 1978. *India's Population*, vol. I and II, Abhinav Publications, New Delhi.

Mohan, R. 1981. Urban Policies and Growth Trends, An Analysis, *Urban India*, Vol.I, pp.9-16.

Mohmood, A. 2001. Urbanization, Migration and Development in Uttar Pradesh. In *Essays in Indian Geography*, R. Gopal Krishnan and Ali Ahmed (eds.), Regency Publications, New Delhi.

Mukerji, A.B. 1976. Small Towns of Uttar Pradesh: An Exploratory Analysis, *Indian Geographical Review,* Vol. LI, No. 1, pp. 33-40.

Munsi, S. K. 1975. The Nature of Indian Urbanization – A Review, *Geographical Review of India,* Vol. XXXVII, No. 4, pp. 287-299.

Myrdal, L.G.1957: *Economic Theory and Under developed regions*, Duckworth and Co., London.

Nangia, S. 1978. Delhi Metropolitan Region – A Profile of Population Growth, *Indian Journal of Regional Science*, Vol. X, No. 1, pp. 68-77.

Noble, A.G. and Dutta, A.K. 1977. *Indian Urbanization and Planning: Vehicles of Modernization*, Tata Mc Graw Hills, New Delhi.

Parveen, S., 1992. Levels Of Urbanization in Uttar Pradesh. In *Environmental Management and Sustainable Development*, Department of Geography, Jamia Millia Islamia, New Delhi.

Parveen, S., 1994. Quality of Life – A Study of Class I Cities of Uttar Pradesh, *The Geographer*, Vol. XLI, No.2, pp. 70-80.

Parveen, S., 1996. Territorial Stress: A Study of Urban Housing in Maharashtra. In *Environmental Management in India*, Majid Husain, and Syed Sajid Husain Zaidi (eds.) Manak Publications Pvt. Ltd., New Delhi.

Parveen, S., 2001. Levels of Living : A Study of Urban Housing in Class I Cities of Uttar Pradesh. In *Essays in Indian Geography*, R. Gopal Krishnan and Ali Ahmed (eds.), Regency Publications, New Delhi.

Pascoe, E.H. 1919. Early History of Indus, Brahamaputra and Ganges. *Quarterly Journal of Geological Society of London,* 75: 138-159.

Patankar, P.G. 1978. *Urban Mobility in Developing Countries*, Popular Prakashan. Bombay.

Pathak, C.R. 1975. Spatial Variation in Urban and Industrial Growth in India, *Indian Journal of Regional Science*, Vol. VII, pp.1-10.

Peet, R. and Thrift, N. 1989. Political Economy and Human Geography. In *New Models in Geography : The Political Economic Perspective*, R. Peet and N.Thrift (eds.), Unwin Hyman London, pp. 3-29.

Pilgrim, G.E. 1919. Suggestions Concerning the History of Northern India. *Journal of Asiatic Society of Bengal,* 15: 81-89.

Popenoe, D. 1965. On the Meaning of Urban in Urban Studies, *Urban Affairs*, Vol. I, No. 1, pp. 20-36.

Prakashsarao, V.L.S. 1982. Urban Population Density Models and Correlates, *Geographical Review of India*, Vol.XLIV, No.2, pp.1-18.

Pred, A. 1977. *City-system in Advanced Economies: Past Growth, Present Process and Future Development Options*. New York: Wiley.

Premi, M.K. 1981. Role of Migration in the Urbanization Process in the Third World Countries – The Case of India, *Social Action*, pp. 291-310.

Preston, S. 1984. A Path Model of Residential Stress and Inertia among Older People, *Urban Geography* 5, pp. 146-64.

Raju S. 1980. The Social Meaning of Urban Neighborhood in India, *Ekistics*, No. 283, pp. 286-289.

Ramachandran, R. 1979. *Urbanization and Urban System in India*, Oxford University Press, New Delhi.

Rapport, A. 1977. *Human Aspects of Urban Form*, Pergamon Press, Oxford.

Ravenstein, E.G. 1885. Laws of Migration, *Journal of the Royal Statistical Society,* Vol. 48, pp. 167-227.

Ravindran, K.T. 1982. Politics of Design, *Urban India*, Vol II, No. 3, pp. 13-17.

Raza, M.and Habeeb, A. 1980. Role of Urban System in National Development – A Case Study of India, In *Urbanization and National Development*, K.Honza and R.P. Mishra (eds.), Nagoya.

Raza, Moonis and A.Kundu, 1977. Spatial Organization and Urbanization in India – A Case Study of Underdevelopment. *Occasional Papers*, 9, Centre for the Study of Regional Development, School of Social Science, Jawaharlal Nehru University, New Delhi.

Reginald, G. G. and Stimson, K.J. 1987. *Analytical Behavioral Geography,* Groom Helm, London.

Reismann, L. 1964. The Urban Process. In *The Study of Urban Geography,* Carter, H. (ed.), Edward Arnold, London.

Renaud, B.M. 1981. *National Urbanization Policy in Developing Countries*, Oxford University Press, New York.

Richard E.S. and Rodney R.W. (eds.), *African Cities in Crisis*, Westview Press, USA, pp. 246-275.

Richardson, H.W. 1977. City Size and National Spatial Strategies in Developing Countries, *World Bank Staff Working Paper*, No. 252, Washington D.C.

Rogers, A. 1980. Migration, Urbanization, Resources and Development, *Ekistics*, 284, pp. 312-324.

Rogerson, P. and Plane, D. 1985. Monitoring Migration Trends, *American Demographics*, Vol. 8, No.2, pp. 27-29.

Schwind, P. 1975. A General Field Theory of Migration : United States, 1955-1960, *Economic Geography*, 51, pp. 1-16.

Shafi, S.S. 1994. Quality of Life and the Indian Metropolitan: A Process of Reverse Acculturation, *Nagarlok*, Vol. XXVI, No. 3, pp. 1-15.

Shafi, M. 1968. Ganga-Yamuna Doab, *India Regional Studies*, pp. 31-35

Sharma, H.S. and Chattopadhyay, S. (eds.) 1998. *Sustainable Development – Issues and Case Studies*, Concept Publishig Company, New Delhi.

Shaw, R., 1985. *Intermetropolitan Migration in Canada : Changing Determinants Over Three Decades*, NC Press, Toronto.

Sheppard, E., 1986. Modelling and Predicting Aggregation Flows. In *The Geography of Urban Transportation*, S.Hanson (ed.), Guildford Press, New York, pp. 91-118.

Sheppard, E.S.1977. Rethinking the Nature of Urban and Regional Interdependencies. In Growth Determinants in the Core-periphery of Korea, H.Lee (1989), *International Regional Science Review*, Vol.12, No.2, pp. 147-63.

Shevky, E. and Bell, W., 1955. *Social Area Analysis*, Stanford University Press, Standford.

Short, J.R., 1989. *An Introduction to Urban Geography*, Routledge, London.

Siddique, M. 1977. The Geography of Literacy in Uttar Pradesh, *Geographical Review of India*, Vol. 39, pp 374-388.

Singh, O.P. 1996. Population Growth in Himalayan Environment : A Case of U.P. Himalayas, *The Geographer*, Vol. XLIII, No.1, pp. 27-35.

Singh, K. and Florien, S. 1996. *Urban India in Crisis*, New Age Industrial Ltd, Publisher, New Delhi.

Singh, N. and Krishan, G. 1996. Urbanization –Emerging Scenario and New Challenges. In *Urban India in Crisis*, K. Singh and F. Steinberg, (eds.), New Age International Publishers, New Delhi, pp. 1-19.

Sinha, V.N.P. and V.S. Phadke, 1980. Declining Towns of India, *Transactions of the Institute of Indian Geographers*, Vol.II, No.2, pp. 1-8.

Sjaastad,L.A.1962. The costs and Returns of Human Migration, *Journal of Political Economy*, 70(5), pp. 80-93.

Slater, P. 1989. A Field Theory of Spatial Interconnection, *Environment and Planning* A 21, pp. 121-6.

Smith, N. 1996. *The New Urban Frontier-Gentrification and the Revanchist City,* Routledge, London.

Sovani, N.V. 1966. *Urbanization and Urban India,* Asia Publishing House, Bombay.

Subramanayam, V.V. and Bawa R.L. 1996. *Urban Economic Development in India,* Galgotia Publishing Co., New Delhi.

Sundaram, K. and Tendulkar, S.D. 1983. Poverty Reduction and Redistribution in Sixth Plan – Population Factor and Rural-urban Equity, *Economic and Political Weekly*, Vol.XVIII, No.38, pp. 1617-32.

Todaro, M.P. 1969. A Model of Labour Migration and Urban Unemployment in Less Developed Countries, *American Economic Review*, 59.

Townroe, P.M. and Keen, D. 1984. Polarization Reversal in the State of Sao Paulo, *Regional Studies,* Brazil, Vol.18, pp. 45-44.

United Nations, 1980. Patterns of Urban and Rural Population Growth, *Population Studies,* No. 68, New York.

Unwin, D. 1981. *Introductory Spatial Analysis*, Methuen, New York.

Williamson, J. 1965. Regional Inequality and the Process of National Development; A Description of Patterns, *Economic Development and cultural change*, vol. 3.

Wirth, L. 1938. *Urbanism as a Way of Life.* Chicago University Press, Chicago, pp. 60-83.

Reports

Carrying Capacity Based Regional Planning, 1996. National Institute of Urban Affairs, New Delhi.

Census of India 1991. *Uttar Prdesh, Series 25*, Office of the Registrar General, India.

Census of India, 1991, *Town directory of Uttar Prdesh, Series 25.*

Census Of India, 1991. *Uttar Pradesh :Regional Divisions of India-A Cartographic Analysis*, B.K.Roy and V.S. Verma (eds.), Series I,Vol.XXII, Office of The Registrar General and Census Commissioner, India

Government of India,1992. *Eighth Five Year Plan* 1992-97, New Delhi

National Commission on Urbanization, 1988. Government of India (ed.*),Main Report*, New Delhi.

*Profiles of States-Uttar Pradesh, 1997.*Centre for Monitoring Indian Economy (CMIE), Private Limited, New Delhi

*Statistical Abstract of Uttar Pradesh, 1994.*Economic and Statistics Division, State Planning Institute, Lucknow.

*The State of Indian Cities 2001.*United Nations Centre for Human Settlement Housing and Urban Development Corporation (HABITAT), New Delhi.

Urban Environmental Management. The Indian Experience (1996). Institute for Housing and Urban Development Studies, Rotterdam, New Delhi.

Urban Environmental Management–The Indian Experience, Human Settlement Management Institute (HUDCO),New Delhi.

Uttar Pradesh Development Report:2000, by A. K. Singh, New Royal Book Depot, Lucknow, Uttar Pradesh.

World Bank 1982: *World Development Report,1982*, Oxford University Press, New York.

World Bank. 1991: *Urban Policy and Economic Development: An Agenda for the 1990s,* Washington DC.

INDEX